A CELTIC KIWI TAPESTRY
A MEMOIR OF RESILIENCE AND HOPE

SABRINA M. G. DOWLING

MELROS PRESS

Copyright © 2025 Sabrina M. G. Dowling

Sabrina M. G. Dowling asserts her moral right to be identified as the author of this work.

All rights reserved. No part of this publication may be reproduced or transmitted in any form or by any means, electronic or mechanical, including photocopying, recording or information storage and retrieval systems, without permission in writing from the copyright holder.

Published by Melros Press
Contact author: sabrinamgdowling@hotmail.com

This book is based on true events, but some names, places and incidents have been changed to protect individuals' identities.

A catalogue record for this book is available from the National Library of New Zealand.

ISBN 978-0-473-74610-0 (paperback)
ISBN 978-0-473-74611-7 (EPUB)

Cover design by Jeroen ten Berge, jeroentenberge.com

CONTENTS

1. When You Have Harrowed What I Have Ploughed! — 1
2. Lui an Talún Agus Déileálacha Shady — 13
3. Sabrina — 23
4. A Move to the Country — 33
5. Farming Life — 51
6. Tragedy Hits — 73
7. The Irish Psyche — 89
8. Just Getting By — 93
9. The Valley of Kidron — 113
10. Escape! — 145
11. Flying the Nest — 159
12. Finding Love — 181
13. Marriage and Travel — 201
14. A New Life in Aotearoa New Zealand — 215
15. Church and Community Life — 229
16. Birth of a Monster — 251
17. The Journey Towards Healing — 265
18. Studying Trauma and the Ryan Report — 277
19. Up Against the Battering Ram — 291
20. 'Amazing' Grace and Other Friends — 311
21. An Interlude in Turkey and Greece — 323
22. Sink or Swim! — 331

Safety Note — 345
About the Author — 347
Acknowledgments — 349

O Wind, if Winter comes, can Spring be far behind?

—Percy Bysshe Shelley
from *Ode to the West Wind*

ONE
WHEN YOU HAVE HARROWED WHAT I HAVE PLOUGHED!

Is áit thagartha é d'am atá caite, ní áit chónaithe.
(The past is a place of reference, not a place of residence.)

—Irish saying

On a bitterly cold February morning in 1912, my grandmother, Maggie Dowling, stood by the small stone window ledge in the kitchen of her farmhouse in Drom, staring past the icicles hanging from the thatch at the frosty day outside. The chill wind carried the distant sound of dogs barking, while, somewhat closer, the cows bellowed from the gate as they waited for hay.

Maggie watched her husband moping around the farmyard. Denis Dowling was a short, portly figure of a man, his dirty old *caipín*, or cap, worn back to front to cover his receding hairline and balding crown. The binding twine that held his shabby trousers up around his waist was loose and trailing in the dung, but he seemed unaware of either the smell or the pattern the twine was making on his breeches. His steel-capped boots had no laces and impeded his progress as he shuffled around the yard, unable to concentrate on his work. From time to time, he would spit a few chewed ends of straw onto the ground, narrowly missing the dog at his heels who appeared to mirror her master's distress.

Usually by this time, Maggie would have fed the pigs, strained the milk, and brought in a few turf sods from the heap in the yard, but this morning she was totally disorganised, suffering from lack of sleep, her eyes as swollen and as heavy as her heart. A cut of bacon still hung on the hook over the fire lintel, and she really needed to rinse the salt off the meat and put it in the skillet pot to cook for hours if there was to be any dinner. The pot, suspended from a soot-stained crane over the fire, held water left over from boiling the duck eggs for last evening's meal.

At her feet, a tin bucket contained spuds that needed to be scrubbed, and a head of cabbage was still on the doorstep waiting to be brought in, washed, and chopped. Dirty dishes from a hurried supper littered the table, surrounding her mother's prized Delft Blue teapot. On a normal morning, Maggie would have emptied the tea leaves into the geranium in the china flowerpot on the windowsill, but there was no time for that now. Baby clothes lay drying on the two stone hobs, the ash beneath still warm from the embers left there when the fire had been cleaned in the early morning.

The flames danced briefly as the downdraft from the chimney circulated smoke around the room, creating pockets of warmth. Next to the fireplace, in a wicker basket propped up on two wooden chairs, lay a baby. Dressed in a long, white gown and bonnet, his small form covered by a knitted, blue blanket, he was gasping for breath and alternately whimpering and coughing as his tiny chest rattled. It was a frightening sound, accompanied as it was by the murmuring of the baby's two religious uncles, who were storming Heaven through prayer and supplication for the life of the child.

'What am I to do with myself, with all this worry?' Maggie pondered. 'And as if that is not enough, I have extra mouths to feed today.'

'Get yerself over here, Missus and grab the babbie,' one of the holy uncles growled at her.

With intimidation now compounding her distress, she found herself promising then and there that if they continued to petition Heaven, the Blessed Virgin, and all the saints to save the life of her firstborn child, Anthony, she would see to it that his life would be dedicated to God. Maggie understood that it would be her responsibility to ensure that, if God answered their prayers and spared the little mite, his life would be one of servitude to the Church. Whether Anthony, to become known as Tony, liked it or not would be of no consequence.

The burden of that promise rested heavily upon Maggie, and she was to bear it, privately, as her cross throughout her life. Deep down, she wondered whether perhaps she had not been a good mother, to have allowed the child to get so sick as a baby. The infant, of course, was unaware of the struggle to keep him in the earthly realm so soon after his birth.

Tony didn't learn of the pledge over his life until his early teens, when he started to show promise as a sportsman and was told that sport was out of the question, his path was already set, and he really had no say in the matter. Looking back, it's easy to see that, had he been left to his own devices, the roadmap of his life may have been different.

Christened Anthony Bernard Dowling, Tony was the eldest of four siblings—three boys and a girl. His two brothers grew up to continue the farming tradition, while his sister, Loo became what was referred to in those days as an 'old maid', meaning she never married and just worked at home in a domestic capacity without payment, or future inheritance, until her death. Tony was the only one of the siblings to marry, which he did at the age of nearly forty. This was considered an incredibly old age for matrimony in the 1950s and 60s.

The old maid's circumstances might have been better had she accepted the match with a farmer in the county, arranged for her by a local matchmaker when she was still of marriageable age. Matchmaking was often the process for meeting a lifelong partner in 'old' Ireland and still goes on to this day in Lisdoonvarna, County Clare, on Ireland's Wild Atlantic Way, where Europe's biggest singles festival takes place every September. The festival comprises music and dancing in every bar in the small settlement of under 1,000 permanent residents — very enjoyable occasion. However, Loo refused the proposal and ended up with little or no quality of life.

In conversations with me later, Tony indicated that the reason for Auntie Loo's refusal was, perhaps, that his sister was of a nervous disposition and was too frightened to marry. After the death of her parents, she spent her days living in a thatched house with her unmarried brother in the capacity of a servant. Her only company was the dog, as she and her brother did not generally converse at that stage of their lives. Auntie Loo used to go to the local chemist and ask for shampoo for short hair, which she probably cut herself. She must have been left some money by her parents, and when she needed to go to the bank, she would usually go on a weekend or after hours. The bank manager in those days lived alongside or above the bank premises, so Auntie Loo would knock at the private residence to get service outside of banking hours.

The story in the family was that after Tony's uncles, Bro. Seamus and Bro. Michael, OMI (Oblates of Mary Immaculate, a religious missionary congregation in the Catholic Church, founded in 1816) prayed for his young life to be spared, his parents vowed that their son would become a priest in thanksgiving for his remarkable recovery. As it turned out, Tony had a high IQ and was extremely academic; he loved Latin, history, and literature. He probably would have been a much happier man as an academic, free to engage himself in his love of sport without feeling guilty.

In order to advance his education and the promise made over his life by others, his parents paid for him to attend the local Christian Brothers secondary school at Baile na Ghlic. Only people with money could get a good secondary school education in Ireland in those days, i.e., between the 1920s and the 1970s. If a person were poor, their academic career would be over before it started, as they would have had to take any job they could find in order to bring some money into the house to support the whole family. In a letter to me dated 23 February 1994, Tony stated, 'I went to Darrigban School with a crook[1] in my hand, which my father cut for me in the fields, so I was fond of hurling[2], you may say from birth.'

Tony had enjoyed the Irish game of hurling from a very early age when he first showed a keen interest in the sport, but it was much frowned upon by the religious orders. Although he initially hoped to go on to play at county, or maybe even national level,

---

1. Crook in this case refers to a rough-cut hurling stick, the origin of the word being Anglo-Norman derived from the old Norse word *krokr*, meaning a hook or a bend. The name was brought to Ireland by Viking settlers during the medieval period.
2. Hurling has prehistoric origins; it has been played for 4,000 years. It is one of Ireland's native Gaelic games and shares several features, such as the field and goals, the number of players and much terminology, with Gaelic football. There is a similar game for women called camogie, which shares a common Gaelic root with the sport shinty, played predominantly in Scotland.

Tony's passion for hurling was considered a distraction from the plans that his family and, in particular, his mother, had decided for him—but that did not stop his enjoyment of the game. Tall and skinny in stature with the physique of an athlete, Tony was also a cross-country and open road runner, a sprinter, and a keen cyclist who loved a variety of sports.

Tony Dowling Scholastic Group in Daingean, 1934 (source: De Mazenod Circle Record No. 2 December 1934)

After leaving school, he was sent away to study in a seminary in order to become a priest; but there his continued interest in hurling was the cause of much dissatisfaction among those in authority. Gripped by a passion for the excitement of the game, Tony would think nothing of cycling a hundred miles to a hurling match. Unfortunately, but perhaps predictably, this would appear as a black mark against him in the eyes of the seminary administrators. In his final year there, he was called into the office by the Superior in charge to be greeted with the words, 'The Fathers and I have decided that you, Tony, have no vocation to the priesthood.' This, according to Tony, was because of his love of hurling.

He was immediately made to leave the seminary, after nearly seven years of studying towards his goal of becoming a priest. Tony was 'turfed out,' with no consideration having been given to the shock and rejection he would feel. No plans had been put in place for his future career after life in the seminary. He had not seen this coming, and it distressed him very much; he never got over the shock of that rejection, which stayed with him for the rest of his life. In a state of dismay and penniless, he left with only the clothes on his back and cycled the hundred miles or so back home, to the disgrace of his family.

Even weeks before he died in 1994, at the age of eighty-two, he would reminisce in his letters to me about the shame he had brought on his family at that time. My last letter to my father advised him to forgive himself and to let go of the past disappointment over the priesthood. I told him that his descendants would bring the 'glory to God' where he had, according to both him and the seminary, missed the mark. (Tony would often discuss his concerns and worries with me, though he used me more as a sounding board rather than seeking my advice. Anyway, I knew that he had already made up his mind before he spoke and sometimes wondered what was the purpose in expressing my views!)

My grandmother, it is understood, was so distressed and

embarrassed by the failure of her eldest son to become a priest that she could not show her face in the community. Old newspaper cuttings, found after her death, revealed that she had kept printed articles on the ordination of Tony's classmates at the seminary. It was said in the family that immediately after being rejected for the priesthood, a match for an arranged marriage was made for Tony, but the prospective bride turned him down. Apparently, the woman did not think much of his prospects, or something like that.

The Dowlings have Irish ancestry, though it is said that they originated in France prior to the 11th century and later settled in Ireland. The family was part of the Irish overlord system[3] and had been farming the land for generations by the time of Tony's birth in 1912. For centuries, the Dowlings had been well-respected farmers in the area by the lough. However, by the 1950s, they had a big problem on their hands: Because he had been promised to the priesthood, their eldest son had not inherited the family farm — the tradition in Ireland at that time. They were left wondering what was to be done about him. Tony's two brothers were each well set up, having a farm apiece, so a discussion would have taken place within the extended family around how they would provide for the eldest son.

It soon became clear that Tony would have to make his own way in life, and he took up a job as an orderly at St Bartholomew's Hospital in Clonlea, in County Ballynagoon. (Although he never discussed such a thing with me, it is possible that he had an accident there while driving an ambulance, as he never again drove a vehicle. After he married, he always depended on his wife to drive.) Luckily for Tony, very shortly after this unfortunate turn

---

3. On 16 October 1175, Henry II of England and High King Ruaidrí agreed to the Treaty of Windsor which divided Ireland into two spheres of influence. Henry was acknowledged as overlord of the Norman-held territory, and Ruaidrí was acknowledged as overlord of the rest of Ireland.

of events, an aunt left him a business which included a pub, a restaurant, some rental accommodation, and stables. And then, not long after receiving that bequest, he also inherited a farm from an uncle. These timely inheritances meant that the nearly 40-year-old Tony's life began looking up, though he was an academic who had no real experience of life outside a seminary. He knew absolutely nothing about running a business or farming.

Fortunately for him, a young woman from a farming family was waiting in the wings. Delphine Lavinia Laughton was descended from Church of Ireland people, Protestant gentry in Ireland. She came from a long line of ancestors who originated in Normandy, France and was a direct Irish descendant of Captain Thomas Laughton and his son John Laughton, born in 1660, who married the sister of an Irish baron. Research suggests that the family were among the invaders who arrived at Pevensey with William the Conqueror in 1066. There was a name change when the family settled near Cannock Chase in Staffordshire, England. Between the 14th and 19th centuries, Laughton ancestors are found in Staffordshire, Shropshire, Derbyshire, Oxfordshire, and Lancashire. They appear in Ireland in the 17th to 19th centuries.

The pedigree of this family is held in England and includes knights, earls, a king's coroner, a mayor, a painter, a botanist, an educationist, parliamentarians, a magistrate for Westminster, a king's goldsmith, a king's banker, a commander of the English forces, and other such people in English history and society. The family is also connected with John Bunyan, author of *The Pilgrim's Progress*. An earldom created in 1621 saw one of Delphine's ancestors marry into a major landowning family with ties to a baronetcy in Wales.

In the early 17th century, the Lower German Palatinate had a vast number of Protestant refugees. These people had arrived in the area from neighbouring lands and settled in the area to escape religious persecution. This Palatinate area was constantly being ravaged by attacks from France during that period. Following a particularly harsh winter, many of these Protestant settlers responded to publicity around the benefits of emigration to America, and the resultant 1709 exodus from the Lower German Palatinate saw many Palatine families head directly for the New World. However, 13,000 of them were routed via Rotterdam, where those who were not Protestant were turned back. The remainder went on to Blackheath, outside London.

At the same time, the landlords of Irish estates sought to increase the Protestant tenant population, a goal supported by Queen Anne of England. Thus, in September 1709, almost 3,000 Palatines were sent to rural Ireland. A further 3,000 were transported to New York, North Carolina, and Canada. Over the next three years, about two-thirds of the Palatines who had settled in Ireland, now known as the Irish Palatines, left Ireland and returned to England or Germany.

The term 'Poor Palatines' referred to the 13,000 Germans who emigrated to England between May and November 1709. The return to England of some of the Palatines who had recently settled in Ireland caused a highly politicised debate over the merits of immigration. (The reason the British had tried to settle the Protestant Palatines in England, Ireland, and North American colonies was to strengthen Britain's position abroad.) Delphine's ancestors were among 3,000 of the 13,000 Palatine refugees who had arrived at Blackheath in 1709 from Alzey in Rhineland-Phaltz, via Rotterdam, and who were subsequently taken in by Sir Thomas Southwell of Castle Matrix near Rathkeale, County Limerick, in Ireland.

Sir Southwell was the most successful landlord in securing government support for the settlement venture, and he took care of many of the refugees' initial needs at his own expense. Sir Thomas was only reimbursed just prior to his death in 1720. In 1711, Southwell had retained only ten families, but, by 1714, this number had substantially increased and a hundred and thirty, families had settled on his lands. The largest concentration of Irish Palatine residents to this day is in Killeheen, Ballingrane, and Courtmatrix in County Limerick. The Irish Palatines did not initially integrate with the local Irish population. They ran their lives as though they were still back in Germany, including the appointment of a Bürgermeister as the master of the town or borough. Today, a museum exists in Rathkeale, County Limerick, dedicated to preserving the history of the Palatine refugees.

During his sixth Irish tour in 1756, John Wesley visited the Palatines in Ballingrane. Wesley described those he met as 'a plain, artless, serious people'. Initially, they were Lutheran, but later became Methodist and then Church of Ireland (Anglican). The refugees were visited several times by the Wesley brothers, which probably led to many of them later becoming Methodists.

Local neighbours recalled that, when they were children, Delphine and her siblings would attend the Church of Ireland service in the village on Sundays and would walk along the road alone. They had minimal interaction with the local community, as they were seen as different because they were Protestant. All of my Laughton ancestors are buried in Methodist and Anglican (Church of Ireland, known as C of I) graveyards, separate from the Catholic burial grounds.

TWO
LUI AN TALÚN AGUS DÉILEÁLACHA SHADY
THE LIE OF THE LAND AND THE SHADY DEALINGS

Forgetting a debt doesn't mean it's paid.

—Irish saying

Delphine was my mother. Her grandparents, Harold and Joya Laughton, purchased a farm in County Ballynagoon and lived there with their children Brendan, Seán Óg, Aine, Harriet, Bella, and Harold Junior (Har) who, in time, became my mother's father. Aine died young; Seán Óg was listed on the census as being a 'lunatic' (a term commonly used in Ireland in those days for anyone who had psychiatric problems, including anxiety and depression) and spent many years of his life in hospital prior to his death. My grandfather, Har, inherited the family farm from his father, Harold. An additional farm, known as Drochta Cottage, at Drochta in County Knocknagarra was then purchased for their other son, Brendan, on a fee farm grant basis[1]

---
1. Unique to Ireland, a fee farm grant is effectively a freehold estate, subject to a

or fee simple (in other words, freehold with some minor costs to the owner.)

Soon after the death of his parents, when Har was in his fifties, he decided to find himself a wife. He met Wilma, his wife-to-be, when she answered his advertisement in the newspaper with a marriage proposal for a Protestant woman. Har was at least thirty-five years Wilma's senior, but it was much more difficult to find a Protestant spouse in Ireland in those days, as the Protestant population was relatively small compared to the Catholic population. After the wedding, Wilma moved into the house where two of Har's unmarried sisters, Bella and Harriet, were still living with him. Although this was a frequent occurrence in Ireland for unmarried siblings, it was a difficult situation for the younger Wilma to cope with — three women in the one kitchen.

At that time, a woman usually remained living at home with her parents until she was 'married off' (the term used in those days), or in circumstances where no marriage had been arranged or accepted. Sometimes, this meant that unmarried women remained at home carrying out domestic or farm duties for the family, free of charge. At other times, however, the easiest way to get a woman out of the family home was to have her committed to a psychiatric institution for the rest of her life, and this was often done with the assistance of the local doctor. Such behaviour was common in Ireland, and it sometimes happened to men when the family wanted to get rid of them for various reasons and in disputes over land inheritance.

There are many stories of families in Ireland getting rid of unwanted, unmarried adult children, either by sending them to a mental institution or by encouraging them to emigrate to places

---

rent. Technically, it is a freehold estate by reason of its perpetual duration. However, its other characteristics are those of a lease.

such as New Zealand. This far-off colony — 'at the other end of the world' — was the preferred place.

Eventually, Har's two unmarried sisters moved to an outhouse on the property after it had been renovated, by the standards of the day, and made it somewhat more comfortable for human habitation. (These dwellings were originally built to house animals during the winter months.)

Sometime later, Har's brother Brendan gave up his professional career in the city and returned to County Knocknagarra to farm the purchased land at Drochta. Harriet and Bella then went to live with him and work on the farm, which was probably much more comfortable than living in a converted outhouse. The two sisters kept house for Brendan and composed music in their spare time. Brendan died, intestate, in 1923, and Harriet and Bella continued to farm the land as their own property — with the help of two workmen or labourers, the Farrell brothers — until the sisters died in 1939 and 1944 respectively.

In 2020, I tried to obtain official information on what had happened to the Laughton family farm in Drochta. The Irish Department of Agriculture responded to my enquiry saying, 'Please be advised that information and/or copy instruments are only available to the registered owner of the folio concerned or to a person authorised to act on their behalf'. This could be construed, in effect, as a gagging order on behalf of the Land Commission/the Irish Department of Agriculture designed to stop an individual or family from researching the department's own past and unethical behaviour.

What I gleaned from another source was that upon Bella's death in 1944, the Irish Land Commission, today known as the Irish Department of Agriculture, took the property and paid £1,000 into a Lawyer's Trust Account for the land and the house in 1945 without consultation with the Laughton next of kin.

Years later after the trust lawyer had located the heirs of the Laughton Estate in Drochta in County Knocknagarra, my mother did inherit a small amount of money from the Laughton estate. However, according to my father, by the time the solicitor was 'finished with the money' only a few pounds were left for each of the four siblings. Mammy, her two sisters, and brother felt that they had been cheated out of their inheritance by both the Solicitor and the Land Commission. This type of behaviour was a common occurrence in Ireland in those times.

This was the property where Brendan's two unmarried sisters, Harriet and Bella Laughton, had farmed the land as their own property for over twenty years after Brendan's death. This is where my mother had been living with her two aunts and working at times on the farm after she had been orphaned.

The estate had at least 500 acres. Mike Farrell received 150 acres and Drochta Cottage, and his brother Pat lived there with him. Local farmers in the area received divided plots of the remaining 350 acres of the Laughton land from the Land Commission.

When Mike Farrell was presumed to be dying in hospital in the 1970s, the local priest, Father Damien Ryan, a good friend of Benny Brien (Mike Farrell's nephew), visited Mike Farrell in Rimelow hospital in the company of Benny's solicitor, Sam Devine. The assumption was that Mike Farrell would soon be deceased, and the priest and solicitor managed, on Mike Farrell's death bed, to legally transfer Mike's 150 acres and the house to Benny Brien, thus leaving Mike impoverished on his death bed. An arrangement was put in place that Pat Farrell would be cared for by Benny.

Benny Brien was delighted with his newfound wealth from his uncle Mike. Pat Farrell was allowed to stay at the Laughton house in Drochta, presumably to help with the day to day running of the farm, which now belonged to his nephew, Benny Brien.

To the surprise of all concerned, Mike Farrell did not die but recovered and eventually ended up in the County Home in Lorna, County Knocknagarra. (In Ireland, 'County Homes' were institutions that replaced workhouses after 1922. They served as a form of social welfare housing for a wide range of deprived people.)

Mike Farrell managed to leave the confines of the County Home in Lorna and ended up sleeping rough in the countryside for a period. In the late 1970s, when Mike regained his physical strength and mental capabilities, he engaged a solicitor in Lorna who took a case to court on Mike's behalf.

Sam Devine, the original transfer solicitor, was reprimanded by the judge, as also was Father Damien Ryan who was criticised for his role in the matter of the land transfer.

Benny Brien had already invested in a new business in the south of the country, believing he was now a wealthy man. However, with the sudden turn of events of the court case, Benny was now under financial pressure in that the Laughton/Mike Farrell/Brien land was then returned to his uncle, Mike Farrell, by order of the court.

Fortunately for Benny Brien, his wife had a professional career and he had a small pension from the cement factory, which saved him from total financial ruin. Benny eventually bought the farm back from his uncle, Mike Farrell.

In Rimelow, the presiding judge was critical of how the transfer had been handled. The court ultimately came to a compromise, being mindful, no doubt, of the financial stakes for the parties concerned.

Eventually, Mike Farrell's land (part of the Laughton estate) was sold around the year 2000 for £104,000 Sterling. (This was before the Euro, which was introduced into Ireland in 2002.) It was considered a respectable price at the time, with keen bidding from a variety of interested parties.

The 150 acres were then sold to a concrete company, Mending Broken Roads Limited, by the Brien family.

Later, Benny Brien was unsuccessful in his efforts to obtain a rental lease for the original Laughton land from Mending Broken Roads Limited.

When my mother left Drochta Cottage, she had taken with her spoons that had belonged to her grandmother, bearing her grandmother's initials, J.O.L. I can remember using these as a child, along with other childhood memories of visiting Drochta Cottage, an impressive, big, old stone house standing in the middle of fields down a long driveway. The chimney smoked; there was a downdraft (when the wind would come down the chimney or when the front door was opened or closed abruptly), and I particularly remember the earthy smell of the old men living there.

The Land Commission was set up in 1881 under the Land Acts to facilitate the transfers of land ownership from large landlord holdings to small farms. It was a law unto itself. Whilst it traditionally grabbed family farms, it often left many families destitute in that process. In the case of the Laughton family, two children had gone into an orphanage, one had been fostered out, and one had been taken in by a previous employee who had worked for her parents, after the confiscation of the Laughton family farm at Drochta, where my mother had been living.

The Land Commission, very generously and at the expense of such families, gave away land to labourers and workmen. Frequently, this was land that did not rightfully belong to the Irish Free State[2] in the first place.

---

2. The Irish Free State, which existed from 6 December 1922 to 29 December

The Irish Land Act of 1909, fostered by Chief Secretary for Ireland, Augustine Birrell, allowed for tenanted land purchase where an owner was unwilling to sell. The land would be forcibly bought by the Land Commission by means of placing a compulsory purchase order on it. In this way, the Land Commission unscrupulously acquired land that was then given to individuals in the local farming communities to turn small farms into larger holdings. The Land Commission used whatever means it had in its power and often worked in conjunction with smaller landowners who hoped to gain from the information they supplied.

Hardworking, larger landholders in the country were seen to be the main target of the Land Commission's activities, and Irish Protestant farmers were often the victims of this practice, as the Land Commission did not consider that Irish Protestants were the 'true' Irish when it came to owning farmland. The Land Commission did not give a damn what happened to the rightful owners, and no consideration or duty of care was expressed by it in these circumstances. Some might say that the Land Commission was no better than the Crown, which had taken Irish land in centuries past and given it to the 'new' settlers. This behaviour was little more than a legitimised form of theft on the part of the Irish Free State.

The Department of Agriculture has the largest, single collection of undisclosed, historical records in the country, and it continues to fight against opening its historical books. If, and

---

1937, was established under the Anglo-Irish Treaty of December 1921. The Treaty ended the three-year Irish War of Independence between the forces of the Irish Republic — the Irish Republican Army (IRA) — and the British Crown forces. The Free State was established as a dominion of the British Empire and comprised 26 of the 32 counties of Ireland. Northern Ireland, made up of the remaining six counties, opted out of the new state, as it was entitled to do under the Treaty.

when, the Land Commission's historical records are finally brought to light — and such disclosure is more likely to happen under the direction of the European Union rather than voluntarily by the Irish Government — there may well be outrage throughout Ireland and abroad, leading to the Irish Government having to compensate 'victims' in respect of the theft and underhand dealings of the Land Commission in Ireland in years past.

In Irish farming families the land is traditionally given to the eldest son, the women in the family get little or no inheritance and are supposed to find a husband. In turn, once married, that husband is expected to provide for his wife.

In ancient times, a bride came with a dowry, the Irish word for which is *spré* meaning, literally, 'fortune'. The definition of a dowry is the transfer of money, goods, or property from parents to their daughter when she marries and is a way in which the bride's family can try to ensure financial security for their daughter in case of either a neglectful or irresponsible husband, or should she be widowed. Her dowry is intended to enable her to continue living in the manner to which she has become accustomed. More usually, however, the dowry went into the household and, therefore, was deemed to belong to the bridegroom. A dowry was seen as something the bride brought to her new husband. Often, a dowry would be agreed between the families of the bride and groom, with the first half being paid on the day of the wedding and the second instalment being paid on the birth of their first child.

My parents were introduced to one another at an agricultural event when Delphine was in her late twenties. They must have hit it off immediately, as they started dating and married in 1951. My father said that he had only five pounds to his name on his wedding day. Before the wedding, my mother had been living in a house with Jock Ryan, at one time a farmhand on her parents' farm in County Ballynagoon. Motivated by kindness and compassion, following the death of her two aunts, Jock had taken her in and put a roof over her head after the Land Commission took Drochta Cottage where she had recently been living.

There were just four people, including the bride and groom, at the wedding. The bridesmaid was a Jenny Crighton, who may have been related to William Crighton, late of Drochta Castle, who died in 1887. It's possible that my mother knew the Crighton family in Drochta when she lived there with her aunts, Harriet and Bella. After the wedding, neither of the extended families supported my parents' union and they were, as a couple, effectively on their own from that day onwards.

The relationship between my mother and her siblings became strained, and her two sisters would not speak to her after she married my father. In the common saying of the time, she had 'turned', a term applied to a person who had changed from Protestant to Catholic.

In those days, if a non-Catholic person married a Catholic, they had to become a Catholic 'on paper' — there was no choice in the matter. The Catholic Church occasionally allowed mixed marriages in a circumstance where the adult concerned refused to become a Catholic, but no matter what the decision, the children had to be brought up as Catholics. My mother was, therefore, confirmed into the Catholic Church, but showed little or no interest in the Church's doctrine thereafter. In fact, throughout her life she maintained her ties with friends in the Church of Ireland, and she also became a member of the ICA (Irish Country Women's Association) which regularly went on outings — the women appearing to have lots of fun. This was the only activity that my mother participated in with friends outside the home, but the connection brought her great pleasure, as it helped her to continue to socialise with other women, mainly of Irish Protestant background.

THREE
SABRINA

'There is always one moment in childhood when the door opens and lets the future in.'

—Graham Greene

I entered the world on 24 July 1954, when my parents were living in the small town of Baile na Ghlic, where my father had inherited a business from his aunt. They named me Sabrina.

As a child, I had fine features and a small mole above my left eye (which older men would refer to as my 'beauty spot') and dark, natural pencil-shaped eyebrows. From around the time I was nine years old, a particular man used to tell me that one day I would 'break some man's heart'.

Some of my earliest memories from around the time that I was between three and four include those of a cattle drover, a man who drove cattle on foot to the town mart and would then come to our family shop and restaurant for his meals. He was referred to as *seanfhear*, which means old man. Years later, I asked my father what the real name of this man had been, and he was amazed that I could recall him.

His real name, my father said, was Donny Melodee. I remember seeing him herding the cattle along the street to the fair day or mart and the distinctive smell of the cattle dung on the street, which was never cleaned up. I also recall Angela, who used to help my parents with the domestic duties around the house when I was a small child.

My parents earned some of their income at this time from rental accommodation above the businesses, where the bedrooms on the first floor over the shop, pub, and restaurant were let to lodgers — mainly working men who had found employment in the town — on a weekly or monthly basis. There was a bathroom with a bath, a washbasin, and a toilet available for the lodgers' use. It was a bustling, industrious environment with many people constantly coming and going.

At times, my father would become distressed over the theft from the house of some of his treasured memorabilia. He and my mother were busy caring for me, as well as running the businesses, and they felt very vulnerable to theft by both their employees and lodgers alike. To this day, I am extremely cautious about my personal belongings when others are around. There were outhouses in the yard for tying up the horses (there is now an historic protection order on those buildings), as well as an outside toilet, which had a long chain that was much too high for me to reach, and a shed where rubbish was disposed of.

As a result of the upstairs rooms' being rented out to paying lodgers, I slept in a downstairs room behind the kitchen. This room was accessed from the kitchen through a door on the left next to the stove, known as the 'range', to the right of which was a hot water press. (The word 'press' comes from the Irish word *prios* meaning an enclosed storage space.) My room could also be accessed from outside via another door beneath the external shed. Once I'd been put to bed, I always tried to stay awake to safeguard myself against unwanted visitors entering the bedroom. I would make the shape of a triangle with my right arm in front of my face to enable me to observe what was going on around me, and I still find this sleeping position comfortable. As a child, I had a fear of the dark, often experiencing bad nightmares and, occasionally, I wet the bed.

Donny Melodee is just one of the characters I remember from those early days. There were also Louie Livewire, an electrician who worked with the Electricity Supply Board and Bill Taffy, a painter and decorator. Another boarder at the property, who according to census information was there between the years 1953 and 1954, was Jimmy Deviouss, a cobbler in the town of Baile na Ghlic, whom I referred to as 'the cripple',[1] because he had one leg shorter than the other and he hobbled along.

Deviouss was a paedophile and was later known around the town as a man who 'interfered' with little children, both boys and girls. My earliest recollections are of this man sneaking into my room at night and waking me up in fear. He would usually do this when my parents were busy working in the shop, restaurant, and pub. From the time that I was very young, the cobbler would touch my body beneath the bedclothes, a terrible harbinger of things to come.

At that stage, my parents never suspected the paedophile's motives. Jimmy Deviouss was more than willing to help whenever the opportunity presented itself, and they would gratefully accept his offer to babysit me. I still have a photograph of him sitting on a blanket with me in the backyard of the property, with a cigarette in

---

1. This culturally insensitive term was used in Ireland until the late 1970s to describe a person who had a physical disability.

his big gob. I can vividly remember the intimidating looks that 'the cripple' would shoot me when I tried to indicate to my parents, in a nonverbal way, what he had been doing to me. His evil expressions succeeded in shutting me up and prevented me from communicating in my childlike way that he had been abusing me at night in my bed.

Then in early May 1958, whilst my mother was in hospital, Deviouss took the opportunity to be of even more assistance to my unsuspecting father during his wife's absence. I recall playing in the backyard while my father was busy with customers in the shop, aware that 'the cripple' was watching me through the kitchen window. I felt uncomfortable, as I was disturbed by his stare, but continued playing, despite being fearful.

Sabrina with Jimmy Deviouss c1955 in Baile Na Ghlic

Prior to this occasion, the cobbler had shown me a mixture of love, affection, aggression, hostility by way of intimidating looks, and physical violence in the way he would grab me by the arm or hand and pull my hair. Not quite four years old, I had no way of understanding that the man was grooming and manipulating me and I found his behaviour utterly confusing. Sometimes he would show me love and then reject me, and he had, of course, been helping himself sexually to me as I slept in my bed.

I can't remember exactly what it was that I'd done on the day of the violent assault, but whatever it was, Jimmy Deviouss decided that I needed to be punished for my behaviour while my father was unaware of the situation. The cobbler grabbed me painfully by the wrists and dragged me up the stairs to a bedroom to be 'disciplined'. As I resisted, he yanked my hair and pulled it hard, which really hurt me and made me cry.

Held close to this brute of a man, I was intensely aware of the stench of his body, and the smell of methylated spirits or something like that; perhaps it was alcohol and cigarettes (I suspect that it was, in fact, the former, which he probably used in his shoe repair business.) As an adult, the smell of methylated spirits still triggers those memories

Sabrina aged almost four years old in 1958 at Baile Na Ghlic. She was abused in May of that year.

of childhood abuse for me. Throughout my life, I have never been a great lover of alcohol either. I would much prefer a good cup of Barry's tea.

The 'discipline' that the cobbler administered to me was unlike anything I had ever experienced in my short life. On previous occasions, my mother had usually not been too far away, and this had been my safeguard when Jimmy Deviouss was hanging around and touching me inappropriately. He had to be very much on his guard at those times but, as his name suggests, he was devious. At the beginning of this 'discipline' session, my head and neck were wrenched by 'the cripple', as he applied force to my head in order that I would comply with his self-gratifying demands.

Choking and gagging, I panicked and started to leave my body to escape the terror as, at some level, I felt that I would not survive the ordeal and that death was near. At the time, I was unaware of Psalm 118:17, 'I will not die but live and will proclaim what the LORD has done.' Now being violently sexually abused by this brute, I sobbed and tried to call for my mammy, but my attacker put his hand over my mouth and no one heard my cries for help. Gasping for breath beneath the man's foul-smelling hand, I had no idea what was going on. I wished that I had not been 'bold', an Irish colloquialism for naughty, or cheeky, but also knew that I didn't deserve to be treated like this for my behaviour, no matter how bad my 'boldness' had been. My overriding memories are of fear, shock, and the horrific pain that I suffered as he raped me. Squashed beneath his weight, suffocated, bleeding, and terrified, I felt utterly abandoned.

I cannot remember for how long I was subjected to this brutality by the cobbler, nor whether my rape and physical assault were later reported to An Garda Síochána (the Irish police force), or our doctor in Baile na Ghlic. I now believe that such incidents were treated as secret because of the shame attached to such an assault. That is how paedophiles were able to operate, unhindered, in Ireland at that time.

On arriving home from hospital two days later, my mother immediately realised that I was in an extremely traumatised state. I tried to show her what our lodger had done to my body, and a horrified Mammy swung into action. She summoned Jimmy Deviouss and asked him to explain what had happened to me in her absence, as my father didn't know what was wrong with me, and I was inconsolable.

What I remember happening next is an altercation between my mother and Deviouss by the hot water press in the family kitchen, while I myself was unable to move, sobbing and shaking. Mammy yelled and shouted at 'the cripple', but he just laughed in her face and tried to belittle her. The rapist was then told explicitly, in forceful, angry words to 'get out of the house and never touch Sabrina again.' I believe that my mother never shared with my father what had happened to me at the hands of the cobbler, in order to protect him from the emotional stress of the situation. My mother carried the burden of her child's rape alone.

Census details show the rapist living in Drury Lane, Baile na Ghlic in the years 1960/1961 in a two-storey, semi-detached house diagonally across the road from the Dowling premises in a cul-de-sac next door to another pub. Later, he went on to purchase a property in another part of the town and started up his cobbling business there, uninterrupted in his paedophilia.

As a girl growing up in Baile na Ghlic, I was aware that mothers in the town would often whisper to one another in conversation that 'Jimmy Deviouss interferes with little children'. This information was widely known, not just among the women but also to An Garda Síochána and those in authority. Years later, some of the cobbler's neighbours told me that Deviouss was often assaulted on the street by mothers with frying pans for interfering with their young children.

It seems that no one was ever aware of, or gave a damn about, the long-term consequences or effects of this molestation on the town's children. In fact, 'the cripple' started renting out rooms over his large property to women who, in those days, were referred to as 'unmarried mothers'. This provided him with the perfect opportunity to have complete and free access to their young children as a babysitter. In most cases, the mothers were unaware that he was a known paedophile.

Years later, there were a number of suicides in the town, and I believe that many of those untimely deaths can be attributed to abuse suffered by the victims at the hands of Jimmy Deviouss when they were young children living with their mothers in his premises. Nothing was ever done by the authorities, especially An Garda Síochána, about the paedophile's behaviour. 'The cripple' just continued to run his shoe repair business and sexually abuse young children, unhindered by the law, which appeared to have turned a blind eye to his crimes.

Although there was shame attached to it, being sexually abused in Ireland in those days also seems to have been treated as some sort of a joke. When I was an adult, my Uncle Bart who, by then, knew about the abuse, used to bring up Jimmy Deviouss' name with me and have a good laugh about his behaviour towards me, saying 'Hey! What about Jimmy Deviouss, eh?' as though it was a highly entertaining thought.

Shortly after the traumatic event, and following my fourth birthday in July, I started primary school at the convent school in the town in September 1958. The route to the school was via the grounds of the Catholic church, and I have fond memories of collecting conkers and kicking through the drifts of leaves with my feet during the autumn, a thing I still like to do to this very day.

This is perhaps one of my happier memories of that time. There had been an outbreak of whooping cough in the country that year, and I was one of those children who had developed the illness. I have clear memories of being held down, screaming, by a parent while I was dosed with quinine, the only remedy available and recommended at that time. In an attempt to distract me from the gruesome process, my parents administered the dose from a blue china teacup, part of the precious doll's tea set that was usually kept under lock and key.

As a result of the epidemic, many of the children in the new entrants' class, called Baby Infants, had begun school later than anticipated, so the new entrants' class at the school, taught by Sr Cuffer (aged in her mid-twenties), was much larger than normal.

At the convent there was one roll book for the whole school. The daily routine was that this book, or attendance register, would be taken from one class to another to register, with the stroke of an ink pen, those children who were present or absent on the day. The book was then returned to the principal's office. To a four-year-old, the register seemed exceptionally large. It had a dark, hardback cover and was barely manageable for a small child to handle.

One day I must have volunteered, or I may have been asked, to take the book to the next classroom after my own class roll had been called. However, as this entailed going up what appeared to me to be a very threatening flight of stairs, I was frightened. I became catatonic with distress and was unable to complete the task; as described in Psalm 143:4, 'I am losing all hope; I am paralysed with fear.' This failure was interpreted by Sr Cuffer as 'wilful disobedience', and, consequently, the nun immediately removed me from the classroom and dragged me by the hand down to the foyer area by the school's entrance door. There, I was taken under the stairs and beaten across the backside and the back of my legs with the leather strap which hung down from Sr Cuffer's long black habit. The shock and terror of this punishment were immeasurable, and the memory of that physical abuse has remained with me throughout my life. I was so distressed that my mother had to be sent for and, when she arrived at the school, she had an enormous row with Sr Cuffer.

Mammy was a woman of power and strength, who certainly didn't mince her words as she shouted at the young nun for the cruelty shown to her child. Following the incident, my mother removed me permanently from that school, and my education wasn't resumed for another six months. The distress of the beating was compounded by my having witnessed the altercation, which had included strong language, between my mother and Sr Cuffer. I felt that the situation was my fault, which added to the trauma of the event. Some sixty years later, I still often have nightmares about my experience at that school; my dreams are usually about not being able to complete the required task, causing me to wake up in a distressed state.

I was always aware, on a certain level of consciousness, of the traumatic events in my early life. However, as the years passed, I thought I had put them out of my head and moved on with life. In reality, I had only suppressed the experiences.

FOUR
A MOVE TO THE COUNTRY

For I know the plans I have for you, declares the LORD,
*plans to prosper you and not to harm you, plans to give you
hope and a future.*

—Jeremiah 29:11

In March 1959, after my father inherited a farm from his uncle, the family moved out to the country. I was almost five years old at the time, and I felt relieved to be moving away from Baile na Ghlic, leaving behind the traumatic events of the first four years of my life.

My memories of the move — about which I was excited — are of being in the Volkswagen ute, or pick-up truck, belonging to Wallace, a neighbour in the country. The vehicle had a flat front like a van and I, who was only used to driving in a car with a bonnet, was gripped by fear of an accident as the ute nosed up to the cast-iron front gates of the farm when we arrived at our destination.

The farmhouse was whitewashed and traditionally thatched with natural reed and grass which, when finely cut, dried, and installed, formed a waterproof roof.[1] Irish thatched cottages are based on a simple, rectangular plan, and the walls were very thick and built with stones found locally, pieced together in interlocking fashion, then covered with a mud plaster and whitewashed. There was an exceptionally large iron key for the front door and a half, or 'stable' door at the back of the house, another traditional feature in Ireland. As I was to discover, the chickens and pigs wandered around freely outside, no doubt hoping that some scraps would be thrown out to them from this half door following a meal.

Released from the somewhat terrifying vehicle, I went inside and looked around the house to check the 'lay of the land', so to speak, as I wanted to ensure my safety in this new environment. Coming inside, I found that the ceiling was thatch. (Sometimes loose bits of the underside of this would fall into the living room.) A long wooden table covered with an oilcloth stood in the middle of the floor. There was a dirty, stained teacup and saucer on it, and *cruiskeens* (jugs) full of souring milk lined the dresser. My first impression was that the smell here was somewhat different from the house in the town.

There was an old man in the house; his name was Jake, and he was my father's maternal uncle, whom the family had come to live with. Uncle Jake continued to reside at the farm and, thinking back, I believe that one of my father's unmarried aunts or uncles must have recently died, leaving Jake alone and that he had decided that it was time to 'look after' his nephew and his family. Uncle Jake was very elderly, but he was a kind and gentle man who grew extremely fond of me. He had never married and was

---

1. The most durable thatching material is water reed (Phragmites australis) which can last up to sixty years, though in Ireland thirty years is a more typical duration.

the last surviving member of his family in that generation. He had his own bedroom in the farmhouse and, later, I used to stand in there and watch in amazement as he shaved with his cut-throat razor, sharpening the blade on a leather strop.

Venturing into the yard to check things out further afield, I glanced around and noticed the lane, ripe with possibilities for further exploration. In summertime, blackberries and blackcurrants as well as wild strawberries and wild peas would grow along the shady lane that led down to fields, known as the 'bottoms'. Here, the soil underfoot had been disturbed where the cattle continually trod on their journeys to and from the milking parlour.

In the yard was a silvery-grey pump, which brought spring water from the well. It wasn't long before I was taught how to prime this pump by putting a small amount of water down, to make the water 'rise'. Vigorous pumping was then required to get the desired results, with the handle of a metal bucket being hooked onto the front of the pump to take the weight of the full bucket as the water was collected. This task was considerably easier for an adult than for a young child — in my case, frantic activity was necessary to start the water flowing.

Our neighbours had an open well, rather than a pump, in their yard. It was round, walled, and deep, and a bucket on a long rope was lowered to collect the drinking water. When the well was not in use, a sheet of roofing tin or iron was put over the opening and kept in place with heavy stones to prevent accidents.

There were no fancy bathrooms in the farmhouse, nor even an outside privy. Chamber pots were used and kept under the beds, and these were emptied and cleaned daily. For ablutions, there was a separate washing room, which had a washstand with a porcelain basin set into a hole in it, and a jug. Nowadays, these washstands, porcelain basins, and jugs are collectible antiques, but they were normal household items of necessity in years gone by.

Water was heated in the cast-iron boiler in the boiler house, an outside lean-to at the end of the cottage. Our family always had a washing machine. This was the old type with a top-mounted mangle, or wringer; clothes had to be fed through the wringer after each wash, achieving the same effect as a spin cycle in an automatic washer. As a teenager, at times, my long hair used to get caught between the rollers of the wringer, which was very painful, and I would have to ask someone to wind the handle backwards to release me! The washing machine also sometimes doubled as a type of early dishwasher for the family, as the dirty dishes were often hidden in it until my mother had time to do the washing-up.

The old stone cottage had an open fire with hobs on either side of the fireplace. A movable crane with hooks attached, from which pots were hung for cooking food and baking the bread, was a permanent fixture over the fireplace. There were two stone seats each side of the fireplace, beneath which were two holes, referred to as the 'ash holes', into which the ash was swept when the embers had cooled. In the beginning, bread was baked on the open fire in the cast iron baker with coals placed on the lid with large, long-handled tongs, to aid the cooking process; both homemade bread and bought white bread were toasted with long toasting forks over the open fire. When the family sat around the fireplace in the evening, we would have to move suddenly when there was a downdraft, otherwise we would all end up coughing from the smoking chimney.

On one occasion, I was peering up the chimney in the fireplace when I saw a large bone lodged in the gloomy space, at a time when the adults were discussing 'blackleg'. Apparently, it was believed among the old farming folk in Ireland that the treatment for blackleg[2] disease in animals was to hang the leg of an animal that had died from the disease, up the chimney. If the animal's leg remained in the chimney, it meant there would be no more cases among the farmer's livestock.

Na tinceiri (tinkers) would often come around in the morning after breakfast looking to mend pots and pans for a small fee and asking for food scraps for their children. A baby was usually carried under the woman's shawl, secured close to the mother's body, similar to being carried in a baby wrap today. These women always appeared to be pregnant; sometimes they must have been, but at other times they'd be carrying their latest newborn. Ten to ten in the morning was known as 'tinkers time'.

My parents were generally self-sufficient. They grew their own vegetables, milked their own cows, and occasionally they would churn butter, so the only thing that was bought for dinner was meat. Hens, ducks, and turkeys were raised on the farm, meaning there were always plenty of eggs to eat.

We had a car, a white Ford Anglia, and I can still remember the registration number, which was FI 3707. My parents and I would pile into the car (no seat belts were worn in those days) when we needed to go to church or on other such outings. I always wanted to be allowed to shut the gate as we left the property. On one occasion, Mammy decided to close the gate herself and, in the process, she stepped on a pair of old-fashioned hand sheep shears that had been left in the long grass, possibly by me. The blade went through her leg, in one side and out the other.

I would often listen in on my parents' conversations and for years I wondered why my father would ask my mother 'are you fond of me?' It was only much later that I understood that what he

---

2. An infectious disease fatal to cattle, sheep, and goats, which is most commonly caused by a gram-positive bacterium, *Clostridium chauvoei*.

had actually been saying to her was, 'Do you follow me?' From what I can recall, most of the conversations were about finances.

My mother came from a highly gifted musical family, and she encouraged me in song and dance. We had a radiogram, or radio, and my mother would also play the harmonica in the car on family outings, even when driving, while I sang along with her on the journey.

My recollection of my mother is of an attractive woman with brown eyes and straight, dark hair that she wore tied up at the back in a bun or similar style. She wore little makeup, just powder and a little rouge, and lipstick. One day, she got fed up with her long hair and just cut it off herself, without going to the hairdresser. I was shocked to see my mother looking so different with her new, short hairdo. She was a woman who took care of her appearance, wearing lace-trimmed blouses and skirts or sometimes what she referred to as a 'costume', which was a skirt with matching jacket — but never trousers — with high-heeled shoes. In keeping with the times, when going to town she would put on a headscarf. She had a fur coat, which she wore in winter with a hat.

Having inherited the farm in addition to the business, my father was, in Irish terminology, 'taken care of' and was considered to be well set up for the future. However, he had little or no experience with farming, even though he had been the eldest child on his parents' farm. Because he had been promised to the priesthood at an early age, his future had been mapped out for him in a different direction. He had grown to be an intellectual who had little or no interest in farming and hardly any experience on the land. So it was that, when our family moved to the country to take up residence on the inherited farm, most of the farming responsibility fell on my mother.

Mammy was industrious and hard-working and had been brought up on a farm so would have been very experienced in its day-to-day running. This was fortunate for Daddy, as he didn't like to get his hands dirty. He used to say that he 'suffered from his nerves'. However, my mother did not keep particularly good health either. She had a heart condition, which she often blamed on the fact that she had been expected to lift a younger sibling, who had developed childhood rheumatoid arthritis, from his bed.

As far as paid work goes, my mother may once have had a live-in housekeeping job for a Church of Ireland (Anglican) family in the south of the county, but that is all I know about her working life outside of her extensive family commitments. My parents would go off to town on the first Tuesday of the month to collect the state-paid children's allowance, or when the regular cheque was issued by the creamery in respect of the milk. As I was quite young, I would stay behind with Uncle Jake on the farm in their absence. Leaving children aged eleven or twelve at home alone was common practice in Ireland then.

Usually, when my parents returned, I would look forward to getting something special to eat such as chocolate or biscuits, or perhaps a new item of clothing. The breadman, Winston, from the village of Kane, came every Tuesday and Friday in the company of his elderly father, making rural deliveries. My mother bought two loaves of white bread and cream buns on both of those days. There was fish on Winston's van on Fridays, and doughnuts as a treat. When I was young, many Irish families would eat fish on a Friday, in keeping with the Catholic tradition of avoiding meat on that day[3]. For some reason, I took a dislike to the breadman and did not

---

3. In 1966, the United States Conference of Catholic Bishops passed Norms II and IV that bound all persons from age 14 to abstain from meat on Fridays of Lent, and throughout the year. Previously, the requirement to abstain from meat on all Fridays of the year had applied to those aged seven and older.

feel safe around him; I was very aware of his facial features and his unpleasant-looking teeth.

Now living in the country, removed from Baile na Ghlic and the convent there, I restarted school at Asher National School (NS). I would often walk the half-mile there and back, and, at other times, my mother would take me in the Anglia, though I suffered terribly from motion sickness. When Mammy was driving, I would often have to have my head out of the car window because I always felt sick, which was very unpleasant for me and everyone around me.

One of my favourite things was sitting on the bonnet of the car as we drove along the country road. My mother did not appear to see any danger in allowing this behaviour; in those days, there were fewer cars on the road and perhaps safety was not such an issue for country people. Soon after the family moved to the country, Mammy had what was referred to as a 'blackout' while driving the car and ran it off the road. I have no memory of how she got home that night after the accident, which was considered to have been her fault. She stopped driving after that, both for health and insurance reasons, and maybe also because the family could not afford to replace the car.

Going to school, the route went up the hill, first past Nelly's, then McNae's ruined house, and then past Tass's and Dillon's shop, which was the original schoolhouse that my mother had attended as a child, then a left turn at the crossroads and down the road, ending up at Asher NS. When I walked to and from school in the summer, the other children and I would forage for wild peas, strawberries, sloes, crab apples, and plums, both the black and greengage variety. All the school children knew what to avoid in the way of anything poisonous.

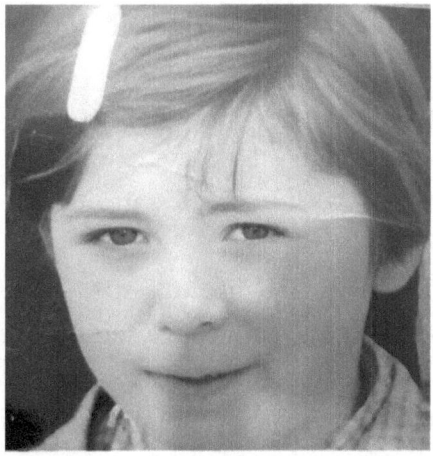

Sabrina in 1959 aged 5 years old when she moved to Asher school

Some of the pupils cycled to school, and I would often meet other, neighbouring children going to and from school, which provided a bit of fun along the way. On one occasion, I was on the back of a bicycle, and the rider went over a small bump on the road, which made me feel sick, so the next time the rider approached the same bump, I jumped off the bicycle first and hit my face on the road, leaving a permanent scar between my nose and upper lip. Another time, again as a passenger on the back of a bike, I caught my heel in the spokes of the rear wheel. I didn't do anything about the injury for a while, and an infection developed and travelled up my leg to the inguinal lymph nodes, making walking very painful. I became quite unwell, running a high temperature, so my mother took me to see Dr O'Dea, who prescribed antibiotics which cured the infection. I was very proud of myself for getting a special reward at the end of that term, for not having missed a day of school, even though I had struggled to walk with my sore heel and leg. The reward was a small figurine ornament that I treasured for many years.

As well as school friends, I would meet different types of

people on the roads in those days, including the busy postman on his bicycle. There was one particular man who had mental health issues, and, when he was released from the psychiatric hospital, he would ride his bicycle along the roads, jumping off the bike every so often to go down on his knees and start praying. Other members of this man's family also had psychiatric problems.

There were many mental health issues in families in Ireland when I was a young child, perhaps caused by intermarriage, as no one appeared to move more than a few miles away to marry, something which went on for many generations. Then again, perhaps such problems could be attributed to poor living conditions, lack of money, social isolation, and a general lack of support in the understanding of depression, anxiety, and family situations. Everyone in the locality appeared to know someone who was 'mad' and avoided them.

At times, vagrants would take up residence in a particular tumbledown house in the countryside, but I was very much aware of my personal safety. I would refuse to pass by the derelict house if I thought there was someone in there and would take the long way round through the fields, avoiding any bulls or cattle, sometimes arriving at school late.

The fields and verges were full of wildflowers, such as snowdrops, cowslips, bluebells, daffodils, white and blackthorn, red and white clover, and *nóiníní*, or daises, in their seasons, as well as brambles, thistles, and nettles. We children played a game that, so we thought, could determine whether or not you liked butter, by holding a buttercup flower beneath the chin. If the flower cast a yellow glow on your skin, that meant that you liked butter. We would also make daisy chains and place them around our ankles and wrists to adorn ourselves.

It was said that nettles were plentiful in an area where someone had been buried in ancient times and that the nettles were, therefore, very nutritious and healthy for human consumption. They were used as a tea or as a green vegetable, prepared like cabbage. When stung by a nettle, my skin would react and produce welts, and I would frantically rub dock leaves on the area to relieve the pain and swelling. I learned that if I quickly pinched the nettle leaf between my fingers, instead of gently touching it, I wouldn't get stung.

The teachers at Asher School were Mrs Liffey, a kind, elderly lady and the headmaster, Mr Jones who, as far as I could make out, seemed to drive a long distance every day to and from school. However, in later years, I discovered that the journey had probably been no longer than 20 minutes by car. When Mrs Liffey retired, Mrs O'Neill became the replacement teacher. She was a widow with three particularly well-dressed, well-nourished children who attended the school. The family lived in a new house outside the local village, on a farm that Mrs O'Neill had 'set', or rented out, to local farmers until the day that her only son would inherit the property.

Asher schoolhouse had two classrooms with a retractable partition dividing them. The partition could be pushed back when required for school gatherings and other such functions. My earliest memories from that time include taking tea to school in old HP glass sauce bottles. The bottles were lined up in front of the safety fender by the open fire, keeping the tea warm until it was drunk at lunchtime.

The open fire was the only form of heating in the school, and during the winter it was lit early in the morning by the caretaker who lived next door so that the teachers and pupils would arrive at school to a warm classroom. Mrs Liffey had what I called 'ABC' legs, mottled with red marks from standing in front of the open fire and, worse, those legs had a distinctive smell which I did not particularly like!

At the beginning of the day, pupils were expected to line up in silence once the bell had been rung and enter class in a line, before hanging a *mala scoile* (school bag) and coat on a peg in the hallway. In class, we sat side by side at wooden desks arranged one behind the other. The desks had built-in inkwells, and we wrote with nibbed pens, using blotting paper to dry the ink on the writing paper. No communication among pupils was allowed in class. As well as the usual primary school subjects like reading, writing, and arithmetic, the girls were taught to sew, knit, and embroider as part of the curriculum, whilst the boys did other tasks that were considered suitably male skills. Perhaps woodwork was one of these, though I do not remember precisely what gender-specific subjects the boys learned.

Lessons were taught in English. Irish or Gaeilge was a separate subject, as were mathematics, geography, history, and singing. There was no art or physical education (PE); children had to use playtime as a form of exercise. In addition, there was Catholic religious instruction which included learning Catechism. Fr O'Rowdy, the diocesan inspector, usually came and examined the children in this subject before such events as First Holy Communion or Confirmation. If one of us got the answer to a question wrong, he would pull that child's cheek, as a form of humiliation — something that once happened to me. In later years, I learned that this Fr O'Rowdy had been accused of sexual misconduct towards children.

Sos, meaning a break or rest time, lasted about ten to fifteen minutes in both the morning and afternoon. There was a half-hour break for lunch, that was known as lunch or lón (lunch in Irish). The girls and boys had separate playgrounds, and they were not allowed to mix except in class. Skipping, Queenio, and rounders[4]

---

4. Rounders has been played in England since Tudor times, with the earliest

were the girls' favourite games. The boys mainly played Cowboys and Indians, as well as lots of fighting and boxing matches. In the game Queenio, a person was picked to be the 'Queenie'. She had to turn her back on everyone else and then throw the ball over her shoulder, and one of the other players had to either catch it or pick it up. Everyone except the Queenie would put their hands behind their backs so that the Queenie couldn't tell who had the ball. The Queenie then turned around to shouts of 'Queenio, Queenio, who has got the ball?'

Often the boys would run along the top of the outside wall of the girls' playground by the meadow, trying to engage with us or annoy us (another 'game' as old as time itself!) The wall between the two playgrounds was about twelve foot in height, whilst the wall next to the meadow was much lower, probably only about five feet high.

I had a good friend called Pam, who was a Lutheran. The Lutheran children had an extra half hour for lunch break, during which time the rest of the class were having Catholic religious instruction. The Lutheran girls had long hair and wore ankle-length dresses; they had no television set at home, and I was told that they spent most of their evenings reading the Bible. Pam was a kind and gentle person, but her brother Aaron used to tease me and referred to my mother as 'Merryman' for some reason. He

---

reference being in 1744 in a book for children, where it was called baseball. In the 19th century, the second edition of *The Boy's Own Book* was published, which included the rules of rounders and the first printed description in English of a bat and ball base-running game played on a diamond.

There are several innings in which the teams take turns at batting and fielding. Each team is made up of nine players and points, or 'rounders', are scored by the batting team when one of their players completes a circuit past four bases without being put 'out'. The batter has to hit the ball and attempt to run a 'round' passing the first, second, and third bases and home to the fourth, though they are allowed to rest at any of the first three.

would recite 'Georgie, Porgie, pudding and pie' to me, which I found upsetting, so I tried to avoid Aaron in order to prevent the teasing.

This wasn't the only teasing I suffered, though. We would have a little playtime before classes started, depending on how early we arrived at school. One day, I must have said something out of place (or perhaps not!) when a big boy named McMurten came into the cloakroom before school started. He punched me in the stomach with his closed fists, like a boxer. I was bent over from the sudden blow, winded, and unable to walk. Such physical bullying was most upsetting, but McMurten was also known to behave in this manner towards other children.

As a form of punishment for minor offences such as talking to one another during class, pupils would be sent to stand outside in the cloakroom for a short time. For major offences, miscreants were sent to the headmaster, who kept a long cane switch (thin stick) in the bottom left-hand drawer of his desk. He would strike the disobedient child with it, usually on the palms of the hands. I can remember the switch being used once on McMurten for some incident involving another student.

Pupils would be sent to the dunce's corner when they took too long to grasp an idea or a concept, or for spelling a word wrongly, or even just if they were slow learners. In the dunce's corner, the child had to face the wall with their back to the rest of the room and not look around or make eye contact with anyone in class for a certain period. Sometimes, their classmates would tease the child at lunchtime by chanting 'Dunce, Duncey D, doesn't know his ABC.'

When it came to being excused, we would have to raise a hand and then stand up to ask the *múinteoir* (teacher) for permission to go to the toilet 'as Gaeilge', '*An bhfuil cead agam dul amach go dtí an leithreas, más é do thoil?'* — 'Do I have permission to go outside to the toilet, if it is your will?' The outside toilets were 'long drops', and the toilet paper consisted of old newspaper pieces cut into squares and threaded onto a bent piece of wire, on a holder attached to the wall. The toilets were very smelly, and there was probably a cold water tap for handwashing after toilet use. Three girls' cubicles were located quite some distance from the classrooms, by the back wall of the playground on the left-hand side of the school building.

Each time I went out there alone, I felt somewhat fearful as I entered the cold, eerie concrete toilet block. I worried that there might be someone hiding in one of the cubicles, waiting to harm or frighten me, which, given my history, was perhaps unsurprising. Luckily, nothing like that ever happened to me, but nevertheless, I was also anxious when walking across the empty playground on my way back to the classroom. On the occasions when I went out to use the toilet, I would carefully survey the school grounds and then take my time in returning to the classroom. I wouldn't hurry back; the teacher did not appear to put a timeframe on my absence from class.

Every summer school holidays *na tinceiri* — gypsies or travellers — would clean out the long drop toilets and bury the waste near the back wall of the boys' playground, within the school grounds. This area of ground was raised higher than the rest of the playing field or playground, because of the waste buried in there, which was covered over with earth. There was little or no concern shown for the safety and wellbeing of young children at that time, and the attitude towards the disposal of the sewerage waste is a good example of this.

There were occasional 'treats' at school, though. A circus or comedy show would occasionally come to the school, and we had to pay to see the entertainment. I thought the tricks (usually the one about the item in the handkerchief or the disappearing egg) were generally pathetic. However, those were also times of great excitement, often the highlight of the school term.

Going to the dentist was another highlight in term time; we were taken by taxi from school into Baile na Ghlic and often given spending money by our parents, particularly if the dental appointment fell immediately after children's allowance day. The taxi driver would stop on the way home at Ora Nay's for chocolate, toffee bars, Billy Bolands, coconut bars, bullseyes, and similar delights — it didn't make any difference whether we had had an extraction or a filling that day, sweets were part of the trip to the dentist!

Despite being keen on sweets — and I always looked forward to the end of school term, as that was when the teacher put sweets on our desks after we had successfully tidied up the classroom before the holiday break — I wasn't fond of sugar-lumps. When the polio vaccine was given at school, it was administered on a lump of sugar, as the authorities believed that, because most children liked sweet things, this would make the administration of the vaccine easier for the Health Department. However, I disliked the taste of the sugar, as it made me feel ill, so I didn't take mine and was not offered an alternative dose. Fortunately, I never contracted polio.

Memories of schooldays often include events that later turned out to have been of historical significance and mine are no different. I can recall Mrs Liffey announcing that Pope John the XXIII had died, though I had no idea who he was, being about eight years old at the time. I also remember being taken to see JFK (John Fitzgerald Kennedy), the thirty-fifth President of the United States of America, as he passed through Wexford on his four-day visit to Ireland in June 1963, just five months before he was assassinated. My mother and I waited with the crowds by the side of the road to wave as the motorcade went by; there was great excitement in Ireland about JFK's visit.

FIVE
FARMING LIFE

The best things in life are the people we love, the places we have been and the memories we've made along the way.

—Oscar Auliq-Ice

Children from farming families were expected to work hard on the farm after school, at weekends, and during the summer and harvest times. The offspring were really the farmhands in most families, and farms depended on and survived because of this free child labour.

In my case, I had to bring in the cows for milking, milk them by hand, clean out cow sheds and the pigsty, wash the creamery tanks, mangle or pulp turnips, snag and thin sugar beet, and cut and pile wood. From time to time, the newborn piglets (known as bonhams in Ireland) and lambs had to be kept alive under a ray lamp or sometimes next to the fire in the house in winter.

Milk was taken to the creamery every day by a large tanker driven by Mackiemo. The creamery tanks, with lids on them, had to be out on the road by the front gate in the morning for collection. Once Mackiemo had completed his collection run, the full cream milk was delivered to the local creamery for processing. Later in the afternoon of the same day, the skimmed milk would be returned, as the creamery wanted only the cream from the milk for making butter, cheese, and cream.

Because my parents were money-conscious, they never kept back the full cream milk for their own use and only drank the skimmed milk, which was frowned upon in those days. In addition, we mostly ate margarine instead of butter, as it was probably cheaper, though again, this habit was generally disapproved of when I was a child. Milk and margarine always graced our family's dinner table, along with heaps of potatoes, as part of the main evening meal.

Potatoes were usually boiled and served in their skins, then peeled on a side plate and cut up or mashed with salt, milk, and margarine for flavour, on the dinner plate. Dinner would also include bacon and cabbage, a typical Irish meal, and, on occasions, cooked nettles, vegetables from the farm, and various cuts of meat such as pork or lamb would be served, though beef was considered to be too expensive. I remember playing with the potatoes on my plate, making patterns of hay trams or hillocks and changing the consistency of the mash by adding more milk or margarine.

In late summer, we had to 'save the hay' to provide winter feed for the animals. This process consisted of first having the green grass cut, and then when dry, turning it over in the fields manually with a two-grain fork to ensure it dried properly on the underside. Then the hay was laid in rows, turned again and, when it was thoroughly dry, put into little haycocks. These haycocks were left to dry further, then turned and, when eventually the hay was ready, it was put into large 'trams'. An older man or more experienced workmen would climb on top of the hay tram, once it reached a height of about five feet, to arrange the hay into the right shape as it was being forked up by others working on the ground. Finally, the tram of hay was tied with binding twine to hold it down and left out in the fields for a period.

In autumn, the hay was brought in on a tram car and put into 'reeks' in the hay barns — work that was labour-intensive for the adults. The reeks were great for playing in during the winter months, and I had hours of fun in there. Sometimes, the hens would make nests in the reeks (as would rodents) and lay their eggs. I would often get ticks on my skin from the grass and hay; these liked to burrow in under my armpits and behind the knees, and, sometimes, I did not notice them until the area got itchy, when my parents would have to remove the offending bloodsucker. Cows also got ticks, and I would crack the fat, blood-laden ones that clung to their udders.

Of course, cutting and saving the hay were weather-dependent, and I would listen to the older people on the farm talking about the weather. Other climate-related topics for discussion included the best time to plant crops, and I became good at watching the sky and predicting what the weather would be like in the next day or so. I still rely on my own 'weather forecasting' skill, acquired all those years ago on the farm. I can recall one threshing event, when all the local farms worked together co-operatively to cut and harvest the grain. This was also a social occasion, men working as a team, children playing and the women supplying the sandwiches, tea, and cakes and sometimes alcohol.

A few years later, combine harvesters were introduced, making the harvesting process more efficient. These machines were expensive to buy, but would be hired from other, wealthier farmers. As the hiring of combine harvesters started to emerge throughout the country, it created employment and increased productivity. However, at the same time, it destroyed what had been a centuries-old annual social event for farming communities.

Once, I fell asleep during the cutting of the grain, and the wheels of the combine harvester almost went over me in the long grass. I can still remember the fear I felt on seeing the big wheel moving towards me, before someone shouted a warning that there was a child asleep in the grass, and, luckily, tragedy was averted. Once the grain had been cut, the stubble was left for the sheep to graze on over the winter. I would run through this sharp stubble and my legs and ankles often bore cuts and scratches as a result.

My parents grew sugar beet on the farm, and this would have to be thinned — the process of getting rid of weeds and leaving a suitable distance between plants to ensure that they would develop into a strong, healthy and well-nourished crop. Later, at harvest time, the adults and I would have to 'snag' the sugar beet, which meant chopping the green or coloured tops off the vegetables and leaving the root to be sent to the mill for processing into sugar. The tops of the vegetables were left in the field and were used as fodder for the animals, especially sheep. A 'snagger' was a large metal or steel knife used by the adults and children alike to do the snagging. Today, for health and safety reasons, children wouldn't be allowed to use such sharp knives, supervised or unsupervised. I was mostly unsupervised on the farm, but, fortunately, I was a careful worker and mainly managed to avoid accidents.

Potatoes were sown in drills and cow dung was put in with the soil, and a suitable distance had to be left between each seed potato or spud; the adults could use their feet to measure the correct distance between the seedlings. Sacking or bags were tied to the knees of adults and children to protect them from the cold, damp soil as they knelt between the drills, but their hands would get very cold while planting and thinning. The remedy for cold hands was to put them in warm water, and this would alleviate some of the intense, numbing pain.

Seven or eight apple trees surrounded our house, and I claimed ownership of one that produced a sweet, red-skinned variety called Beauty of Bath. There were also other types of eating apples and cooking apples, as well as blackcurrant and gooseberry bushes, all of which provided fruit for the family. I knew every plum tree and crab apple tree on the land and devoured both ripe and unripe fruit; I also collected mushrooms in the late summer and autumn. I knew when to avoid eating the blackberries in the hedges, as there were often tiny maggots in them at the end of the season. However, on one occasion when I did eat one of those maggoty blackberries in error, I was surprised to find the fruit sweeter to taste.

Carrots, parsnips, potatoes, and other root vegetables were kept in pits above ground to provide winter food for both family and animals. These pits were covered first with sacking, then with straw, followed by earth over the top to keep the stored vegetables at the correct temperature and away from light during the winter months; they were opened when food for the family, or fodder for the cattle, was required.

Rats were often attracted to the pits for food once they were opened, and it was common, even for me, to kill the rodents with a two-pronged fork, without batting an eyelid. My father had a Pierce Pulper — the family called it a 'mangler' — for mincing up vegetables, to be used as fodder, which was fed to the pigs, mainly in winter. Over the coldest months, farm animals had to be kept indoors, protected from the harsh winter conditions and fed fodder and hay in the barns.

My mother loved dahlias, and in summer she would have a beautiful display of various colours in the front garden. Old tractor tyres lying flat on the ground and filled with soil served as permanent planters on the lawns, where the dahlias flowered in season in a profusion of reds, pinks, golds, and yellows. Mammy would lift the bulbs before the winter came on and store them to protect them from the hard frost and then re-plant the bulbs in spring. On at least one occasion, she left the bulbs in the ground over the winter months, covered with large, compacted 'forks of straw' for warmth. There was also what she called a 'rock garden' with different varieties of flowers growing among the stones, as well as sweet peas and wallflowers, which she loved, in another part of the garden. A type of perfumed wild rose grew on the property, which was more for show because of the thorns that made taming it difficult.

One of my fondest memories of my mother is of her great love for her dogs. When we lived in Baile na Ghlic, the family had Gowey, a gentle female dog. Then, when we moved to the country, there was a male dog named Fellow, who may have been Gowey's pup. I have no recollection of Gowey dying. Fellow would become aggressive when I teased him from inside the house through the open window, and, at other times, he would growl if I came too close to him. One day Fellow disappeared, and my mother and I went out in the car to look for him.

We found him lying dead near my school, his lifeless body under a closed farm gate, visible to passersby. He had been poisoned, and I clearly remember my mother's distress on finding the dead dog. He may have wandered onto farmland belonging to the neighbours, who had 'Poison' notices displayed on their land in hopes of protecting their livestock from attacks by packs of roaming dogs, which were common. In the country, barking could always be heard in the distance, and the sound gave me a sense of security which, to this day, I still associate with feeling safe.

The Christmas presents that I remember being given were a doll's tea set, a draughts board game, snakes and ladders, and necklaces and rings. These were usually bought at Hickey's, a quaint old shop in the town where everything was cheap and the elderly gentleman was kind to me.

Christmas chocolates would arrive from my mother's sister, who lived in the city, and they were given pride of place on the top of the sideboard in the parlour, probably far out of my reach — for good reason. Like many children, I was told that Santa would come down the chimney on Christmas Eve. Mammy would leave him a slice of Christmas cake and a bottle of porter or stout.

At Christmastime, my parents and I would visit some distant relatives that my father referred to as 'the cock and the hen'. This couple had no children and would often be seen riding their bikes together along the country roads, like lovers. I was always given Christmas cake and a mineral (soft drink) there, whilst my parents and other visitors were usually offered sherry, tea, and cake. There was Tommy Lyon, 'the egg and spoon man', which distinguished him from another Tommy Lyon, of The Hollow. The egg and spoon man was a distant relative of my father, and there would be visits to his home, when his wife would bake delicious cakes for us. He and his wife were in their sixties at that time and had no children or grandchildren. I was extremely interested in the fowl that Tommy kept, as well as the number of eggs that had to be collected from the hens every day.

There were frequent visits to Molly Tiff's in the local village. Molly lived with her husband, Tommy, near the village square in a thatched house with a stone floor and an open fire, and I would be given treats by Molly whenever I visited with my mother. Molly and my mother had been friends, living on the same street in the village prior to my parents' marriage. Molly always wore an apron and seemed incredibly old to my young eyes, though she was probably aged in her late fifties or early sixties at the time.

It was the custom then for the man or husband always to be

known by his first name, whilst his wife was usually referred to only as missus and no first name was used. You would often hear the greeting, 'hello, Johnny!' and 'hello, missus!' called out on the street. Then, when a woman became widowed, she was often referred to as the Widow Smith, Widow Hogan, and the like. The Widow Rye, who owned a pub in the town, was another character to whom my father was related in some way. On one occasion, I was there with my parents having a mineral in the company of other children when one child, who was about five years old, accidentally took a bite out of the tall, slender glass, which broke in her mouth. Fortunately, she was not seriously injured by the broken glass, but I was somewhat traumatised by what happened to her.

There was not a lot of time for hobbies on the farm, but I remember my mother weaving a green and cream plastic lamp base cover over a nicely shaped green glass bottle. Whenever she got an opportunity, Mammy would do a little work towards the completion of the project. She also wove a stool seat for the house. Family recreation mainly consisted of learning to dance and sing, and I attended singing lessons in the local village.

The singing teacher was Laureen, who had left a religious order in 'the Great Southern Land' and returned to Ireland. In those days, many young adults in Ireland entered the priesthood or became nuns because the church would provide for them throughout life. Many had no vocation; it was seen as a way out of poverty for many whilst, on the other hand, it was also considered to be a status symbol to have a nun or a priest (or a doctor) in the family. Laureen was now back living with her mother and was trying to make a living for herself. She later moved to East Anglia, in England, where she married a candlestick maker and raised a family. I still send her a Christmas card every year.

One of the songs that Laureen taught me was *The Little Shoemaker* (though she called it 'In the Shoemaker's Shop'), based on a French song, *Le Petit Cordonnier* by Rudi Revil. The original French lyric was written by Francis Lemarque in 1917. The English language lyrics were written by Geoffrey Claremont Parsons, Nathan Korb, and John Turner, and the song was recorded by Petula Clark in 1954, when it reached number seven in the UK charts, becoming Clark's first UK hit single.

As an eight-year-old, I was amazed at how I could remember most of the words of this song so clearly and wondered what significance it held for me. Perhaps it was that the shoemaker in the song was a kind gentleman, unlike the cobbler I had known!

Encouraged by my parents, I would attend Fleadh Cheoil (Music Festival) and enter singing competitions. I won many prizes, taking awards for traditional Irish singing in both English and Gaeilge. It was exciting travelling with my family to different parts of Ireland to enjoy the best of traditional music, both on the streets and at indoor venues. I earned some beautiful certificates, inscribed in Irish with calligraphy, at the festivals, and these remain in my possession after nearly sixty years.

Dancing lessons were another of the week's highlights for me. The teacher, Mrs Doyle and her daughter, Doreen, came out from Rimelow each week to teach Irish dancing to the children of the village and surrounding areas. The teacher always collected the fee in cash from the parents prior to the start of the lesson. At the end of each term, we would perform what we had learnt to a packed audience in the village hall. The evening would consist of song and dance, with tea, cake, and sandwiches being served afterwards, making it quite a social event in the life of the village.

Most of the time, I had little time for play, as I was expected to contribute to the farm chores. I used to play a ball game which consisted of throwing a ball against the upper boiler house wall and trying to catch it. This was one of my favourite pastimes, but I was constantly on alert waiting to hear the call to come inside, as my mother would not let me play there for long if there was still work that needed to be done.

Sometimes, I used old boxes and tin cans for playing shop on makeshift shelves; I would dress up in my mother's old clothes and shoes and get carried away with all sorts of games including shopping and other imaginary play, which I enjoyed very much. I owned few dolls, but I do remember having two that Mammy had named Nina and Frederick. Then, one day, I became curious and wanted to see what was behind Nina's face. I pulled the hand-painted plastic face off the doll, which was made of cloth filled with sawdust, and that destroyed it — something I never owned up to!

On another occasion, I pulled the photograph off an 'In Memoriam' card dedicated to one of my mother's close friends who had passed away. I remember Mammy being upset about this, but, again, I never owned up to the damage as I had only wanted to see what the photograph had underneath it, and I hadn't done it with destructive motives. Of course, on both of these occasions, my mother must have known that it was me who had caused the damage, but she never challenged me on it.

I was not allowed to have any friends at our house to play, and neither was I let outside the gate once I came home from school. Our home was strictly private, though there was one person with whom I would play informally. Rick Dudley was the school caretaker who lived next door in the schoolhouse in Asher with his wife and they had a son, Keeley. He was, in fact, their grandson, being the illegitimate child of their daughter, so the Dudleys cared for him, as their daughter lived overseas. Keeley was a friendly sort of chap, but had an intellectual disability. He would follow me home after school and come and ride with me down the hills in the fields on the wheels of an old pram frame. I would go up to the top of a hill and get a push down from someone else; this equipment had neither a steering device nor any brakes, and the feeling of careering down the hill at high speed was exhilarating.

Adult visitors to the house were the insurance man, who came to collect weekly or monthly insurance policy money, and the occasional relative. I remember the greeting that the insurance man used to give on arrival, which was 'God Bless all here' as he just walked into the house.

If a relative turned up unexpectedly, Mammy would immediately bake a sponge cake. She was good at making these, beating the eggs and margarine by hand. (I did not inherit that trait and have never been able to make a good sponge cake, even with an electric mixer.) However, the insurance man did not warrant cake; only relatives were honoured with that. The family did not welcome the sight of the insurance man arriving because that meant parting with some of the little money we had. Often, families were manipulated into taking out insurance policies that they couldn't afford, and the only way to ensure that the premiums were paid was for the agent to go around to the policyholder's house with an insurance book to collect the money in cash.

One day, two of my cousin Sarah's adult children arrived at the farmhouse. The brother and sister stayed until evening and my mother fed them throughout the day. When they decided to leave, she took them up to the main road so that they could hitch a ride back the twenty or so miles to their home. They wanted her to buy them cigarettes, but she did not, as she hadn't the money for such a luxury item. The siblings said that they would be happy to spend hours waiting for a ride home, as long as they had cigarettes. For some time after that visit, my mother would often say, when referring to what the cousins had said to her, 'If I had a fag, I'd stay under a bush all day.' She was not impressed by their 'cadging' attitude!

One special occasion for my mother was when her friend Kitty arrived at the farm in a Rolls Royce. It was a big, beautiful, gleaming black car. I was wearing a lacy lemon dress, a new pair of white ankle socks with lace on the tops, and my shiny black patent leather shoes, all of which Kitty had given to me as a present. The shoes were quite different from my usual everyday footwear. In winter, I wore wellingtons (gumboots), which were replaced in the summer by plastic sandals that made my feet sweat, as I wore them without socks. I had a white pair with straps and a buckle; however, there may have been coloured ones, too, as the colour faded in the summer sun.

Baile na Ghlic had no such things as the 'Op' or Opportunity shops which exist today. The equivalent in Ireland nowadays is charity shops, but back then the second-hand shops were often disgusting places to visit; the clothes in them were frequently filthy and smelled bad. When I was young, second-hand items were for the poor, and no decent Irish person would let it be known that they had purchased such items for their family.

The alternative to second-hand clothing shops were jumble sales, and, consequently, many of the less well-off in Ireland would go to these to pick up household items and clothing for their families. The jumble sales were often outside their locality, but it was desirable to go a little further afield as one could never be seen wearing a garment that had possibly belonged to another person in the town or village. To avoid such a situation, the purchased item would first be dyed a different colour and then altered in some way to change the finished appearance. The leather shoes found in jumble sales were generally either too big, too small, or too tight for a child's foot, but were worn anyway.

It was a well-known fact that jumble sales put on by the Church of Ireland and other Protestant groups had superior quality items for sale, and there were more good bargains to be had at those sales. My mother would often travel around the county to the Church of Ireland jumble sales in search of bargains, with me in tow. I remember finding a white furry toy rabbit at one of these sales near Boherlahan, (the Anglicised version of the town's name which, in Gaeilge, was An Bothar Leathan, literally meaning 'wide road'). I must have picked up that rabbit and put it down so many times that the lady at the stall eventually gave it to me for free, as I had no money with which to buy it in the first place.

I used to get what was known in our family as 'ire', a painful rash at the back of my knees, in winter. The rash seemed to occur on the skin that was exposed to the winter elements, just above where the tops of the wellington boots ended and between where the hem of my skirt or dress came to. This rash was most likely caused by the cold winter weather and wind, especially when walking to school in the autumn and winter months of the year. That wasn't the only irritant I had to deal with — developing ringworm as a result of contact with livestock is a hazard for children growing up on farms, and I was no exception. A homemade remedy would be purchased from a local 'quack'[1] and put on my skin, as well as on that of the cattle, to deal with the fungal infection. The smell of the potion, which was something akin to sour milk mixed with turpentine and vinegar, was something not easily forgotten.

There were also the usual childhood illnesses. In addition to the whooping cough that I contracted when I was very young, prior to starting school, I became quite ill with the measles,

---

1. A person who pretends, professionally or publicly, to have skill, knowledge, qualification or credentials they do not possess.

running a high fever. I wasn't vaccinated against the illness, as the measles vaccine was only introduced into Ireland in 1985. I was also left with scars on my left thigh, as well as some on my forearms, so at some stage I must have had chickenpox too.

My mother was always rushing and running late, as her life was so busy with the farm, her husband, and child. On one occasion, I remember her speeding into the local village to get me to my First Holy Communion service on time. I was around six or seven years old and really had no idea what Communion was all about, so I just copied what the other children were doing and then felt bad because I had chewed on the host, or communion wafer, in my mouth.

Sabrina aged 7 in her communion dress

The Irish custom at that time was that people would give money to children on special occasions such as their First Holy Communion and Confirmation. I remember Mammy taking my gift money off me, as I would have lost it anyway. The usual amount of money given was a half-crown (two shillings and sixpence, pre-decimalisation).

In church, the women sat on the left-hand side of the aisle, wearing mantillas or headscarves, as tradition demanded that their heads should be covered when attending church services. The men sat in the pews on the right-hand side, though many of them did not enter the church at all, but congregated outside, with their left knee bent. The *caipín* was removed from the man's head as a sign of respect and placed on the right knee for the duration of the service. The men's presence outside the church was enough to satisfy the clergy that they had attended the service, which was conducted in Latin, a language hardly anyone understood — certainly not children like me.

The local grocery shops did a good trade on Sundays, as everyone would buy sweets, biscuits and ice-creams on their way home from church, especially in the summer. Often the teenage boys would ride their bicycles to the service and hang around in their Sunday best trying to make conversation with some of the young ladies outside the church. Other regular opportunities for such romantic forays were the supervised 'socials' (dances) which were often held at the local hall which, along with the church, were focal points for the community. Drama classes were also held in the hall, as well as cake and jam stalls and the jumble sales. On other nights, people would gather there to play card games such as 'forty-five' or whist, a forerunner to bridge known as 'English solo', or 'solo'.

The local GAA (Gaelic Athletic Association) was an important meeting-place for the young men. Nearly all the boys in Ireland learned hurling from an early age and played for their local village against other community teams.

On my way home from school, I would sometimes drop in to visit a spinster named Nelly, who lived up the road from us, for a drink of water or milk. Nelly lived alone in a slate-roofed, pebble-dashed house with a concrete pathway up to the front door. It probably had one bedroom, a combined kitchen and living room, and a parlour, which was used in Ireland for visitors and where most of the nice furniture and ornaments were kept.

I didn't know very much about Nelly and cannot now recall how the visits started. I have no idea whether Nelly had brothers or sisters, though I think that the woman did have a nephew who later inherited her property. All I knew was that Nelly lived alone in the house and had no car, nor any other form of transport. She had a farm which was 'set', or rented out, to a local farmer, and she lived on the income from that rent.

There was a large clock on the wall, and I liked the comforting, ticking sound it made. I used to talk to Nelly about school and other such things, enjoying the undivided attention from someone other than my parents. I was a chatterbox and used to sit on a bench called a forma (pronounced 'fur-rum') at the long wooden kitchen table which had an oilcloth on it, the edges of which were tacked up underneath the table. Often, I would run my fingers along the underside of the table, feeling the tacks. I would stay for about twenty minutes, just enough time for a quick chat and a refreshing drink, and I would then leave to go home.

One day when I was about six years old, I made my entrance after school and sat down at the table, waiting for the usual snack and chat. Out of the blue, Nelly went crazy and started shouting at me, accusing me of stealing a pound from her purse. I had no idea what she was talking about and was so upset by the angry outburst that I went into shock. I left the house crying and never went back there again. Eventually, I learned that my occasional playmate, Keeley, had made up a story and told Nelly the lie that I had stolen some money. It appeared that he was jealous of my visits and tried to replace them with visits of his own (which did not work out) but, sadly, my relationship with Nelly was ruined after that.

That wasn't the only friendship that came to grief. Nelly used to get a lift to town once a week with her neighbour, Tass. On those days, Nelly had her washing ritual: With a basin of water and soap ready and waiting, she would remove her top garments down to her bra and then put a towel around her waist. When I was still on friendly terms with Nelly, I had liked to watch her do this and was fascinated by the number of 'ribs' in Nelly's bra and the construction of the old-fashioned garment. At some point, Nelly told my mother that Tass had tried to take advantage of her during one of those expeditions to town, which upset her very much. Nelly then had to discontinue the trips with him and make alternative arrangements for shopping.

Tass was unmarried and owned the adjoining farm to ours. He would go to the creamery in the morning and then call in at the pub on the way home and not return until late in the evening, driving home very drunk along the country roads. The skimmed milk that had sat in the unrefrigerated tanks all day was, in his case, fed to the animals and not for human consumption, so it did not matter much what state it was in at the end of the day. His housekeeper, Fiona, and her daughter lived with him. It was rumoured that Tass and Fiona — a married woman — were in a relationship and that Tass was probably the girl's real father. This type of liaison was naturally disapproved of by the community, so the solution in those days was for the woman to be employed as a housekeeper by the man to make it look more respectable. There was always plenty to eat at Tass' house, and certainly Fiona's daughter was very well cared for in terms of food and clothing. Fiona's husband, Shay, was a labourer on Tass's farm. I used to meet Shay on the way home from school on occasions, and I would stop and chat with him as he was engaged in fencing on the road boundary or some other similar task. He used to ask me to sing songs for him, and I would happily oblige, as I liked to perform.

Years later, when I was in my forties, whilst on a trip back to Ireland, I visited Fiona and Shay, who were by then in their eighties and living together as husband and wife again. Shay told me that I had been a chatterbox and remembered that, as a young child, I was always friendly and that I had liked to sing for him.

Sometime afterwards, I was shocked to hear that, apparently, Fiona had set up the rape of a woman in the local turf bog back in the 1960s. It was understood that the young woman was alone in the bog, footing turf[2], and Fiona informed the rapist that there was an opportunity to commit the offence. Fiona was a terrible woman when it came to men; she was sex-crazed and was always chasing after them despite her rotten teeth (which were revealed when she opened her red-lipsticked mouth) and the fact that she drank heavily. She had a number of children, all with different fathers. The woman whom she set up became pregnant as a result of the bog rape, and the child was brought up by someone else.

Entire families often helped to cut turf in the bogs. Despite the hard work, cutting turf was often a very social occasion — picnics were brought and people came together in the warm, sunny weather — before the turf was transported home and stored in sheds. Originally, it was burned on the open fire and, later, put in ranges for fuel. For centuries, each local farming family had been allocated a portion of a bogland to provide them with fuel for the household. My parents had inherited a portion of the Smilingham Bog, near Larnedore Estate. The bogs could be extremely dangerous places for children, as they were full of bog holes (about six feet deep at bedrock level, before the hole filled with water) and other hidden threats, and I remember wild raspberry canes growing there, too. Many people dumped their household rubbish on the lanes leading to the boglands, and I often spent time sifting through the rubbish looking for items to take home.

Our near neighbours were the Butterworth family, who had two daughters very much older than me and who had left school

---

2. Today in Ireland the bogs are protected areas, but, in the past, people heated their homes and cooked their food using turf, taken from the bog, as fuel. For many generations, turf was cut by hand, using a two-sided spade called a *sleán*. Once cut, saving the turf involved turning each sod of turf to ensure the sun and wind could help in the drying process (similar to drying the hay). The turf was then placed upright or 'footed' for further drying. Footing the turf was a back-breaking job and involved placing five or six heavy sods of turf upright and leaning against each other.

by the time I started at Asher School. Every summer, the Butterworths had visitors from the city who travelled by pony and trap from the local railway station in the town. In later years, they would come in a motor car with a swing or crank handle in the front, which Mr Butterworth had to swing to start it. The doors of this car opened upwards.

When I was nearly twelve, an event occurred which is etched on my memory — attending the fiftieth anniversary of the 1916 Uprising, also known as the Easter Rising. This requires a short history lesson: In 1800 the Acts of Union were passed meaning that Ireland, which had been under some form of English control since the 12th century, merged with Great Britain to form the United Kingdom of Great Britain and Ireland. As a result, Ireland lost its parliament in Dublin and was governed by a united parliament from Westminster in London. During the 19th century, groups of Irish nationalists opposed this arrangement to varying degrees, with matters coming to a head during the First World War.

On Easter Monday, 24 April 1916, a group of Irish nationalists proclaimed the establishment of the Irish Republic and, along with some 1,600 followers, staged a rebellion against the British Government in Ireland. The rebels seized prominent buildings in Dublin and clashed with British troops. Within a week, the insurrection had been suppressed and more than 2,000 people were dead or injured. The leaders of the rebellion were executed. Initially, there was little support from the Irish people for the Easter Rising; however, public opinion later shifted, and the executed leaders were hailed as martyrs. Thomas Stanislaus MacDonagh (Gaeilge: Tomás Anéislis MacDonnchadha), born in Cloughjordan, County Tipperary in 1878, was court martialled and executed by firing squad on 3 May 1916, aged thirty-eight. He was the third signatory to the Proclamation to be shot, at Dublin's Kilmainham Gaol, for his part in the 1916 Uprising.

MacDonagh, a member of the Gaelic League, *Conradh na Gaeilge*[3], was an assistant headmaster at St Enda's School, *Scoil Eanna*, and a lecturer in English at University College Dublin. He was well known for his poetry and plays and was a prominent figure in the Dublin literary world. He is commemorated in several poems by W.B. Yeats, as well as in his friend Francis Ledwidge's *Lament for Thomas MacDonagh*. In a poem rich with allegory, the 'Dark Cow' alludes to an 18th-century symbol of Ireland. Ledwidge wrote:

> He shall not hear the bittern cry
> In the wild sky where he is lain,
> Nor voices of the sweeter birds
> Above the wailing of the rain.
> Nor shall he know when loud March blows
> Thro' slanting snows her fanfare shrill,
> Blowing to flame the golden cup
> Of many an upset daffodil.
> But when the Dark Cow leaves the moor
> And pastures poor with greedy weeds,
> Perhaps he'll hear her low at morn,
> Lifting her horn in pleasant meads.

In his poem 'Easter 1916', Yeats wrote of MacDonagh:

---

3. The Gaelic League had been established in 1893 by Eoin MacNeill and other enthusiasts of Gaelic language and culture. Its first president was Douglas Hyde. The objective of the League was to encourage the use of Irish in everyday life in order to counter the ongoing Anglicisation of the country.

> This other, his helper and friend
> Was coming into his force;
> He might have won fame in the end,
> So sensitive his nature seemed,
> So daring and sweet his thought.

MacDonagh's birthplace of Cloughjordan was chosen for the anniversary celebrations in 1966. The Minister for Fisheries and Agriculture at the time, Charles Haughey, was there. He was later to serve as *Taoiseach,* or Prime Minister of Ireland, on three occasions between 1979 and 1992; he became the dominant, as well as the most controversial, politician of his generation. Lieutenant Michael Joseph Costello, who took part in the War of Independence of 1919–1921 and fought in the Irish Civil War of 1922–1923, gave the oration.

The anniversary was marked on Sunday 10 April with a parade and, as it was raining that day, my school friends and I took shelter under the makeshift stage during the main part of the event. The sides had been removed from a lorry, providing an elevated wooden platform from where the national anthem was sung, poems read, speeches made, and music played. Hidden beneath it, I remember nothing of the formal addresses, which were in the Irish language, but the atmosphere with such illustrious people in attendance must have been charged, and the occasion was televised by RTE (Radio Telefis Eireann, the national broadcasting corporation).

From a young girl's perspective, much of the excitement came from the marching bands and the music; many of the children had been given flags to carry and the pubs in Cloughjordan were doing a roaring trade. With no money in my pocket to spend, I watched the festivities around me and enjoyed being in the thick of it with my friends. I have no memory of how I got there that day, but it was probably the last time I was a relatively happy, carefree child.

SIX
TRAGEDY HITS

Had I the heavens' embroidered cloths,
Enwrought with golden and silver light,
The blue and the dim and the dark cloths
Of night and light and the half light,
I would spread the cloths under your feet:
But I, being poor, have only my dreams;
I have spread my dreams under your feet;
Tread softly because you tread on my dreams.

—WILLIAM BUTLER YEATS

My mother had been diagnosed with a faulty heart valve when I was nearly four years old and we were still living in town. My memories of this are vague; I remember that an aunt came to the house to help look after me while Mammy was in hospital following a cardiac arrest, around mid-1958.

My mother suffered a second cardiac event sometime after the family had moved to live in the country. I can't remember much about that either, except that neighbours told me that my mother was unwell and would 'be home from hospital soon'. At that time, Mammy was under the care of Dr Leonard at the local hospital and was on prescribed medication for her heart condition.

The only way by which I can roughly date that event is a seemingly insignificant thing: I had accidentally left a pink comb and cover on the left pillar by the entrance gate to our house and forgotten about it because of Mammy's illness. When I later found it, the sun had faded the comb to a paler pink, so the second heart attack must have occurred in the summertime.

Neither of these events, however, had prepared our family for the tragedy that was to come out of the blue one June evening in 1966. That morning, my mother had got a car ride to town with Mr Heath, a gentleman from the village whom she had known since her Church of Ireland days, to do grocery shopping, as by now we had no motor car following an earlier crash.

Earlier in the day, my mother had made a swipe at me with her hand for being cheeky, or 'back answering' her as it was known — I was almost twelve at the time. Mammy missed hitting me on the hand and only clipped the little finger on my right hand in the process, which stung a little. That evening, Mammy complained about a pain in her left arm, but went out to the fields to do some work.

I was busy with my own farm chores, feeding the pigs followed by setting the table for supper. (Dinner was usually eaten around midday on weekends on the farm.) I would always follow a process for setting the table, repeating to myself, 'bread, butter, milk, sugar, salt, pepper, knife, fork, spoon' so that I'd remember to put everything that was needed on the table. As it had been my mother's shopping day, I had helped myself to some biscuits when no one was watching and felt a little guilty for having eaten them without permission.

Then a neighbouring farmer, Mr Wallace, knocked at the door, saying he wanted to pay my mother for an animal he had recently purchased from her. This presented me with a dilemma. I knew that Mammy would want the money, but she did not like to be seen doing farm work, as it would, in her own words, 'show up' my father and embarrass him, something she didn't want to do to her husband.

However, I decided to take Wallace down the field anyway to find my mother, in order that he could hand over the welcome cash. On the way down, we had just met my father driving a horse and cart, when we became aware of a commotion in a distant field. Still wondering whether I was doing the right thing, I started humming a song to drown the noise, as I thought that the disturbance might be Mammy singing while working, which she often did, and I didn't want to identify where she might be.

Suddenly, my father broke into a run, throwing the reins to me as he did so, causing the horse to bolt with the cart which got stuck in a drain. I panicked and, unable to help the frightened horse, took off towards the commotion in the field. I arrived to find an extremely distressing scene. My father was on the ground, holding Mammy, who had blood trickling from the back of her head. My mother had collapsed, hitting her head on a rock during the fall, after uttering the words 'I'm going to die.' My father, now holding his wife's limp body in his arms, asked me to come and kiss my mother, and then said 'she's gone.'

Absolutely terrified and in a state of denial, I cried 'No, no, no!' as I whirled around and took off, running blindly through our own farm and then across a neighbouring farm to the nearest house, to raise the alarm. I covered a distance of about half a mile in my distress and arrived at Tass and Mrs Fiona's house to inform them that my mother was lying dead in the field.

Fiona tried to reassure me by insisting that everything would be fine, saying Mammy had probably just fainted and would be better by tomorrow. I, distraught, was adamant that this was not the case and kept insisting, 'No, no, no, she is dead.' Fiona continued assuring me that my mother would be home from hospital tomorrow, but I knew better and did not believe her, and Fiona's insistence that Mammy would be fine only added to my despair. I remained at Tass and Fiona's house until late that evening and clearly remember staring at the rail on the front of the cream-coloured AGA cooking range which was also used for drying tea towels or airing clothes. I must have been gazing at it in a traumatised state, for hours, all alone in the house, as the occupants had gone to help my father. Later that night, I found myself back in my own home, but with no memory of how I'd got there. Of course, I wanted to know whether my mother had indeed died, or just fainted, and was told that she had died.

A dark, heavy weight descended on me as the enormity of the situation sank in. Apparently, I then started screaming, my emotions having taken over. Later, I thought to myself that lying to children, trying to hide the truth from them in such circumstances, was not the best reaction. The next thing I remember is my father sitting on the settle bed (a wooden sofa box that could be converted into a bed at night) by the kitchen table, with tears streaming down his face. He appeared to be in shock and consumed with grief.

The horse and cart were used to bring Mammy up from the fields to the yard, where an ambulance was waiting. Her body had been thrown on the back of the cart, like a dead animal, with her legs dangling over the back; no effort had been made to lie her down nicely. Eamon Fraillen, the head paramedic at the local hospital, seemed to be in control of the situation at the farm. However, during this time, the jewellery that my mother had been wearing was removed and was never returned to us; it's possible that those responsible for dealing with the body robbed the dead. When my father later made enquiries about the whereabouts of his wife's jewellery, he was told that all of it, including her wedding ring, her mother's ring, and other items of jewellery, had been buried with her. I have never believed this version of events and am convinced that someone stole the jewellery, something that may have influenced my own lifelong love of jewellery. (I have a keen eye for exceptionally good second-hand jewellery, which I have had remodelled into modern pieces.)

Mammy's body was taken to the County Hospital and, following a post-mortem, was transferred to the mortuary where I saw her for the last time, on the day of the funeral. I was keen to see my mother, but children were not usually allowed to view the deceased laid out. So, when the opportunity arose, I slipped inside the mortuary, and there I found my mother, lying on a white marble slab with a raised area resembling a pillow. The pallor of Mammy's skin contrasted starkly with her short dark hair, which had been nicely combed. She was in a pale blue and white shroud, with her hands folded on her tummy.

This image of my mother resting in peace was somewhat different from the one I had been carrying around in my head since the awful scene in the field a few days earlier, and I have always been grateful that I was able to see her like that; why did the adults not consider that this might have been a healing experience for me? I wept, but left without touching my mother or saying goodbye.

Ironically, the catchy Irish rock'n'roll number *Don't Lose your Hucklebuck Shoes* by Brendan Bowyer was playing on the car radio as we travelled to the mortuary viewing that day, with Bowyer and his Royal Showband singing about 'dancing your blues away'[1]. That this cheerful song should have accompanied the family to such a sad event has stuck with me all my life. I had prepared for my mother's funeral by visiting Crier's shop in the village to buy black nylon stockings to wear.

The wearing of black has, of course, long been associated with mourning and the grief of the family following bereavements. In earlier times, black clothes were worn so that the mourner was seen in 'shadow', rather than substance, so that the spirit of the dead person could not enter their body. In Ireland at that time, women wore black clothing, stockings, and shoes for months after a death in the family, while men had a black diamond-shaped patch sewn on the outside of the upper left sleeve of the jacket or coat. These symbols were recognisable signs to others to be respectful and show tolerance for those going through the grieving process for a loved one. The wearing of normal coloured clothes was resumed at the end of the mourning period, which took anything from months to years. Irish people would greet each other at a funeral by shaking hands and saying 'Sorry for your trouble.' The word trouble comes directly from the Irish word *'triobló¡d'*. The Irish language has no word for 'bereavement'.

I walked behind the hearse as the funeral cortège progressed down the street in Baile na Ghlic where my family had once lived and where I had been sexually violated, passing the front door of our now-defunct business. The custom of drawing all the curtains on the street where a funeral procession is about to pass is still

---

1. Bowyer had taken part in the 1965 Irish National Song Contest for a chance to represent Ireland at the Eurovision Song Contest with that song (though he didn't win; that honour went to Butch Moore with 'Walking the Streets in the Rain', Ireland's first-ever Eurovision entry). Bowyer had five number one hits in Ireland and was renowned for having had The Beatles open for his Royal Showband at a concert on 2 April 1962 at the Pavilion Theatre in Liverpool, some six months before the release of their first single *Love Me Do*, in October 1962.

common in Ireland. This is said to prevent the spirit of the dead person from entering the house, but many people have a kinder interpretation, saying the curtains are drawn out of respect for the funeral cortège so that the grieving family will not feel they are being 'gawped' at by the townspeople.

Mr O'Brien, who was said to like his drink, came out of his house to see the funeral procession and tripped over the milk bottles that had been put out on the threshold to indicate to the milkman, who made his daily deliveries with a horse and cart, how much milk the household required that day. Mr O'Brien sent the empty glass bottles rolling down the street in front of the cortège, which made me laugh despite the sadness of the occasion.

Custom required that a woman, once married, would join her husband's family in the graveyard when she died. Accordingly, Mammy was laid to rest with my father's family within the ruins of a medieval church where the Dowling family had been buried since the 11th century. I noticed the bones of my ancestors scattered among the freshly excavated, heaped soil waiting to be shovelled back on top of my mother's coffin to fill the grave. (Under Brehon law[2], my father's forebears were part of the Irish

---

2. Brehon law (from the old Irish word *breithimh*, meaning judge) comprised the statutes which governed life in Ireland in the early medieval period. They fell into decline after the Norman Invasion, but underwent a resurgence between the 13th and 17th centuries and survived into early modern Ireland, alongside English law. Early Irish law was often mixed with Christian influence and juristic variation. These secular laws existed in parallel, and occasionally in conflict, with canon law throughout the early Christian period.

The laws were a civil code governing the payment of compensation for harm done and the regulation of property, inheritance and contracts. The concept of state-administered punishment for crime was foreign to Ireland's early jurists. Brehon law shows that Ireland in the early medieval period was a hierarchical society, as great care was taken to define social status and its' associated rights and duties, according to property, and the relationships between lords and their patrons and serfs.

overlords; it was a tradition in that cemetery that the deceased be interred facing east, a practice stretching back in time to the pagans, who buried their dead so they would face the rising sun.)

Sabrina's family ancestral graveyard near Drom, Ireland

My memories of the funeral after leaving the graveside are vague; I think my father hired a local hackney cab (taxi) to take us to and from the church service and burial. In old Ireland, merrymaking formed a large part of farewelling the dearly departed right across the rituals, which included the wake, the funeral, and the burial. In early Christianity, merrymaking, despite being frowned upon by the Church, went on regardless. According to the people, this was the right way to pay tribute to the departed and involved taking snuff, smoking clay pipes, using plug tobacco, playing games and riddles, drinking, and singing, even as the tears flowed. Clocks were stopped at the time of death and mirrors were either turned to face the wall or covered. There was no wake or gathering after my mother's funeral; my father — who did not drink alcohol — and I just returned to the sad, quiet house to get on with our lives that now lacked a wife and mother.

Once the funeral was over, Daddy and I were left to fend for ourselves, both physically and emotionally. Sad and empty feelings consumed me; I missed my mother terribly, particularly at mealtimes and had to adjust the table settings after Mammy's death to one less place. I continually regretted the trouble that I had caused my mother on the day she died, for 'back answering'. The grief was unbearable, but I had to cope as best I could; my father and I were alone, and no outside help was available or offered to us, as counselling was not a concept that was known in Irish society at that time. My father did the best he could under the tragic circumstances, but I was more concerned for his wellbeing than my own grieving process at that stage.

Life slowly returned to normal — or rather, to the 'new normal'. After my mother's death, involvement in music ceased, as there was no form of transport, and my father did not drive. He tried to arrange for me to attend some local events, but when he organised the transport, the neighbours always let him down. I also noticed that I had lost the confidence to sing in public, something that greatly upset me after my earlier successes at the festivals. I never took up singing again, though I often thought about returning to singing lessons. I sought out a job for myself thinning beet on a neighbouring farm, working long hours. The child pay rate was poor, but I was pleased to be earning money even though I was under-age for employment purposes and was probably being exploited.

. . .

Shortly before his sister's death, my Uncle Bart had gone back to Drochta Cottage and removed the personal belongings that she had left in the loft there when their aunts, Harriet and Bella died. These included a suitcase containing sheet music[3], photographs and letters, all of which Bart kept. When he informed my mother of what he had done, she had voiced her displeasure, leading to a disagreement, but Bart had refused to return her property to her. An argument took place in the front yard of our home, just outside the kitchen window, through which I saw and heard everything. Sadly, Mammy and her brother Bart were not on speaking terms at the time of her death.

When I visited Uncle Bart's house in later years, he would often produce a photograph or some other memorabilia which had originally belonged to my mother and show it to me. Although I recalled what had gone on all those years earlier with the suitcase, I never mentioned what I knew about the items on display. Ironically, because of the strange turn of events, many of these things fortunately survived as family heirlooms for inclusion in a family genealogy book. It's possible that if my mother's belongings had been returned to her as she had wished, they might have been lost in transit when our family moved back to town, or even disposed of by other members of my mother's family, either at the time of her death or later on. Although I had not much interest in my family history at that time, I still have an old gold-plated copper bangle that had belonged to my grandmother[4], Mammy's

---

3. It is understood that many years after their deaths, a professional opinion on the importance of unpublished music by the Aunties was sought from a man known as Mankie Rankie. Instead of giving his professional opinion on it as requested, Mankie took out copyright on the music as belonging to himself; some people are a law unto themself and no one will ever challenge their unethical behaviour.

4. My grandmother's bangle appears on the cover of this book.

mother, which I found a long time afterwards buried in the yard at the house in town.

A major challenge for me following my mother's death, and for many years afterwards, was dealing with my father's mood swings. It's uncertain what triggered his depression; I'm not sure whether it started with his rejection from the priesthood and became more severe after the loss of his wife, or whether he was always prone to feeling 'down'. I think that he may have had a genetic predisposition to anxiety and depression, and that the traumatic events in his life caused Daddy to sink into a seriously depressed state. He and my mother had been married for about fifteen years when she died. Following her death, my father became what would now be recognised as clinically depressed. The mention of my mother's name would cause him to become upset and cry, so I made a conscious effort to avoid talking about her in order to protect my father's emotions. No psychological assistance was offered to either me or my father by anyone in authority following our bereavement. The prevailing attitude in Ireland at the time was that such tragedies were the victims' lot in life, and that they should 'just get on with it'. The misfortunes of others were of little or no concern to anyone else; it was almost as if such events befell those who deserved them.

On two occasions my father was hospitalised for depression and administered ECT (electroconvulsive therapy), which involves a brief electrical stimulation of the brain while the patient is under anaesthesia. After that, I noticed that his right hand would move involuntarily against his right thigh as if he were speed writing, though at the time, I doubted that he was even aware of the movement. Following the ECT treatments, he took prescribed sleeping tablets until the end of his life. Sometimes I would look at the exceptionally large supply of red pills (which appeared more like Smarties or Pebbles than medication) in the living room cupboard. Aged about sixteen at the time, I would often wonder to myself whether replacing them with the chocolate-centred sweets that they resembled would make any difference. I suspected the sleeping tablets had become simply a habit for Daddy and that it was more the ritual around taking them, rather than the tablets themselves, that was therapeutic.

Based on my father's supply of sleeping pills, I decided then and there that, as far as possible, I would avoid using medication throughout my life. In later years, I took out health insurance in New Zealand and, as part of the assessment, I informed the insurance company that my father had become depressed after my mother's death and had been administered ECT. The insurance agent said that he would not put down any reference to that depression, because, in his view, anyone, including himself, who found themselves in my father's circumstances would also have become depressed.

Adding to the stress of the situation in the aftermath of our family's bereavement was a showdown with the Land Commission. The very words 'Land Commission' could arouse fear and terror in the minds of decent people in Ireland — apart, of course, from those who were on the receiving end of their land thefts. In Ireland, as in many other cultures, land is extremely important to its people and, thus, it is often the cause of many family arguments and rifts that carry on from one generation to the next. The tradition is that land must stay in the family and, consequently, it is usually passed on to the eldest son.

After my mother's death, the neighbouring farmers, including her only — and estranged — brother, Bart, got together and collectively approached the Land Commission in an attempt to get the Dowling farm taken off my father. They hoped that, ultimately, it would be divided among themselves, increasing the size of each farm holding for a minimum fee. The group of local farmers stated that the reason for this request was that the farm in question was 'not being utilised to its full capacity', or similar words, as required by the Land Commission. The group encouraged the Commission to remove the land from Dowling ownership by enacting a compulsory sale process. Investigations by the Land Commission did take place, but I don't remember the discussions or visits to our home by their agents. Despite the tremendous pressure from the neighbours, which caused Daddy a great deal of unnecessary anguish and mental strain, my father succeeded in retaining his farm. It had been in the family for generations, having been purchased with money sent back by relatives who had emigrated to Australia and had been given to my father in about 1959 by his maternal uncle.

One evening, I was in the cowshed, baling the cows (putting the cows' heads in the bales for milking; this was followed by sweeping up dung with a yard brush to clean the floor) when my father came into the shed, crying.

'Imagine what these men are trying to do to me; they are trying to destroy me and get the land taken off me. My wife is dead, and I have a child to take care of. What am I to do?' he said.

I was extremely upset to see my father in tears and horrified to hear the story he told me, which made me feel sad, angry, and helpless. Now aged twelve, I was trying to cope not only with my mother's death, but also my father's increasing distress. Somehow, I managed to stay strong for Daddy, showing little or no emotion around him so as not to upset him further.

The neighbouring farmers probably never knew that I was fully aware of their avaricious intents. They would not have imagined that my father would discuss such things with me and, from that day onwards, the subject of the Land Commission was never discussed when I met any members of the group of farming families. The appalling behaviour by the neighbours remained my secret over the years. Although most of the men concerned are now dead and their children and grandchildren are running the same farms in County Ballynagoon, I will never forget their greed and the uncaring way they treated my father and me back in 1966.

Farmer Wallace had used his truck to help our family move to the country in 1959, and he was there with me on the summer evening that Mammy died in the fields. He was one of the men in the group that contacted the Land Commission, trying to get his hands on the land. When that proved unsuccessful, Wallace tried another tactic to get my father's land off him cheaply. He approached my father directly himself, saying, 'Tony, you are stuck (with a long drawn-out 'stuuuuck'), your wife is dead and you have a young daughter to care for. I implore you to take the six thousand pound I am offering you and walk away.'

This new approach further upset my father, putting him under tremendous pressure. He was at breaking point and felt he had no support from anyone; people were just out to take advantage of him in the unfortunate position in which he now found himself. Saddled with my own grief and feeling responsible for my father's mental health, I was unable to offer any assistance, but what I did offer was a listening ear, which was more than he got from anyone else. Daddy's trust in humanity was shattered, and he felt that no-one gave a toss about him or his daughter. The only thing that these so-called neighbours cared about was feathering their own nests.

Eventually, he 'set' the farm (the term used for renting the land out to another farmer for grazing cattle or growing crops), to a man named Slimy, who paid a minimal rent in cash. The amount he paid was well below the market value for rent on acreage at the time, as it was a private deal. From my memory, Daddy got a figure of around one hundred pounds (pre-decimalisation) every quarter. Slimy would appear, snake-like, at our home in Baile na Ghlic with the money inside an envelope for my father. Slimy had warned him in no uncertain terms that the tax department must not be informed about the amount of money that was being paid in cash. My father complied with the request. (In Ireland at that time, a farmer was considered to have no income, and, consequently, many would marry professional women — such as school teachers, nurses and the like — with good incomes, who could help them out financially.)

In effect, Slimy was blackmailing — emotionally, at any rate — my father. It was made abundantly clear to him that if he breached this so-called 'confidential agreement', he would be considered by Slimy to be an informer, similar to the times of the regime under the Black and Tans.[5] Having been born in 1912, Daddy well-remembered the Black and Tans. He told me that a schoolteacher at his local school had been shot in front of the class, during the war known as the Irish War of Independence, or the Anglo-Irish war.

If suffering brings wisdom, I would wish to be less wise.

—William Butler Yeats

---

5. The Black and Tans were constables recruited into the Royal Irish Constabulary (RIC) as reinforcements during the Irish War of Independence. Recruitment began in Great Britain in January 1920 and about ten thousand men enlisted during the conflict. They were mostly ex-servicemen who had served in World War I, and they all wore khakis and dark shirts. By 1921, Black and Tans made up almost half of the RIC in County Ballynagoon. The Black and Tans gained a reputation for police brutality and became notorious for reprisal attacks on both civilians and civilian property, including extrajudicial killings, arson, and looting. Their actions further swayed Irish public opinion against British rule, though the actions of the Black and Tans were also condemned in Britain.

SEVEN
THE IRISH PSYCHE

For the love of money is a root of all kinds of evil. Some people, eager for money, have wandered from the faith and pierced themselves with many griefs. But you, man of God, flee from all this, and pursue righteousness, godliness, faith, love, endurance and gentleness.

—Timothy 6:10-11

A word needs to be said at this point about the Irish psyche and the effect that the actions of the Land Commission have had on many families. For centuries, the Irish population suffered injustices at the hands of the British. After British Rule was overturned, this situation was followed by further injustices perpetrated by the Land Commission, whereby hardworking Irish families found themselves victims of land grabs. Many of these victims were Irish Protestant landowners and, in particular, families of landowners without offspring, who had died intestate. Neither their wealth nor land assets were distributed to members of their extended family and, in many cases, the land was taken over by the Land Commission and became an asset of the State.

In other instances where the Land Commission perceived, or was informed by the local, neighbouring landowners, that the land was not being farmed to its full potential, the Land Commission took the land and generously distributed it to others, as it saw fit. The Irish State gave the impression that it also believed that Protestants were not the 'true' Irish, as they did not follow the Catholic Church.

In the Ireland of old, tradition within families held that the eldest son was favoured by the family and usually given land or the family farm. This ensured that the family name lived on through a son and that the wealth was not split up. In other circumstances, outside the farming community, the same thing happened, with one 'entitled' child believing that everything that the family owned should go to him. This was often felt by the other siblings to be unfair, as they wondered why one child should get all the assets. Did the parents only love and care about the wellbeing of one of their offspring? It appeared that every child in the family wanted to be the favourite, or special, child. In Ireland, that favoured child often has a very strong sense of entitlement and greed, with fairness or equity having no say in the dealings.

> *... for I, the Lord your God, am a jealous God, punishing the children for the sin of the parents to the third and fourth generation of those who hate me.* —Exodus 20:5.

Emigration was often at the heart of such family conflicts in situations where those who inherited nothing believed the only way they could cope with the discord was to leave the country of their birth and start a new life elsewhere. Centuries of bitterness and family feuds are ingrained in the Irish psyche. This behaviour is not peculiarly Irish, however, as the same thing happens in other cultures, to a greater or lesser degree.

In 2023, there remains under the skin of most Irish families a degree of generational hurt, bitterness, injustice, and pain in which disenfranchised siblings feel that they have missed out on material wealth at the expense of a favoured, or self-entitled, member in the family. These perceived injustices lie at the heart of countless fractured interpersonal relationships and, sadly, feelings of resentment and unforgiveness are often the root cause of fragile, Irish family dynamics.

Throughout history, and even in recent times, family members have killed one another over such matters. Under the surface, all is not well in Ireland, despite the vast wealth it has accumulated over the years. (Ireland ranked as the third richest country in the world in 2023.) The country and its people need to repent so that the Irish population can have the healing it so desperately needs!

EIGHT
JUST GETTING BY

Come away, O human child!
To the waters and the wild
With a faery, hand in hand,
For the world's more full of
weeping than you can
understand.

—WILLIAM BUTLER YEATS

The period after my mother's death was a lonely one for me, and with the feeling of emptiness around the house I now found myself in a strange sort of suspended state when I wasn't in school or working at my various chores. There was no television in the house, which might have offered a distraction, but there was a way of watching it that I discovered and it was thanks to the Missions.

Missionary organisations around the world were heavily reliant upon the Irish population to collect money for them. They would target schools in Ireland and get the young children involved in collecting donations, using a method called 'penny prod' cards. The children would go door-to-door in their neighbourhoods and, for every penny collected, their cards would be pricked with a pin. When a card was completely full of holes or 'prods', the card and money would be returned by the child to the school for the overseas missionaries (according to Irish terminology, 'out foreign', meaning outside of Ireland).

This penny prod card activity allowed me the opportunity to visit the neighbours. Farmer Wallace and his family had a television set, and I was often invited in by his wife for a snack and allowed to watch television for a short time. Watching TV was a novelty for me — I can still remember some of the advertisements, like the one for MiWadi orange juice, with the oranges from 'sunny California'; Squadron shoes, 'the shoes with the six months' guarantee', and Brylcreem, with 'the touch, the personality' and the famous 'Brylcreem bounce'.

Another good deed that earned me the reward of watching television at around that time was walking a young boy named Fergal home from school. On arrival at his house, I was sometimes asked inside and offered refreshments by his parents.

There was also Niamh, my godmother, who made me feel welcome. Godparents or sponsors usually came in pairs, one male and one female, and were asked by the parents to 'stand for' their child at baptism. The role of the sponsor was to make the Profession of Faith in the child's name and to accept the responsibility of instructing the child in the faith, especially if the parents failed in this duty. Very few people in Ireland took this responsibility seriously; most people 'stood' for numerous children, and it meant little or nothing to them, just an honour in front of the parish priest at the time of the baptism. Niamh, a distant relative of my father, lived down the road in a house that she shared with her unmarried sister, Orla. Niamh was always kind, and I would be invited in and occasionally given the sisters' nearly empty lipstick tubes and power compacts to take home. I would wear the lipstick — which was usually red in colour — as I walked along the road, feeling very grown up.

Niamh worked in an office in town, and, in happier times, my mother had sometimes called in to see her there. Niamh would dash out to the shop and buy me sixpence-worth of sweets. Later, Niamh moved in with the owner of the business, and they lived near Softly-Softly Bog in a prefabricated house. She ended up becoming an alcoholic, but I was always very fond of her in the Baile na Ghlic days, for she was an exceedingly kind godmother. Orla and Niamh used to tell me how they remembered my mother's family and that they had been 'well-to-do' Protestants in the vicinity.

After my mother's death, I was once again able to visit Dillon's shop at the crossroads. There must have been a falling-out between the owner and my mother at some time, because I wasn't allowed to go there when Mammy was alive. The shop was separate from the house, with no internal access. If you went to the shop, you had to knock on the entrance door to the house and wait for the owner to go and open the shop to attend to you.

Sometimes, I would wait in the owner's kitchen while she completed the house chores before attending to her young customer. This kitchen-living room was an interesting place to be in, for there were clothes drying, fruit being bottled, money strewn around, food cooking on the range, and deliveries dumped on the kitchen floor, as well as dirty dishes waiting to be washed. Cartons of Sweet Afton and Players Please cigarettes were also there on display. One of the sweet treats that I remember was a tuppeny chocolate-covered toffee bar with coconut in the chocolate. Then, there were sweetie cigarettes with vivid red tips that suggested they were alight, and I would use the red colouring as lipstick. Inside the packets of sweetie cigarettes were cards that I collected and swapped at school. Other varieties of sweets on offer included bullseyes and sherbet dabs that came with a lollipop inside the bag. Lucozade was a popular fizzy drink and many of the local teenage boys, arriving on their bicycles, appeared to have plenty of money to spend. There wasn't a fridge or freezer in this little country shop, so there were no ice-creams; perishables had to come from the local village.

Our farm had a river running through it, bordering the neighbouring farm. I would often go there to catch 'brickeens' (like minnows — members of the carp family) using a tin with a hole punched in it near the rim. Binding twine was wrapped around the outside upper rim of the tin and then threaded through a hole, and this was used as a lure. The fun was purely in the catching, for once the brickeens were caught, they were released back into the water again. Another pastime would be to find shallow pools of water on some poorly-drained areas of the farm in which there was ample frogspawn. Frogs, which can breed at two and three years old, often return to the pond where they were spawned. The males attract females by croaking, the sound of which would guide me to the spots where the females had laid their spawn in shady, well-vegetated, shallow ponds. Here, the eggs would mature into clusters of swollen spawn floating on the surface of the water. I would wade through this spawn in my bare feet, a feeling that was like walking through jelly.

After my mother died, I would go down to the river in the summer, to a particular area known locally as 'the bridge gap'. This part of the river had a square area cut out, where the depth of the water was about five feet. The local children would swim and play there, unsupervised, getting a good wash in the process. It was a social time for the youngsters, and my memories are that the weather was always sunny as we splashed about in the river.

For most of this time, I was unsupervised on the farm and would make my own amusement by catching sheep by the horns and, in the summertime when I had bare feet, I would catch a cow by the tail and get pulled along through the field, trying to jump into cow patties (known as cow cakes) for fun. There was a donkey on the farm called Teddy, but he was extremely stubborn and had a habit of running into the hawthorn bushes as soon as I climbed onto his back — a very scratchy experience!

Every year on my birthday, my father would take me to drink water from the local holy well. The ancient Druidic religion placed emphasis on earth, air, fire, and water; great lakes, waterways, and springs are built into many legends and place names in Ireland. In the area where I grew up, the local saint is St Coolan (Conlon), and his feast day is celebrated on 24 July, which also happened to be the date of my birth.

The significance of the ritual of drinking from holy wells is probably rooted in both paganism and Christianity, as the ancient Celts believed that many spirits and divine beings inhabited the world around them and that humans could communicate with these beings through ritual and offerings. The pagan Celts perceived the presence of the supernatural as interwoven with the material world. Every mountain, river, spring, marsh, tree, and rocky outcrop was believed to have its own particular spirit, and the Celts venerated the spirits who inhabited the natural features of their world. To them, certain animals were seen as messengers of the spirits or gods. Sacred spaces, often in natural locations, such as groves, wells, or lakes separated from the ordinary world, were considered to be sanctuaries.

There is evidence that the Celts and their Bronze Age

forebears revered water in particular. In the pre-Roman Iron Age, special offerings of metalwork or wooden objects were often left at lakes, rivers, springs, and bogs, while animals and, occasionally, humans would be sacrificed to the gods of such places. The goddesses Boann and Sionnan give their names to the Irish rivers Boyne and Shannon, whose original stories are intertwined with the tales of these goddesses. The goddess Brighid, who is considered to be a triple deity because of her association with poetry, healing, and domesticated animals such as horses, is also associated with a number of holy wells throughout Ireland. Brighid and the Christian saint of the same name may well have been one and the same, due to a combining of the different belief systems regarding this particular deity.

During the period 1536–1691, Ireland saw its first, full conquest by England and its colonisation with Protestant settlers from Great Britain. Irish society was transformed from a locally driven, intertribal, clan-based[1] Gaelic structure to a monarchical, state-governed society similar to those found elsewhere in Europe. This established two central themes that would echo down the generations in Irish history: subordination of the country to London-based governments, and sectarian animosity between Catholics and Protestants.

In Ireland, as in most colonised countries, the colonisers and the colonised have become intertwined over generations. A quick look at the surnames in Irish communities today shows that both groups are represented. There is much talk these days about the effects of colonisation, which has produced a new offspring made up of a mixture of both those who *colonised* and those who *were*

---

1. A clan is a group of people united by actual (blood relationship) or perceived kinship, through social ties that are neither by blood nor marriage (affinal) and through descent.

colonised. In recent times, the global trend has been for people to become more vocal about blaming all their current problems on colonisation. I believe that this new, 'hybrid' offspring is really part of both the problem and the solution, being descended from both sides of the coin. Perhaps it's time for the 'blame game' to stop and for society to move forward, focusing on who we are now, as a whole, and not as segmented individuals.

In the depressed economic era of my childhood, there was no such thing as neighbourhood support — everyone was just struggling to survive. Most people worked hard to make ends meet, and there was nothing much to spare for anyone else outside the nuclear family. With my mother gone, once my father had set the farm, we had to move back into the house in town. Daddy still retained the public house licence, which he later sold to another publican, as the pub and shop were no longer functioning as a business. (No new pub licences were then being issued by the National Excise Licence Office, so a person who wanted to operate such an establishment somewhere in the country had to seek out and buy an existing licence that was no longer in use.) The house in which I had been raped as a small child was where I now found myself living again.

Shortly after arriving back in the house, something about it upset me and I became hysterical.

'I never wanted to be born; I never asked to be born; I don't want to go on living,' I said to my father.

Whatever it was that had happened must have triggered memories of the events that had taken place in the house years earlier, and I was now being re-traumatised by having returned to live there. I was so upset that my father had to hold me tight in his arms until I calmed down and my emotions had subsided. Another time, I was in the kitchen when it appeared to me that the kitchen light had been turned off from the upstairs landing. I became hysterical again and insisted that there was someone upstairs, the distress only fading once my father had checked throughout the house and found no one else there.

On arrival at the Baile na Ghlic house, I found a packet of powder which I mixed up with water and then put it in a large glass, leaving it overnight. The next day, I went to look for the glass and found to my surprise it now contained set concrete. The powder had in fact been cement, and the glass had cracked! Another memory from that time involves a kitten that was either given to me, or which belonged to someone else. For some reason, I washed the kitten and dried it with a towel, which — perhaps unsurprisingly! — made it terribly angry or unhappy with me, so I cuddled it in my arms in my bed. I really loved the kitten, though what happened to it after that, or who it belonged to, remains a mystery.

After my father and I returned to live in town, a neighbour suggested that Daddy might like to consider an arranged marriage to an elderly spinster, Florence, who was still living with her three, unmarried brothers, Tom, Jep, and Joe, a few doors away. Two of the men ran a shop and the pub, while Joe had his own shop selling small items, such as yard brushes, buckets, shovels, and seeds. Although his premises had a separate entrance door, this was always locked, meaning the only access to the shop was by way of the pub. Joe had what I described as 'wandering hands', and no woman felt safe going into his shop alone.

Apparently, Florence would not allow her siblings to bring a partner into the house, though one of the men was 'great' (meaning in a relationship) with a woman across the road. Whenever Joe met a girl on the street, his conversation was sexually suggestive. I had heard that he had a habit of molesting young women when he took them out in his car for a date, having parked somewhere secluded. Most of the school girls would avoid him because of his reputation, and I tried to do the same whenever I could. If I required something from his shop, I made sure that business was conducted in the pub area for safety. Daddy used to refer to the brothers in a derogatory term, because he considered them very mean by nature. He was horrified by the suggestion that he marry Florence, and the subject was never mentioned again.

There was a family down the road whose mother had also died, and it was said that one of the daughters got pregnant by her father. The two girls in the family always looked very dejected, while the father was a drunk and known to frequent the homes of women that he treated like prostitutes. There were such women in the surrounding area who the local men would visit for sex, though they were not necessarily prostituting themselves.

Our immediate neighbour was a spinster named Lacey, who wore bright lipstick and had a very hairy upper lip with long hairs growing out of a dark mole. Lacey did not talk to me, but would just stare at me whenever we passed on the street. Then, there was Lacey's friend, Sally, a spinster, and her brother, Hack. Daddy warned me to avoid Sally, as he said that she had 'a terrible tongue on her'. In other words, she was a malicious gossip.

The house on the other side of ours was generally vacant, and my father told me that it was because of something that had happened there years earlier. Seemingly, in the late 1940s, in what was devoutly Catholic Ireland at that time, Mrs Pincher had caused her husband great distress by having an affair with one of his work colleagues. Mr Pincher committed suicide in the neighbouring house, and from then on no-one wanted to live there. His widow always had a man in tow, though she never remarried. Mrs Pincher was extremely glamorous and wore expensive clothes and would often try to converse with me when our paths crossed in the town. However, I was wary of her because of what my father had said about 'that woman'.

About eighteen months after my mother's death, my father lost his brother, Ken, to cancer. The news came to me while I was enjoying a day out with friends attending the local annual show. I was unaware that my uncle had even been ill in the first place; his passing had little or no effect on me then, and I didn't go to his funeral. In earlier times, I used to see Uncle Ken by the hay barn, at my father's family's home farm by the lough, when I would sing him songs and have long chats with him. Ken never went inside the old family home, where his unmarried brother, Uncle Sett and sister, Auntie Loo, still lived. I thought that was odd; perhaps there had been some rift or falling out between the elderly siblings (possibly again over land — the usual story in Ireland). Uncle Ken once gave me a mustard-coloured box which I kept on the shelf above the range in the kitchen for years, and it was a treasured memory of him. Sadly, it was later thrown away when I was living in London.

I don't know whether my father was ever told the true facts surrounding his brother's death in 1968. Ken had been diagnosed with stomach cancer and was sent home from hospital, with no pain relief, to die alone. Adding to Ken's distress was the fact that, shortly before his death, his first cousin, Sarah (who felt that she had missed out on a family inheritance) decided to make a hastily-arranged 'match' or marriage between him and one of her young daughters. Sarah was fully aware that Ken was terminally ill and didn't have long to live and arranged the marriage so that her daughter could inherit his farm after his death. Our family considered this to have been a cunning ploy on Sarah's behalf. For reasons unknown, the marriage union never took place and Uncle Ken's farm passed to Uncle Sett; possibly my father and Auntie Loo got a pay-out from Uncle Sett.

It's unclear what effect this marriage proposal had on Uncle Ken's wellbeing, or whether it hastened his demise. Some thirty years later, Dr Tellus informed me that Uncle Ken had actually taken his own life, but that it was not put on the death certificate. At that time, a person who had committed suicide was not allowed to be buried in the family plot, as burial grounds were consecrated ground and suicide victims were exempt from being buried on land that had been consecrated. Likewise, stillborn babies were also not allowed to be buried there, because they had not been baptised in the Catholic faith. A *cillín*[2] is an historic, alternative burial site that was used primarily for stillborn babies and unbaptised children, but these sites also included other groups, such as the mentally disabled, beggars, executed criminals, shipwreck victims, and those who had died by suicide, none of whom were permitted to be buried in consecrated churchyards. For many families suffering such tragedies, this situation of the burial protocol would have been impossible to deal with at such a sad time. Where would they bury their loved one, the one they were grieving for? The best thing to do was to say nothing and hope the doctor would agree to conspire with the family. This is what many people did where suicides were concerned.

Despite a childhood spent splashing about in rivers, both on the farm and at the bridge gap, I didn't know how to swim properly until I taught myself, at the local outdoor swimming pool, when I

---

2. It is reported that there are well over 1,444 *cillíní* in Ireland. The earliest record of a *cillín* is in the 1500s and they continued until the mid-1800s when the 1863 Act for the Registration of Births and Deaths in Ireland obligated parents to register the birth and death of their children. There would be no more hidden burials without the penalty of a fine. Priests were also undergoing change by the late 1800s.

was twelve years old. Although I wasn't particularly good at swimming, I loved meeting other children there, and the socialising was important to me. One summer's day, I went to the local river in town to sunbathe, but accidentally fell asleep. When I woke up, I was extremely sunburnt. That night, I was very unwell and had to continually put cold compresses on my forehead to stop the burning and lower my temperature.

On another occasion while I was there, I was with some friends on the riverbank when I noticed that a man known as Finch was stalking me. This man had a reputation in the town for abusing women. I immediately left the river and went back inside the supervised pool, but I had been frightened by the ordeal. There were many such 'creeps' always hanging around young girls. A child such as myself, who had little or no adult supervision or protection from a parent, was an especially easy target.

Obviously, Finch was aware of me and, another time, he tried to get into our house. He wedged his foot in the open doorway, but I managed to close it on him, feeling immensely relieved to be safely inside the house with the creep on the outside. Sometime after the door incident, I learned that Finch and his wife once went out together to a function, leaving a babysitter in charge of their children. However, Finch returned during the evening without his wife's knowledge and raped the babysitter. No legal proceedings were ever taken against him for his behaviour, though people were aware of his bad reputation.

I often had to get the groceries, which were referred to as 'messages', for myself and Daddy. The word messages was used in different ways such as 'getting a few messages' or a person having 'messages' to do, and encompassed anything from buying groceries to running errands, such as going to the post office, the chemist, or the bank. During the hard economic times that rural Ireland was experiencing, just paying for the weekly messages could often pose a problem. To help less well-off families, a grocery shop called Pastelles (which was probably more expensive than the bigger shops) would accommodate budgeting families on a regular basis. Grocery items such as butter could be bought by the slice from a pound slab; a few pence-worth of loose tea could also be purchased as well as half a loaf of bread. Many families were grateful for that arrangement.

At Eimear's smaller shop on the street where we lived, most of the groceries were purchased 'on the tick', as it was called, or on credit. This meant that my father would usually pay the bill when he received the grazing money from farmer Slimy. Eimear seemed old to me. She wore a wraparound apron, tied on the left side of her block-shaped body, over her everyday clothes. With her hairnet keeping her hair in order, she presented rather a grim appearance — she never smiled and only ever had one, stern expression on her face. Eimear used to record the items sold 'on the tick' by keeping lists on old scraps of cardboard, which she added to with a pencil that she kept behind her ear and would often sharpen the pencil with a penknife. The bundles of paper and cardboard were stored on a very untidy stone recess in the wall until such time as the bill was paid; I was always fascinated by the way in which Eimear could immediately locate the right bundle of cardboard scraps when it came to paying the bill. Everything was added up in Eimear's head. A strong smell of paraffin oil pervaded the shop, perhaps because of Eimear's rather careless way of dealing with the stuff. A customer would arrive with an empty tin can, and Eimear would go out the back of the shop and pour the paraffin oil from a big barrel into a measuring jug, then funnel it into the tin can, often spilling some of the paraffin in the process. She would return the can to the customer, never washing her hands between paraffin oil fills and serving groceries, sweets, and chocolate bars.

There was a gas stove connected to a Calor gas bottle in our house. When the gas was empty, the bottle had to be swapped out and exchanged, the cost for a replacement bottle being in the region of one pound.

I learned to eke out the last bit of gas by lying the bottle on its side on a chair, and, in this way, we would probably get another few days out of it. The gas cylinder took up more space in that position, but the inconvenience was worth the saving in money. In addition to the gas stove, there was an open fire in the living room (which I referred to as the dining room, as this had been the dining room when the business operated). Briquettes of compressed turf were burnt on the fire, and Daddy would buy a bundle at a time to keep us warm during the harsh winter months. This was the only form of heating used in the house. Although many of the bedrooms had fireplaces with mantlepieces above them, fires were rarely lit. During the school term, I would come home for lunch. Lunchtime meals consisted of a packet of instant soup and white bread or, sometimes, cheese, ham, and tomatoes. Occasionally, tea leaves inadvertently ended up in the soup, as my father would have made a pot of tea at the same time; I would scoop out the leaves without any comment, as I was pleased that my father had made the effort to provide for me.

Following the trauma of my mother's death, I had to return to the primary school in Baile na Ghlic where I had been beaten by Sr Cuffer some eight years earlier and from which I had been permanently removed at the time. Now everyone there knew that I had no mother. It seemed to me that there was something in the Irish psyche that caused the other students to look down on me because of the calamity in my life, instead of showing care and compassion. To me, it felt as though people thought that my father had done something wrong to deserve being in this tragic situation.

On one occasion, as I was walking back to school after lunch, my headscarf got saturated in the rain, so I draped it over the radiator in the classroom to dry. (It was common for girls in Ireland to wear headscarves then.) Sr Constantia entered the room and enquired as to whom the scarf belonged, and I said it was mine. Sr Constantia asked for it to be immediately removed, saying that there was no way that she would allow me to turn the classroom into a 'tenement house'. As tenement houses were run-down and often overcrowded state apartment buildings meeting minimum standards of sanitation, safety, and comfort found in poor sections of large cities such as Dublin, I found the nun's attitude and comment deeply offensive.

After my mother's death, I struggled at school, both emotionally and academically, being unable to concentrate or focus on my schoolwork. Every term, each child in the class was given an academic ranking. If there were thirty children in the class, each student was given a number from one to thirty, based on their overall achievement. Of course, no one, including me, wanted to come last. It was humiliating and embarrassing for those children who came near the bottom of the class ranking when they heard their names being read out in front of their classmates. Not long after returning to the school in Baile na Ghlic, I was the recipient of a 'special' prize from my teacher, Sr Devlin, for coming last in class. The overwhelming feelings of horror, embarrassment, and shame, along with the sense of failure and sheer despair that I felt as I heard the announcement, are with me to this day. Once that had happened, no one wanted to talk to me or be friends with me anymore.

The school's weekly physical education (PE) lessons were

conducted in the main hall on the wooden floor, with rubber mats for protection, and the required outfit consisted of navy culottes, a t-shirt and white, knee-length stockings. I neither liked nor enjoyed PE. I never looked forward to that class, as the more physical children at the school appeared to me to be showing off and seemed to take over the activity, giving little or no opportunity to the more physically timid students.

I would often go to my aunt and uncle's house when I went down to swim in the water of the lough in the summer months, sometimes bringing friends with me who were also made to feel welcome. There was always bread with ham and tomatoes to eat, as well as an ample supply of biscuits and cake washed down with tea or minerals. Uncle Sett was a very jovial person, but he used to call me 'Stump', saying that I 'forgot to grow'. In my own view, Uncle Sett was short and fat himself and in no position to criticise me, though I never said that to him. In fact, Uncle Sett had rheumatoid arthritis in his knees that caused him to walk with a waddle, and his heart was also affected by the condition. Occasionally, he would be admitted to hospital in the city for treatment before returning to the cold, damp house once again.

He would sometimes meet me in town or in the public bar in the local village and buy me Tayto crisps and a Club Orange drink, and I have always been grateful that he took an interest in me, treating me in such a kind manner. Other times, I would actively seek out Uncle Sett by checking to see whether his car was parked nearby, in which case I'd go into the pub to meet up with him to be 'spoilt'. Sett was very generous to me and would slip me money and special treats whenever our paths crossed. Each Christmas, Uncle Sett would buy an unplucked turkey with the head still attached. The carcass would hang on the back of the dining room door until I got up enough courage to chop the head off and clean out the turkey with my bare hands, in order to get it ready for cooking. Uncle Sett and Auntie Loo's home in Drom (the house where my father had been born and promised to God) still had the open fire with hobs on each side of the fireplace. The lintel above the fireplace, covered with linoleum tacked to the wall, still had the metal hooks where large pieces of cured bacon hung, waiting to be removed when ready and required for consumption.

Years later, when I married, my husband and I took our best man, Billy T.P. Hunt, and my in-laws from New Zealand to the house for afternoon tea. For this special occasion, Uncle Sett had bought a new tablecloth for the New Zealanders' visit; I noticed that the price tag was still on it when tea was served. Uncle Sett was very sociable and made a gift to my mother-in-law of two cups and saucers, heirlooms from the family home in Ireland, to take back with her to New Zealand, where they are now in my possession.

Auntie Loo never spoke to visitors or to her brother (though she would occasionally ask me questions about the clothes I was wearing because she wanted to know the correct names for the garments). She was always positioned on the sidelines, watching and waiting, teapot in hand. As soon as she saw that a teacup was about half empty, she would immediately spring into action and refill it. My husband had to explain to his best man, Billy, that the only way he could win that game with Auntie Loo was to leave a full cup of tea (or glass of whiskey, which she also served) on the table. It worked! When there were no visitors and Auntie Loo was otherwise occupied and not watching the teacups like a hawk, if Uncle Sett required a refill he would simply tap on the side of his cup with the teaspoon and his needs would be immediately met by his sister. All conversation between the siblings was channelled through their dog, Cheeky. I thought this behaviour strange, but as a child, it was always nice to go to the house where there was lots of food and I was made to feel welcome, something that became increasingly important after the loss of my mother. When my father went to Clonlea Hospital to receive ECT treatment, I was sent to Auntie Loo and Uncle Sett's house to be cared for. I shared Auntie's bed, which had wire springs; the bedroom was cold, dark, and felt old-fashioned and dingy.

Auntie used to cycle most places, even though Sett had a car. Her main outing was to church on a Sunday, when she went on her bicycle which I nicknamed her 'High Nelly,' whilst her brother travelled to the same service in his car. In the summer evenings, Auntie would often walk down the road to watch the water and to chat to the people she met along the way. On the odd occasion she would go to town, and in the days when my mother was still alive, she pedalled the twelve miles out into the country once or twice a year to see us on the farm, bringing sweets for me; probably about sixpence-worth was all she could afford. She would stay for a few hours and then cycle back home again on her High Nelly. In fact, Auntie Loo visited my parents and me the day before my mother passed away; Mammy had baked a sponge cake for the occasion of her visit.

Uncle Sett died in 1985, and I received a monetary inheritance from his estate. After his death, Auntie Loo, now living alone on the farm, became paranoid about such things as the gas stove. Apparently, one day she turned it on without immediately lighting it. When she eventually struck the match, the gas exploded and she was thrown across the floor, the shock of which affected her psychologically. A while later, Auntie went to live in a psychiatric hospital facility. Sometimes, she would be in good form but at other times she would use foul language and I would have to tell her, in a stern voice, to 'stop that' and she would immediately comply.

Throughout her life, Auntie Loo had had no niceties or luxuries and no earning power. However, after her death at the age of eighty-three, the Irish government discovered an error by the establishment where she had been resident for several years in the deductions for her keep from her pension contributions. As a result of an investigation, the Irish Pension Fund was found to have made a miscalculation in her contribution. The error amounted to 30,000 euros, in favour of Auntie Loo's estate. Auntie Loo had had the last laugh! (The Irish government suggested that if the money were 'not required' then they could use it elsewhere, on a more deserving project. That was not an option, as far as I was concerned.)

NINE

THE VALLEY OF KIDRON

Looking back on my childhood, what a brave and courageous person I have been to survive.

—Sabrina M. G. Dowling

Within weeks of my return to Baile na Ghlic with my father, two nuns from the local convent, in their capacity as social workers, started coming to the door with gifts. They were never allowed inside and must have concluded from those visits that things in the family needed to change. One of these nuns was called Sr Lynch and, as she featured in my subsequent removal to a state-funded residential school[1], the conclusion I have come to is

---

1. The Industrial Schools Act of 1857 was intended to solve problems of juvenile vagrancy in England, by removing poor and neglected children from their home environments to a boarding school. The Act allowed magistrates to send disorderly children to a residential industrial school. Similar industrial schools were established in Ireland under the Industrial Schools Act of 1868 to care for 'neglected, orphaned and abandoned children'. By 1884, there were 5,049 children

that the pair were behind the removal. I remember travelling in a car with two nuns (one being Sr Lynch) one evening and being excited to see the bright lights of the city ahead. I was on my way to the residential, or industrial, school. Blissfully unaware of what that situation would mean for me, I enjoyed the drive.

Shortly after that, I was made a ward of the state (a ward of court) and was committed to The Valley of Kidron until the age of sixteen. While this did not seem to bother me too much, at the time, it must have devastated my father.

An Chúirt Dúiche (The District Court), Inspector, I.S.P.C.C. (The Irish Society for the Prevention of Cruelty to Children) as Complainant

and Sabrina Dowling, as Defendant

There is a Court Order of Detention in a Certified Industrial School, under the Children Acts, 1908 and 1957. Wherein, Sabrina Dowling who appears to the Court to be a child under the age of fifteen years (having been born, as far as has been ascertained, on 24th July 1954), and who resides at Baile na Ghlic in the County of Ballynagoon has been found in Baile na Ghlic, aforesaid having a parent or guardian who does not exercise proper guardianship.
It is hereby ordered that the said child shall be sent to the Certified Industrial School at The Valley of Kidron being a school conducted in accordance with the Doctrines of the

---

in such institutions throughout the country. Former industrial and reformatory schools in the Republic of Ireland were later referred to as children detention schools.

Catholic Church, the Managers wherefore are willing to receive her to be therefore detained until, but not including (3) the 24th day of July 1970. Given under my hand, this 10th day of March 1967, Justice of the District Court Assigned.

The Courthouse in Baile Na Ghlic where in 1967 Sabrina was sent to the Certified Industrial School at The Valley of Kidron, under the Children Acts, 1908 and 1957

When referring to me, the entry log at The Valley of Kidron states, regarding circumstances and other particulars, that 'The mother of the above-named child, Sabrina, died suddenly and her father was not able to look after her, so she came into care'. Other details given on the form are my name, my date of birth, admission date, date of committal, my general health — and there is then a section headed 'Sentence Expires'. The only information about my medical history during my entire time in residential school care states that, in March 1967, I measured four feet eleven inches in height and that I weighed six stone and seven pounds:

Condition on Admission, date of examination 2-3-1967, Physical Condition–Satisfactory, Diseases–none, eyes healthy, ears healthy, speech normal, mouth, throat, nose– healthy, lungs–healthy, heart and circulation, nervous system and mental condition–all normal. Generally, Sabrina had no tuberculosis, rickets, deformities or defects and no marks of injury or violence.

This was the sum of the information that was available for the duration of my stay in The Valley of Kidron, which lasted for approximately three years. The Irish State paid the Sisters of St Germaine for my keep in The Valley of Kidron. In addition, my father had also to pay a contribution for me, which was based on the valuation of the land and other property that he owned. The Valley of Kidron also collected the state-provided children's allowance for me. All up, the school was financially well provided-for from these three sources.

Whilst the residential school that I ended up in was predominantly for girls, very young boys were also allowed to live there as part of their family unit. Once these boys passed their fifth or sixth birthdays, however, they were sent away to a residential school for boys. It is understood that many of them were eventually sexually abused in homes run by the Christian Brothers.

On arrival at the residential school, I learned that there were three dormitories: St Prop's for children between twelve and sixteen years old; St Enzo's for children between the ages of eight and twelve years old, and St Quenche's for infants up to eight years old. I was put in St Prop's dormitory under the care of May during the day and supervised by Sr Turner at night. Macy was a lay worker in the school who looked after St Quenche's and the young children. She had originally been a resident herself when she was young and had never left the confines of the institutional care facility.

A photo of the Valley-of-Kidron residential school taken by Sabrina on a recent visit to Ireland. Little has changed since Sabrina's time there.

For me, as a girl in St Prop's dormitory, the day consisted of being woken up at approximately 6am to the sound of a loud, clanging hand bell. I would jump out of bed, having been catapulted suddenly into wakefulness, then fall to my knees beside the bed to start the day in prayer before hurriedly getting dressed and rolling back the bedclothes, as I had been taught, in order to air my bed for a few hours before making it later (after church and breakfast). Then, I could go to the bathroom.

From Monday to Friday, we dressed in our school uniform, but on Saturday and Sunday we were allowed to wear ordinary clothes underneath our housecoats. The housecoat was a type of apron that kept our clothes clean. These garments were made of synthetic material (a type of nylon) and, once wearing them, each child looked the same. These housecoats always had to be worn when we were in residence.

Once the dormitory doors were unlocked, we would descend the three or four flights of stairs in silence and wait for the next door to be unlocked ahead of us, so that we would be allowed out to attend daily church. Initially, we went to church at the convent chapel, but, as some children were very disruptive, that changed shortly after my arrival. The new arrangement was that we had to walk down the street at around 6.15am, winter or summer, attend church and then walk back and wait outside a locked door, prior to breakfast, regardless of the weather conditions.

In cold weather, overcoats would be handed out from a motley selection — no one owned their own outdoor clothes at The Valley of Kidron. The coats were hung up on pegs in the basement where there were also shoe compartments in homemade box shelves, marked with each child's name, where shoes and slippers were interchanged. This dark, damp area was underneath a staircase in the basement. The occasional cockroach would make an appearance, and often this was marked by screams when a child put her foot into a shoe that had a roach in it, or as one scurried from the shoe.

Housecoats were again donned after arriving back from church and, after breakfast, I had to make my bed and then perform my allocated domestic duty. I had many different duties during my three-year stay at the school: Sweeping and polishing the front stairs, cutting the bread with a manual bread slicer, cleaning the secondary school classrooms, and sweeping and scrubbing corridors were just some of the tasks I performed. Saturday mornings were spent working at the same duties, but in more depth. In so doing, a more thorough job took about three to four hours longer at the weekend than during the week. These tasks served a purpose in keeping us children busy and occupied on Saturday mornings, as well as ensuring that a comprehensive clean was regularly accomplished.

Perhaps because of my upbringing, I didn't mind working hard and was always diligent and conscientious about my work; I did not need to be supervised, as many of the other children had to be. All I needed to know was what was required, and I took pride in doing the job properly — an attitude I have carried with me throughout my life. My attitude towards the nuns was somewhat different, however.

I felt very hostile towards anyone who was a nun, because of the experience I had suffered at the hands of Sr Cuffer when I was four years old. So, in my mind, my unspoken position was 'Don't you dare, *ever*, put a finger on me again — or else!' I made it clear that I hated and despised the nuns and treated them with contempt, never addressing them by name or looking at them when spoken to. As a result of this, I was often materially and emotionally disadvantaged by the residential school. I was not given clothing, such as stockings, underwear, dresses, or similar items that other children received. The children who were favourites with the nuns (because, according to me and others, 'they played up to the bloody creeps') were referred to in The Valley of Kidron as 'mockies'. I had no intention of ever being a mocky.

Attached to the residential school were the regular primary and secondary schools, attended by children from the wider community and surrounding country areas. These students were known as 'day pupils', while the residential school children were known as 'house children'. The secondary school principal at that time was Sr Prydecock, and she would often remove the house children from class and direct them to pick up rubbish in the school yards or to do other such menial jobs. I felt this behaviour belittled them and, in a way, demonstrated to the day pupils at the school that the house children were subordinate to them. At one point, vending machines were installed in the school selling soup, hot chocolate, and tea to the day pupils. No bin liners were used in the rubbish receptacles, and I had to wash out, by hand, the dirty bins containing the dregs and slops, without wearing gloves. Another of my duties was cleaning the classrooms at the secondary school every morning, in addition to the three or four hours' cleaning on Saturdays.

When a new, larger secondary school was built, I was joined by another girl called Gemma, who helped me with the cleaning duties. No cleaners were employed by the Irish Ministry of Education, and the residential school children were part of the army of almost unpaid cleaners there. In fact, on weekend duty, I had to use an electric scrubber to clean the school linoleum and corridors before polishing the vinyl floors with a polisher. Gemma and I were paid one shilling each per week for our six-days-a-week cleaning job. This virtually free labour probably saved the secondary school, the Ministry of Education, and the Sisters of St Germaine a great amount of money over those years, at the expense of myself and other house children. In addition, many of the house children were sent out to work in bed and breakfast accommodation facilities at weekends and to babysit during the summer holidays for various professionals who 'needed' free labour. These girls were never paid a penny for their services. The general attitude was that the families were doing the house children a great favour, rather than the other way around. Organisations would also enlist the house children to help with 'volunteer' work or missionary work, some of which entailed putting literature in envelopes, addressing, and stamping the envelopes.

I was taken out on a Sunday evening, along with others, to provide free labour in the home of a Mrs Gaunt in a neighbouring county. As compensation, we were given a cup of tea or a cold drink and something sweet to eat. We were accompanied on these trips by a priest who had bad breath. Our 'hostess' had a nice house, but we were all kept in one room and transported back again after we had completed several hours' work in silence and, of course, free of charge.

It would embarrass me when one of my teachers (who wore black academic gowns when teaching) showed up at school early in the morning in time to catch sight of me working as a cleaner prior to attending class. Once, I unwittingly put methylated spirits on the blackboards in an effort to clean them, but it made them shiny. When one of the teachers tried to write on the blackboard, the chalk just kept slipping, but I said nothing and was not prepared to own up to my misguided efforts in my capacity as a cleaner.

After school every day we would arrive at the locked basement door and either a lay worker or Sr Turner (often referred to, among ourselves, as 'Turnkey') with her bunch of rattling keys, would eventually let us inside. Sometimes we were handed out a piece of fruit or a doughnut from a table set up outside; this was the only sustenance we were given between lunch at noon and dinner at around 6.15pm. I disliked doughnuts, because of the sugar on them and could not bring myself to eat them for many years after that. Following the light snack after school, we went immediately to the study room where we were supervised, usually by an elderly nun called Sr Ignatia, who was always mending bloomers (long-legged knickers) for the other nuns. We were not allowed to look up from our desks or speak during study time. At 6pm Sr Turner would arrive and relieve Sr Ignatia, and the Angelus[2] was said

---

2. Church historians agree that the Angelus can be traced to 11th century Italy, where Franciscan monks would say three Hail Marys during night prayers, at the

with Sr Turner. Following the Angelus, the other house children and I would walk and wait, in silence, in the basement corridor outside the dining room until the bell was rung, which meant that we could file into the dining room. Grace was said before and after meals. The tables were laid with strong-smelling, cheap, white plastic cups, saucers, side plates, cereal bowls, and dinner plates. The cutlery, however, was metal.

Sr Crabb would sometimes relieve Sr Turner, and her job mainly entailed locking and unlocking doors in order to allow us to enter or exit the dormitories. Sr Crabb was a miserable woman with a face on her that was 'as long as a wet week'. Obviously, she did not want to do this job and made sure that we saw, and felt, her resentment. As children will, we came up with a nickname for Sr Crabb; we called her 'The Invader', owing to the way her little finger protruded as she held onto the handrail while going down the flights of stairs. The nickname came from a popular television series at the time called *The Invaders*, which was about alien beings from a dying planet who had come to take over Earth and who — presumably, so the audience could easily identify them — could not bend their little fingers properly.

Years later, I went back on a visit to The Valley of Kidron and was met at the convent reception by Sisters Crabb and Prydecock, who both came across as charming and delightful to speak to — in other words, they seemed almost human! Sr Crabb was reminiscing about how lovely and charming I had been as a girl, but I stopped her in her tracks and said, 'No, you did not think that I was lovely all those years ago; you considered me to be nothing but trouble, and you never communicated with me, either.' Sr

---

last bell of the day. This practice of devotion soon spread to other parts of Christendom, including England and Ireland. In Ireland, a recording of the Angelus bell is broadcast before the evening news at 6pm on both RTÉ1 (TV) and Radio 1.

Prydecock was as arrogant and aloof as ever, and still spoke in her condescending manner.

Mrs Fatchatt was the cook, and no one was allowed across the threshold of her kitchen except the children who were responsible for helping with food preparation and washing the cooking utensils. In the three years that I resided at The Valley of Kidron, I was only inside the kitchen once; I wasn't supposed to be in there, but I wanted to have a look at it, because I was curious as to what the large kitchen area was like.

After dinner, the routine duties began again; plastic dinnerware was washed in sinks next to the dining room — the washing-up water looked more like tea than water. The children performing this duty would first collect the used utensils in large square stainless steel trays, then throw the cups, including the slops of tea, straight into the water where they would be sloshed around — that was the extent of the cleaning process. There was a girl called Mandela, who had a cleft palate. She was apparently told that she was no good at school, and I remember her having to wash tray after tray of dirty, muddy potatoes under a cold tap in an outside area as part of the daily dinner preparation for the nuns and the children. This unfortunate young woman was always cold and shivering in the winter months as she performed her thankless task. Some of the girls who were not considered academic by the secondary school were given domestic jobs such as looking after the old and infirm nuns and that was the end of those children's education.

When the last duty of the evening was finished, we had to strip down to our underwear and line up, wash bag in hand, at the hand basins for wash bag inspection by Sr Turner. Wash bags and toiletries were always being stolen from the more vulnerable children who, on inspection, would end up being punished for not having the right personal supplies.

On retiring to the workroom after the washing routine, we would gather for a game or, in later years, a few hours of television. The chairs were lined up in rows one behind one another such as in a hall for a performance, and we had to sit in silence and wait for the television set to be turned on. Sometimes we were just left waiting in the corridors, because Sr Turner was busy on a telephone call or something similar or had been called by her Mother Superior to go into the convent to attend to personal matters.

The short flight of stairs that led to the convent was off-limits to us children. Often, a nun would open the door and ask the nearest available child if they knew where Sr Turner was. That child was then expected to immediately abandon her assigned duty and say, 'I will find her for you, Sister,' which frequently resulted in the child getting into trouble later for not having completed her duty on time.

My standard answer to that question was, 'I have no idea where she is,' as I continued to ignore the nun. I had no intention of doing anything for the nuns, as I despised them all. The only reaction to this behaviour was that I would be ignored and given dirty looks by the nuns, who I knew must have discussed my attitude among themselves, because they would sometimes make nasty comments to me such as, 'We all know about you.'

At breakfast time, cornflakes which had been soaked in milk overnight and kept in large, square stainless steel trays, were served. The soaked cornflakes looked more like the slop that I had fed to the pigs on the farm in the country. Everyone had to line up, table by table, to receive the mush, then return to their appointed table to eat it. After the unappetising cornflakes, there was tea, which was served by older girls from large, commercial stainless steel teapots, and slices of bread and butter.

I would have carefully counted out the slices of bread the evening before and left them uncovered on the table overnight, along with one small sliver of butter per child. The school had a 'one size fits all' approach to the wellbeing of the children, and there was no such thing as second helpings or anything else to eat. If a child was still hungry at the end of a meal, so be it.

No conversation was allowed at the dining table and Sr Turner would sit at the rostrum and watch the children while they ate, occasionally glancing over her half-moon spectacles when there was a slight disturbance. In the room where I had to cut the bread, there was a small, top-opening window for ventilation, and I would often pass out whole loaves of bread or Sally Lunn (a type of fruit bread) to my friends.

Later in the day, we would sit together on the metal fire escape staircase at the back of the building and enjoy an evening snack, which was very much a social event for us. For many years after leaving the residential school, I could not eat bread, because the smell of it triggered memories of the countless loaves I had had to cut and provide for the other children, as well as bringing back other, associated memories of that time. Everything, except for the actual cooking, had to be done by the children for themselves.

Birthdays were sad occasions for me and the other pupils, as they were not celebrated or acknowledged in The Valley of Kidron. My father would send a postal order[3] in the sum of half-a-crown to me each year on my birthday, and I would go to the post office and cash the money order shortly after receiving it; the

---

3. A postal order is a type of money order used to send money through the mail. In the UK, they can be purchased at a Post Office and carry the name of the payee and the sum to be paid and may be redeemed at a Post Office. Irish Postal Orders were withdrawn in 2001, prior to Ireland adopting the Euro.

proceeds would be spent on sweets, which I would share with a friend. I often reflected on my emotions around my birthday, feeling acutely the sadness and loneliness of the unmarked event; this was when I felt the loss of my mother most. The girls at The Valley of Kidron never discussed their birthdays among themselves, so the only recognition of my special day came from my father.

All items of clothing, including underwear and socks, had to have the owner's name written on them with a black permanent ink pen for identification. Clothing went to the convent laundry about once a fortnight, and the older children then had to sort out the returned, clean items and distribute them to their owners.

When the white nylon school uniform shirt or blouse began to look grubby between laundry washes, a bar of soap and a nail brush were used to scrub the collar, and it was left to dry overnight ready for wearing the next day. The collar was the only part of the uniform that we were allowed to wash between the official fortnightly laundry times. However, I often washed my clothes in the dormitory hand basin between laundry days. I would wash my socks and underwear sneakily and found that I could get a faster rinse by holding the garments in the toilet flush, rather than in the hand basin. I managed to dry these garments at night between my bedclothes, which was a trifle damp, but went unnoticed by the nuns.

Toilets and hand basins were located mainly outside the dormitory sleeping area on the same floor, but the dormitory doors were locked at night. The house children were locked into their dormitories overnight, in most cases with no access to the toilets. (St Enzo's was the only dormitory with a toilet located on the same floor which the children could access at night.) As a result, many of the younger children wet their beds, and there was an ever-present smell of urine in their dormitory. The older girls had to strip the wet beds in the morning and remake the beds. Rubber sheets, as they were called, were placed on the beds to prevent the urine from soaking into the mattress. Children who had wet the bed would be referred to as 'sops' in conversation. In desperation, some of the older children would sometimes open the sash windows on the third or fourth floors at night and stick their bottoms out to do 'wees'.

The laundry was another place where children who showed little or no academic promise were put to work, cleaning sheets and clothes for the public as well as for the residential school and the convent. Most of this work was initially extremely labour intensive, and the children had to work hard there, in silence.

In addition to the children and their domestic duties, there were some lay staff at The Valley of Kidron too. One of these was an ex-Kidron resident called Natarleen (pronounced by the children as Natar l-e—e—n), who was in charge of the garden, the hens, and collecting the eggs. Natarleen was not an attractive woman, having buck teeth and auburn hair which, judging by its terribly shaped style, she probably cut herself. The children thought she looked more like a man than a woman and used to make fun of her behind her back. Perhaps unsurprisingly, she did not communicate with the children very much and only appeared to growl. In hindsight, it's possible that Natarleen may have had some sort of intellectual disability, but this was not something we considered at the time.

It seemed to me that the house children who had no input into their lives from extended family were often disadvantaged and got a raw deal. Those who were lucky enough to have family and the occasional visitor fared better, probably because the nuns would be more accountable for how these children were ultimately treated. When visitors were announced, the relevant child or children would be suitably 'dressed to impress' for the supervised visit. This would take place in the convent parlour, where tea and nice treats would be served to the visitors as well as to the children.

The majority of those in the residential school came from dysfunctional families such as those with alcoholic parents. Some were children who had been abandoned. Most of the girls, however, were classified as being illegitimate, or 'bastards', by the terminology of the day. These children did not know where they fitted into their family, or whether their sister was really their sister. (In most cases, she was their mother.) In such circumstances, the grandparents would be referred to as the parents, a situation that must have been extremely confusing for those children.

Many had just been dumped in The Valley of Kidron, and some never had any extended family visits or outside concern for their existence. There were no psychological services on offer at Kidron, no matter what the background or problems a child may have arrived with or developed whilst there. Such matters were of no consequence to the Sisters of St Germaine. Children had to deal with whatever had led to them being alone in the residential school, where they just had to get on with life.

When the girls reached the age of sixteen, they were turfed out into the big wide world and left to their own devices. Many of them ended up in the same predicament as their mothers a generation before, as pregnant teenagers, meaning the cycle was repeated all over again. Fortunately, for me, this was not the case. I had a family and, once I left The Valley of Kidron, I fitted back into wider society without any problems and went on to lead a relatively normal, healthy life to the fullest, with no pregnancies outside marriage, no broken marriage, or divorce.

Macy oversaw the small children, or the 'babies', as they were known. After their evening meal each night, the best these little ones had to look forward to was having their hair checked for lice and nits. As part of their so-called health and wellbeing check-ups, they had to sit around on wooden benches, arranged in a square, to have their hair fine-combed. Macy would often whack the children who disobeyed her (by talking to one another, or similar misdemeanours) with the hairbrush, which she carried under her armpit. Sometimes, she would ask, 'Where's my brush?' and the quick-witted older child assisting her would immediately say, 'Under your armpit!' causing the little ones to laugh. That was what passed for entertainment, though sometimes it was worse, such as when the older children bullied the little ones by giving them the opportunity to entertain them by singing or dancing. The young children took pride in their performances, but as a reward for their efforts sometimes these bullies would just slap the smaller children in the face. The looks of shock on their little faces were horrific; the cruelty meted out by their elders was probably a reflection of the treatment that the bullies had themselves received.

There was a Miss Brile who used to live, on and off, in a room off St Prop's dormitory on the top floor. On evenings when she was there, she would fill her hot water bottle with boiling water from the kitchen and pass by the girls in St Prop's, en route to her bedroom. I understood that this hot water bottle had a dual purpose: Firstly, it was to keep Miss Brile warm at night, and secondly, some of the water could be used for making herself a cup of tea, as she was not allowed to have food or drink in her room at any time, as per the convent rules for nuns. It was unclear what Miss Brile's connection was to The Valley of Kidron, or whether she was related to some of the nuns there, but she was a spinster who didn't seem to like children much.

I did not trust this woman, as she had once promised me and my friend Kareen that we could perform at a concert she had arranged in the workroom. However, when it came to our turn to perform, Miss Brile just ignored Kareen and me and didn't allow us onto the stage. We were waiting by the side of the stage, ready to go on, but it appeared that Miss Brile had run out of time for any further performances that evening. No consideration had been given to the amount of time, effort, and practice that we had put into trying to perfect our item. No explanation was ever given, but to say we were disappointed is an understatement — it was probably every bit as much of a 'slap in the face' as the real slaps that the older bullies would give to the little ones.

Macy, Natarleen, and May were the lay staff and did not eat with the children. May did not live on site and was the partner of the father of two of the house children. It seemed that these three women, who had their own private dining room called Montrents, were given much nicer food than we were, including thicker slices of roast beef and stuffed pork loins on a Sunday, followed by dessert. I and other children would often volunteer to serve them, in the hope that there might be some decent scraps left on the plates, but nothing much was ever left over. Supposedly the lay staff were employed to be of service to the children but, in reality, the children had to be of service to them, especially on Sundays. Mr Reilly was the maintenance man or painter, and I never saw him eating lunch with the three female staff members; I believed he was having intimate relations with some of the older girls. I avoided him and would not engage with him or communicate with him, as I once saw him 'misbehaving' with Margree in one of the wardrobes.

There was an elderly lady known as Miss Sorling, who died in a room off St Prop's dormitory. She was old and infirm, but I never knew much about her or why she was there, living in a residential school at the end of her life.

. . .

Sr Turner, as the nun in charge, had a lockup stockroom where she kept clothing, shoes, toiletries, and other such items for the resident children. I was once given a brown and beige woollen dress with brass buttons on each shoulder, which I referred to as my 'army' dress. Then one day, the dress mysteriously went missing and could not be found. On another occasion when my cousins from the United States visited The Valley of Kidron, I received a lovely top, but that evening the garment disappeared without my ever having worn it, never to be seen again.

Many of the children stole items belonging to the others; it was not a safe environment. It didn't appear to matter where one hid something, someone else would inevitably find it, and it would vanish without a trace. Some of the children were referred to as kleptomaniacs. Once, when Sr Turner went to answer the telephone leaving the stockroom unlocked, I went inside and helped myself to a pair of nylon stockings — I told no one about what I had done. We were always being reminded about the importance of cleanliness and modesty and, in a way, we were expected to emulate the life of a nun. We used to say among ourselves that most of the nuns had probably been jilted by men and then ended up frustrated and jealous 'old bags'.

In addition to the stockroom, Sr Turner had a lockup telephone kiosk, and she was the only person allowed to use the telephone. A big bunch of keys swung from her leather belt, and she kept sweets tucked inside her nun's habit under the scapular — but they weren't for the children; she would be chewing on sweets herself most of the time in front of us. Her waddling footsteps and the jingling of her keys always alerted us to her imminent presence, giving us enough time to disappear, if necessary, or pretend to be working hard upon her arrival, when we had in fact been merely messing about.

Sometimes, on a Sunday night, Sr Turner would open yet

another locked press, or cupboard, situated at the back of the room where I had to cut the bread. The press contained a variety of sweets and edible goodies and Sr Turner would occasionally get some of the more mature, sensible girls to hand these out as a special treat. As soon as the cupboard was opened, word would get around very quickly, as no one wanted to miss out.

Sr Turner lived in a private room on the upper floor, just outside St Prop's dormitory, where she supervised the children at night. When the telephone rang, its loud bell would echo around the residential school, alerting Sr Turner, who would have to go downstairs to the kiosk to answer it. One evening, I took advantage of an opportunity that presented itself. On this occasion we were already in bed, so things were quiet and I knew where Sr Turner was going. As the nun disappeared down three or four flights of stairs to answer a call, we were able to peep over the bannister rail and see whereabouts she was on the stairs. Once she was safely out of range, I decided to have a look inside her bedroom to see what it was like and how she lived.

To my horror and surprise, what I found disturbed me. The room was totally unkempt, with an unmade, messy bed. Brand new children's clothes with the labels still attached had been thrown around all over the place; sweet papers were strewn everywhere, and the rubbish was about six inches deep across the floor. Sr Turner's room was like a tip. The thing that surprised me most, though, was the amount of cash everywhere. There were bundles of notes on the dresser, on the mantelpiece, and more money lying around the room in different places. I thought to myself, 'How *dare* you preach to us about cleanliness and tidiness, when you live in a pigsty yourself? So much for the preaching and teaching!' I also wondered where all that cash had come from. And why was it being stored in this nun's private room, to which no one else had access? I didn't share what I had seen with anyone, as I was not supposed to have been in the room in the first place and would have got into serious trouble if Sr Turner had found out that I had dared to enter her residence. I realised what a hypocrite this nun was and had even less respect for her from that day onwards. I would often ignore Sr Turner when spoken to and would treat her with hostility. No one ever enquired as to the reason, or was in the least bit bothered about why I did not like the nuns.

Each girl had a bath once a fortnight, 'whether she needed it or not'! One week it was St Prop's dormitory and the next week it was St Enzo's dormitory's turn for baths. Naturally, there was a pecking order to the bathing process with the older, bossy girls having their baths first. They got the clean water, and then the younger ones took their turns — in the dirty water — last. Most of the senior girls had secretly washed their hair and their clothes in the original bathwater, when it was first drawn. No shampoo was provided to us; however, we would use an egg-cupful of T.Pol, an industrial cleaner and degreaser used for cleaning floors, as shampoo. This chemical gave a fantastic reddish sheen to the hair.

None of us ever complained about the process for bathing at the school. Perhaps we thought that if we did, we would risk missing out on our once-fortnightly scrub. Time in the bath was limited to between ten and fifteen minutes, and each girl had an allocated time slot. The basement cubicles where the baths were located had been partitioned off, but it was easy to look over the tops of the partitions.

On Sundays, the normal routines were observed. After church came breakfast and duties, religious instruction, and then choir practice. I cannot remember what this 'religious instruction' was about; sometimes, the time was used to highlight a problem with a particular girl, or an incident, and sometimes it was more of a generalised telling-off session. The nun who took choir practice, Sr O'Toole, was an unpleasant character and extremely aggressive in manner with most of the children, often hitting them, though she never struck me. Choir practice was followed by Sunday lunch, which was really dinner. This consisted of a Sunday roast followed by what was called jelly and cream; the cream looked more like milk, which perhaps it was. Taken from an economic stance, it probably wasn't cream, but we considered it a real treat.

Once duties were completed, reliable, older girls were put in charge of the Sunday walk. The children were arranged in pairs one behind another and we followed a specific route towards the hospital and back again, which was quite a long walk. Pocket money was given to each of us to spend at the sweet shop near the hospital. The amount was not much, but the other girls appeared to be happy with it, though many of them would steal from the sweet shop, despite having been given money. I never stole anything from the shop and was very compliant on my walks. In addition to this somewhat regimented Sunday outing, the usual daily routines of meals and duties were followed until bedtime. Every door, both ahead and behind us, was constantly locked. We spent many hours standing, in silence, in corridors or behind locked doors, waiting to be let in or out.

Occasionally, we were allowed out in the playground, mainly unsupervised. The only piece of play equipment was a maypole, and we would make up games or use the time to talk, as silence had to be observed most of the other times.

One day, I saw a small child being beaten up by an older pupil named Patty. This triggered something in me — I was not going to allow the little girl to be treated like that. Angrily, I grabbed Patty by the hair and pulled it hard, hitting her until she cried. I expected that I would be in serious trouble and waited to be reprimanded, but it never happened. Sr Turner just gave me a dirty look of disapproval when she saw me later. In the residential school, the term 'giving the side eyes' was always treated as a threat.

It's doubtful whether any injuries resulting from such scraps or playground accidents would have been treated kindly by the nun who was the resident nurse. This was Sr Hennessy, who was not given to displays of kindness or compassion towards children who were ill. When a sick child went to see her for a medical consultation, Sr Hennessy would often say, after examination, 'There is nothing wrong with you!' followed by a slap in the face. This approach appeared to have the effect of keeping the girls mainly fit and healthy and not requiring much in the way of medical treatment. To Sr Hennessy, an unwell child was just a nuisance that she would not tolerate.

On one occasion, when Sr Turner went away overnight, a few of the older girls got together and held what we called a 'midnight party'. We had a record player with one record, *The Mighty Quinn*, which was played repeatedly as we ate the food we had set aside at dinnertime that day. It was really more of an effort to be a bit rebellious, by staying up beyond midnight!

I was good at maths, but did not like French; I had a French teacher called Miss Middle. One day, another house child bully in my French class copied my homework. Miss Middle accused me of copying, but I was too afraid to say anything because of my fear of being beaten up after school by the bully or her gang group. I remained quiet when wrongly accused, despite being terribly upset by the way that Miss Middle had spoken to me. As a result of the incident, I was sent to the principal's office. Sr Prydecock, known among the children as 'Peacock', reprimanded me for something that, of course, I had not done. Sr Prydecock was regularly seen out walking with the priest who said daily Mass for the nuns at the convent. We children observed this and would comment that they were 'having an affair'; this may or may not have been true. I don't recall what was actually said or done by the principal about the supposed homework copying, but later that evening I ran away from the residential school.

Having managed to escape the confines of The Valley of Kidron, I walked through the city until I reached the main road to Gorren, where I hitch-hiked, or 'thumbed', back to my father's house — a twenty-five-mile journey — getting rides in various lorries along the way. It was late into the evening when I arrived home in Baile na Ghlic. By then, Sr Turner had rung the pub across the road from our house, and the bar staff had sent for my father. He was informed that his daughter had run away, and Sr Turner issued him with strict instructions. When I reached what I thought would be the safety of my father's house, instead of being made to feel welcome and comforted, Daddy was angry with me for running away, as he himself had already been harassed by Sr Turner on the telephone.

My father had been instructed during that phone call to send his child back to the residential school immediately, on the next day's train. When I found myself in the city once more, I walked the considerable distance from the railway station to my school. I have no memory of what the reception was like when I returned, but I immediately resumed my studies in the secondary school, and there were no more incidents with that particular class bully.

There were many other bullies in the residential school, though. Some had many followers or 'gang members' who did all their dirty work for them. Sometimes, fights would break out, and I remember one older girl having her earring ripped out, leaving the ear completely torn. Three girls from one family were the main bullies, and most of the children at our school lived in fear of them.

As I progressed through the school, I was moved to a cubicle in the dormitory for older girls. One of the girls, Bronagh, who had long red hair, would often throw her shoe at anyone who snored during the night. The unfortunate snorer would suddenly find herself woken from a deep sleep, having been hit hard by flying footwear. Rudely awakened and in a frightened state, she would try to work out what had happened. Bronagh and her friend, Nessa were responsible for this type of behaviour on many occasions — despite the fact that they both snored themselves, though no one dared to tell them.

At night, when everyone was in bed, some of the older girls would sneak out to meet boys. Some of the local lads would meet these girls either by the laundry within the grounds of the residential school, or further afield in the city. Nessa, Bronagh, Kaggie, and Letty were some of the girls that sneaked out in the evenings. When they went on these clandestine outings, they would put pillows down their beds so that, on inspection, the nun in charge would think they were tucked up in their beds asleep. At other times, they would recruit the younger children to sleep in their beds for them. This arrangement was nearly always agreed to by the younger girls out of fear of intimidation or physical violence by the older ones.

I observed that Bronagh was not a very pleasant character to be around; she was rather intolerant of anyone whom she decided was not her 'friend' and always wanted to call the shots. A day came when Bronagh asked me to go out with her on a Saturday afternoon. I was pleased to be considered and included in her circle of friends; it was good for my self-esteem, or so I thought, as I was somewhat afraid of Bronagh and Kaggie and had, myself, been a victim of the flying shoe. However, I did not like Bronagh. When I had come back from my summer holidays with shoes that I had bought with my hard-earned money, Bronagh initially borrowed them, but never returned them. I was too afraid to say anything to her, or to ask for them back.

On the day in question, Bronagh had arranged to meet a man who had only one leg and who had a bad reputation with women in the city. It appeared that she had promised that she would bring along another girl for his cousin, Len, but that day none of her regular friends could go out with her. I, however, was unaware of this arrangement when I agreed at short notice to accompany Bronagh. We duly met the two men, who drove us out into fields. Bronagh and her man took themselves off, some distance away from me and Len. Unsurprisingly, since this had been the point of the exercise as far as he was concerned, Len then started to make advances towards me. I rebuffed him, saying I was not interested and had just obliged Bronagh in going out with her on her date. Disappointed that I had no interest in him, Len became annoyed with me. On the return journey, he showed his anger in the way he drove the Mini Minor very erratically through the fields and over the railway line before letting Bronagh and me out somewhere near our school. On reflection, years later, I understood that I had been extremely vulnerable to being assaulted by Len, with no one else around in the field. After that experience, I never again went out with any of the older girls and avoided them, for my own safety.

During my stay in The Valley of Kidron, another small residential school in a different county closed down, and about six of the remaining children were then transferred to our school. For some reason, the new children were treated very well by Sr Turner. I was friendly with two of these girls, Nora and Priscilla. Nora had few eyelashes, and the other children called her unkind names. Priscilla was a small, square-shouldered, big busted girl. She was highly intelligent and always achieved excellent results in every subject, without having to put too much effort into studying.

In later years, I ran into Priscilla in London. She had married an Englishman and went on to be academically successful.

I had one particularly good friend at the residential school, Kareen. According to others at the school, her mother was classified as an alcoholic and was living with a man who was not her husband. (The couple had a child together and that child was now also living in the school.) This type of behaviour was not accepted in Ireland in those days, and often such women were treated as outcasts by society. Kareen and her siblings were only permitted to visit their mother on Sundays. Their father had served with the Army, and she had lots of interesting stories to tell me about the places they had lived in on his postings.

An artistic girl, Kareen was particularly good at colour co-ordinating outfits, and I admired her flair and style. On one occasion, Kareen and I went on a 'mystery' train ride together and met two boys, Kevin and Barry. Both boys played in a brass band, and I communicated with Kevin for years afterwards. These relationships were more like friendships than romances; I was ill at ease with boys at that age. Another time, Kareen and I got hold of a pair of bicycles and made the twenty-two-mile journey together to visit my aunt and cousins. Having rested at my aunt's house for a little while and eaten a meal in the company of my relatives, the thought of the twenty-two-mile return journey, which had to be completed before it got dark, was rather wearying.

That wasn't the only adventure we girls got up to; a group of three or four of us went down to a river near the residential school once and attempted to get into a small boat which was moored there. Priscilla, who had just been given a new pair of beautiful patent leather shoes, got stuck in the mud. Even though the weather was cold, we had brought our swimming gear with us, but never got to use them after the mishap, as Priscilla was so upset about ruining her shoes that we just went quickly back to the school.

Kareen and I attended the School of Music for violin lessons, and that meant walking alone through rough and unsafe areas of the city late in the evening. Sometimes, I was aware of being followed by older men or 'creeps', as I thought of them, as I walked back to the residential school. The convent had a gatehouse at the entrance, with no street lighting around it, and one evening when I arrived back, I caught a glimpse of what I believed to be the shadow of a man waiting in the bushes. I was afraid to pass the bushes to enter the property and waited around anxiously until someone I knew arrived who was also heading into the convent. For my own safety, I walked in with that person.

Once inside, late and distressed by the incident, I told Sr Turner about what had happened. Instead of my tale being received with sympathy, I was instead reprimanded for telling lies.

'You are making this up!' the nun accused me. 'Other children have come back in the evening and nothing has happened to them, so why do you think anyone would be more interested in you than them?' she asked, leaving me feeling betrayed.

A social highlight of my time at The Valley of Kidron was when the older girls were invited to a supervised social (dance) with the nearby Redemptorist school for boys. I persuaded a friend to put ringlets in my hair for me, using strips of rag to get the required style, and I borrowed an orange dress from another girl. Looking at my reflection before the event, I was pleased with my appearance and felt good about myself. There was a boy at the dance called Sandy who took a shine to me. Following that occasion he would often be at the church service in the morning, just to see me there. That was as far as that early romance, if one could call it that, went.

Many of the girls were told about what were generally referred to as 'the facts of life' by Sr Turner, but she did not instruct me; I had to learn about such things from the other girls or by reading books. I felt that because I had an underlying hostility towards the nuns, I was, therefore, mistreated and ignored in turn. Luckily for me, shortly after my mother had died, when I was about twelve years old and still living on the farm, I had mentioned to Mrs Fiona that I had a pain in my tummy. Mrs Fiona told me that I might soon menstruate and went on to explain what this meant. Although I was somewhat horrified by what Fiona had told me and found the conversation unpleasant, I was later glad that it had taken place before I ended up in the so-called 'care' of the nuns.

I would go back home for the summer holidays, which gave me the opportunity to find employment during the vacation and earn some money for when I went back to the residential school in the autumn. My first job was in a sewing factory where I wove belt loops, with fine thread, for dresses. I would sit at a table for eight hours a day, attending to this task without speaking to anyone, and earned about three pounds a week.

Another summer, I worked in a factory using a machine that put steam vents in the lids of teapots and kettles, for which my weekly wage was five pounds. I attracted the attention of many of my male co-workers in the teapot factory, but I wouldn't talk to any of them, as I was extremely shy and blushed easily. I found it hard to engage with boys generally but, despite feeling myself awkward, young men nevertheless showed interest in dating me. When I was about fifteen years old, I went for a walk with one young lad named Freddy whom I had met at the local carnival or fairground. Relationships like these were innocent in nature, but never appeared to work out for me — perhaps I was too cautious about men.

However, I did meet a nice boy, Jason, whom I thought at the time had the most beautiful blue eyes I had ever seen — but one of my friends also liked him, too. He and I went out together on a few dates, and I took quite a shine to him. Then, one Sunday night when I was supposed to be meeting Jason to go to a carnival dance with him, he never showed up. These summer dances were usually held in a marquee or large, tent-like structure, with a live band, and I knew that my friends would be there. In the end, I decided to go to the dance anyway, without my expected date. To my surprise, Jason was there when I arrived, but neither of us spoke to each other. That was the end of that relationship and, deep down, I was extremely hurt by the way Jason had treated me. It took me a long time to get over what I perceived as a rejection. Some thirty years later, I came across Jason again at my father's funeral, where he was one of the grave diggers. He tried to make conversation with me, but I was not interested in engaging with him after the knock he'd given to my confidence when I was a teenager.

At the age of sixteen, I landed a summer job at the local hospital and clearly recall one particular event that happened there. I was responsible for the medical administration department's postal dispatch service each day, which entailed carefully wrapping up and packing specimens, as well as the regular post, for dispatch. That day, it seemed a mastectomy had been performed at the hospital, as the package I found myself handling, without gloves, contained the breast of a woman. It was moist, heavy, and wet. This incident had a long-lasting effect on me, and I often wondered who the breast had belonged to and whether the woman was alive or dead, hoping she had survived and was doing well in life. None of the staff ever spoke to one another in that job. That was the way employment operated in

Ireland in those days; such opportunities were hard to come by and the work environment was very formal.

One thing that I noticed was that the Sisters of St Germaine never offered my father any monetary assistance during the time that he had full care of me over the summer holidays, which lasted between two and three months each year. He was offered neither the children's allowance, nor a reduction in his own contribution for my keep in The Valley of Kidron during the times that I was back home under his roof. In effect, the Sisters of St Germaine were receiving the full twelve-month compensation from the state for my care, including for the quarter of the year when I wasn't even staying in the residential school.

TEN
ESCAPE!

Níl aon tinteán mar do thinteán féin
(There's no fireside like your own fireside)

—Irish saying

It took five years to complete secondary school through to university level. When I was about a month away from completing my third year of secondary education, I was told by Sr Turner to 'get out and don't come back.' This sudden turn of events was precipitated by something seemingly quite minor. One evening at dinner time, someone had attempted to play a prank by putting salt in the sugar on the table where I was sitting. At first, I said politely (though probably in a somewhat irritated tone of voice) to Sr Turner who was sitting at her rostrum, 'Excuse me Sister, someone has put salt in the sugar.' Sr Turner ignored me, making no eye contact with me as I spoke, and neither did she respond to the comment. Again, I repeated the same lines, in a louder tone:

'Excuse me Sister, *someone has put salt in the sugar!*'

Again, I was ignored by Sr Turner.

Now feeling distinctly annoyed, I stood up at the dining room table and shouted loudly at the nun, for the third time,

'Someone has put salt in the sugar!'

'GET OUT, AND DON'T COME BACK!' was Sr Turner's startling, hissed response.

And that is exactly what I did; I packed up my belongings and, alone, hitch-hiked the twenty-five miles to Baile na Ghlic, arriving at my father's house late that night. This time, Daddy welcomed me.

From then on, he would walk me to the bus stop each morning to catch the bus to school, giving me what little money he had. He could only afford the fare for a one-way journey each day, but he was determined that I would complete my Intermediate Certificate (Inter. Cert.) at the secondary school attached to the residential school, and indeed I passed the seven subjects taken. For the month or so after arriving back from The Valley of Kidron, I caught the early morning bus at around 7am from Monday to Friday, riding to the city to attend school. However, as I suffered badly from motion sickness and disliked the smell of the diesel or petrol, I would be extremely nauseated on my arrival at school at 8.30am.

After school each day, I would hitch-hike home and then continue studying after the evening meal. The hitch-hiking was far from ideal, and I had many scary experiences with male drivers; once I jumped out of a moving car, and, another time, I held a man's hand so that he would have to drive with the other hand and could not molest me.

There were other such incidents such as the time I got into a car in which the inside door handle on the passenger side had been removed so that the passenger was unable to open the door. The driver had to stop the car and go around to the passenger's side of the car and open it on the outside to let me out. However, I felt capable of talking my way out of most situations and was never afraid, harmed, or sexually molested during those hitch-hiking encounters, no matter how scary they were. I was a 'risk taker', and at least I was free of The Valley of Kidron.

From the age of about sixteen onwards, after I had left the residential school, I worked from six in the evening until ten at night, three evenings a week and every second Sunday at a veterinary practice in Baile na Ghlic. I was paid three pounds a week, in cash, for the nineteen hours of work at the office.

This job saw me administering tablets for sick animals to farmers and taking telephone calls for the veterinary surgeons in the evening. I would contact the on-call vet remotely, using a radio telephone system in the office. Working at the practice meant I got to know the locality well and also the names of many different farming families and how those with common surnames were distinguished from each other by the use of nicknames. For company in the evenings, there was a television set mounted up high on the wall in the office. As it wasn't usually very busy, I was able to complete my study without too much interruption.

While working there I met Toss, a farmer's son who was home from university for the summer months and helping the vet with the annual cattle testing. He asked me out on a date, and I went to dances with him a few times. One Sunday night, he let me down and didn't turn up; I never saw him again. Years later, when reading the death notices in the local paper on one of my visits back to Ireland, I came across a death notice for Toss's wife — he was listed as being a professor, so obviously he had obtained a good education.

One of the regular but odd features of my evening job was that I received almost-weekly propositions from elderly farmers looking for a wife. One of them put it to me bluntly as, 'All I want is someone like you, maybe a little older, to keep the house tidy and put a bit of grub on the table. That is all I want; do you have any older sisters?' I also had to field my fair share of the town's 'characters'. Once, a man visited the office who wanted to discuss his theories on life and death with me; I had no understanding of the theory he was trying to prove or disprove. I was a sitting duck for people like that and would just nod my head, while having no interest whatsoever in the conversation. Later, I heard that this particular man had been diagnosed with schizophrenia. I also got to know a young man called Simon while he was working at a local factory in Baile na Ghlic in his teenage years. Later, Simon went on to be ordained as a priest. The pair of us got on well together and the friendship has endured throughout our lives, with us writing to one another every Christmas and always catching up when I am back in Ireland.

The vet's office was in a converted stable at the rear of a Victorian house. There was no lighting down the back driveway to the modern office, which had an outside toilet next door. My father would be standing on the street looking out for me when I finished work at 10pm and we would walk home together. When I locked up, turned off the lights and walked from the back yard out onto the road I would be relieved to see my father there waiting for me, as I was afraid of leaving the office in the dark, and his presence made me feel secure. We would chat on the way home about the evening's events in the office.

I had a good relationship with my father and enjoyed listening to his stories about when he was a young man. He told me one story in particular about people being followed by spirits. It was said, according to my father, that the only way to get rid of a menacing spirit was to jump over a running stream, because spirits did not like water and would then leave the person alone. He would never tell me what to do; the most he would say was, 'If you would take my advice, don't do that'. On one occasion, I encountered an older man somewhere who wanted me to meet him at the Ball Alley, about three miles away from our town, in a remote area of the countryside. However, when I told my father about this invitation, he advised me against meeting the man and said that this man was known to be 'dangerous'. Daddy did not elaborate any further and I didn't ask any questions either, but I took heed of my father's warning and didn't go.

I completed my final two years of secondary school in Baile na Ghlic. However, when I first started attending the new school, having left The Valley of Kidron, one of the nuns made the comment, 'We have heard everything about you'. I did not enquire what she meant by that and went about my studies as well as working at my evening job. I was totally focused on my future and wasn't interested in looking back, or in small talk.

Getting up in the morning was a struggle for me, as I often found it extremely hard to face the day. I felt as though I had to work twice as hard academically as anyone else to retain information, because of my lack of concentration. There were so many things going on inside my head that I found it hard to study, but I was determined to make the best of things.

At my new school I met Sr Angela, who was the art teacher. This was to be the only positive relationship or experience that I ever had with 'penguins', as nuns were sometimes known. Sr Angela was relatively normal and treated me with respect and courtesy, to the extent that I often felt that my teacher was almost able to see into my spirit. We had an exceptionally good relationship and later, Sr Angela corresponded with me for years, even after she had left the convent and renounced her vows.

One of the positive things about being back at school in Baile na Ghlic was that I made some good friends who were from more stable families than those of most of the children in the residential school. One of these was Connie, whose family always made me welcome when I went to their house. Connie later became a highly respected member of society in the city as a High Court judge, but for about forty years we lost contact until I recognised my old friend at a local restaurant on one of my visits to Ireland. Connie, who by then had changed her name to Sylvia, was extremely surprised that I had remembered her. Later that evening, we spent time reminiscing about the carnival dances we had attended together all those years earlier. It felt as though time had stood still and we were back in our teenage years again — no information on our lifetime careers or families was exchanged — so strong had our friendship been.

Carnival dances were one of the things my friends and I enjoyed. One evening we went to a carnival dance by the lough, and I and another girl spent the evening dancing with two lads, Liam and Shane. After the dance, we continued socialising on a boat belonging to Shane until it got so late that all the local traffic had departed. Liam and Shane borrowed a motorbike from their friend Harry and put a wooden plank along the seat (this was commonly used as a sort of extension to the seat), and the four of us rode back to Baile na Ghlic on it. We girls were dropped off outside the post office at 3am and then we walked the short distance to our homes, our families never being any the wiser about our rather bizarre transport arrangement!

I never invited my girlfriends into our home. Perhaps I learned this behaviour from my mother, who had not allowed me to have friends in the house after school. I would usually meet them at

O'Leary's Hotel, where I enjoyed having coffee with cream on the top of it. I was amazed at the bartender's precision when he poured the cream over the back of a spoon onto the surface of the coffee, achieving a perfect creation. I did not like alcohol and privately had an exceptionally low opinion of people who drank; I was twenty-one years old before I tasted alcohol, but kept my dislike of alcohol to myself and was always very sociable and friendly. Despite being good at making conversation, privately I felt that I was in some way a 'fraud' because no one really knew the deep burden I carried but was unable to articulate. I felt different on the inside because of the traumatic events in my life thus far.

During my final years at school, I thought that I might like to become a beautician and went back to studying Latin, which was a requirement for the course. I had earlier dropped Latin as a subject in my Intermediate Certificate, but took it up again for my Leaving Certificate and, to my surprise, I passed it at the higher level.

Soon after the Leaving Certificate results came out, I bumped into Sr Constantia — who had taught me Latin — on the street, and the nun commented, 'I was surprised that you managed to pass your exam!' I just smirked and walked away without further comment. When I finished school, I decided that I would never again set foot inside a church because of the hypocrites I had come across during my years in the residential school. However, during the summer while I was waiting for the Leaving Certificate examination results to be announced, I decided to go into the local church to pray and to ask God to help me cope. While I was there praying, I had a very, very strange experience that frightened me; it was as if the presence of God was with me. I felt surrounded by a spiritual force that appeared to be communicating with me and heard a voice say, 'I hear the cry of your heart and I am here to help you and walk with you.'

No matter where I went in the world later in life, I knew that I could always return to my father's house and find him there, sitting by the fire, happy to see me and eager for a chat. Often when I would try to leave the house, Daddy would say, 'Wait till I tell you'. He never had anything whatsoever to tell me — he just wanted me to stay and talk a little while longer. I believe that this relationship with my father had a profound and stabilising effect on my life, even though I knew I had 'something' seriously wrong within myself. Every night before my father went to bed, he would open the front door of the house and count the number of cars on the street, as this gave him an idea of how many people were breaking the law by still drinking in the local pub after closing time. He never touched alcohol throughout his life, even though he had inherited a pub from his Aunt Chrissy. In our home there was never any alcohol, no cigarettes, no television, no telephone, and no foul language. When Daddy was thinking about my mother, he would sometimes say to me that 'to meet, to love and then to part, is the greatest sorrow of the human heart'.

My father had, at some stage in his early life, been part of the Civil Defence Force in the town, and sometimes I would ask him to do a military drill for me. This would entail his standing to attention with the upturned sweeping brush handle under his raised arm, before he proceeded to march around the room for me. This was always a time when we both had a good laugh together. Another amusement that we shared was reciting poems. My father had a wide repertoire that he would recite for me; some pieces may have been local folklore, others were poems written throughout history, concerning traumatic events such as TB.[1] He would recite the first couple of verses from the poem *The Dying Girl* by Richard D'Alton Williams (1822–1862), but after the first few verses, I would lose interest. Nevertheless, Daddy would continue with the recitation, with no one listening, as though he were challenging himself to remember all the words!

THE DYING GIRL

From a Munster vale they brought her,
From the pure and balmy air;
An Ormond peasant's daughter,
With blue eyes and golden hair.
They brought her to the city
And she faded slowly there –
Consumption has no pity
For blue eyes and golden hair.

When I saw her first reclining
Her lips were mov'd in prayer,
And the setting sun was shining
On her loosen'd golden hair.
When our kindly glances met her,
Deadly brilliant was her eye;
And she said that she was better,

---

1. Tuberculosis, or TB, is an infectious disease usually caused by Mycobacterium tuberculosis (MTB) bacteria, which generally attacks the lungs but can also affect other parts of the body. Most infections show no symptoms, which is known as latent tuberculosis. The disease was commonly known as consumption, and at the start of the 20th century it was the leading cause of death in many countries including the USA — the disease can affect anyone regardless of age, sex, or class and thus was a much-feared illness.

While we knew that she must die.

She speaks of Munster valleys,
The pattern, dance, and fair,
And her thin hand feebly dallies
With her scattered golden hair.
When silently we listen'd
To her breath with quiet care,
Her eyes with wonder glisten'd,
And she asked us, 'What was there?'

The poor thing smiled to ask it,
And her pretty mouth laid bare,
Like gems within a casket,
A string of pearlets rare,
We said that we were trying
By the gushing of her blood
And the time she took in sighing
To know if she were good.

Well, she smil'd and chatted gaily,
Though we saw in mute despair
The hectic brighter daily,
And the death-dew on her hair.
And oft her wasted fingers
Beating time upon the bed:
O'er some old tune she lingers,
And she bows her golden head.

At length the harp is broken.
And the spirit in its strings,
As the last decree is spoken,

To its source exulting springs.
Descending swiftly from the skies
Her guardian angel came,
He struck God's lightning from her eyes,
And bore Him back the flame.

Before the sun had risen
Through the lark-loved morning air,
Her young soul left its prison,
Undefiled by sin or care.
I stood beside the couch in tears
Where pale and calm she slept,
And though I've gazed on death for years,
I blush not that I wept.

I check'd with effort pity's sighs
And left the matron there,
To close the curtains of her eyes
And bind her golden hair.

Some of the other pieces that my father knew by heart, and which I still remember, were as follows:

A publican stood at the Golden Gate
His head was bent and low
He meekly asked the Man of God
Which way he should go.
What have you done? St Peter said,
'To seek admission here?
'I kept a pub on Earth
For many a long year'.
St Peter opened wide the gate

And beamed on him as well,
Come in, he said,
And choose a harp,
You've had your share of Hell.

—THE PUBLICAN'S JUDGEMENT DAY,
UNKNOWN

My name is Ma-gee Dooley and I'm Dinny Dooley's niece,
I was courted by McNamara, Sub-inspector of Police.
He promised for to wed me and make me his dear wife,
Saying hand in hand together we'll jog along through life.
But he was removed from Naana town, my curse upon that day,
And likewise on the scoundrel who sent my love away
And left me to the mercy of traitors and of knaves.
And now, I must leave my native town and sail across the waves.

Barney you're a devil, Barney you're a rogue,
You are killing me by inches for you know I am your slave,
But you mean [pronounced 'mane'] old scut when you are dead
I'll dance upon your grave.

—UNKNOWN

When I finished my secondary schooling, I had no idea what to do with my life, though my main priority was to earn money in order to support myself. I had decided against the idea of becoming a beautician, but there was no career guidance available in those days and no one to advise me. I was accepted into art school, but decided I didn't want to be a poor, struggling artist all my life, so that was crossed off my list. Despite having had a lifelong love for music and, in particular, chamber music, I did not apply for a music degree.

Instead, I applied for and was accepted to train as a psychiatric nurse, but I then thought to myself that if I pursued that career, I would probably end up as a patient. Despite coming tenth out of about 250 applicants in the examination for psychiatric nursing, I discounted that as well. I still had my evening job at the veterinary surgeon's office and, in the end, I completed a one-year secretarial course at the local school and was then accepted for a clerical position in the National Television Studio, RTE (Radio Telefís Éireann). However, when it came to it, I decided not to take that position either.

During this period, I also attended an evening art class, where I met a friend of my father's family. This man was a local historian, Samuel K. Lighthouse, and eventually he and I became lifelong friends until his death in 2015. I had forgotten about my earlier friendship with him but, when my father died, Lighthouse approached me at the graveside and asked if I remembered him. Having just arrived back in the country from New Zealand, initially I couldn't place Sam, but after further conversation I remembered the evening classes, the art teacher at the school, and the pleasant hours we'd spent in each other's company.

The conversation at my father's funeral led to my renewing my friendship with Lighthouse, who was much younger than my own father. Sam was a bachelor and lived on a farm with his unmarried sister, a good friend of Auntie Loo's at school — both families had attended the same primary school in Darrigban. Sam Lighthouse was the author of many historical books. I would always call and see him when I was back in Ireland, and we would spend time reminiscing and discussing local folklore. I once turned up at the retirement home where Sam was living on what happened to be his eightieth birthday. The old man thought that I had made the journey especially for him and was extremely excited. By then, Sam was in a wheelchair, but he was delighted to have his photograph taken with me on his special day and told me that my visit had 'made his eightieth birthday very special'. I have always had a great rapport with both the elderly and young children, being able to relate to them very well. I never forgot my friends and always joined them for a cuppa and a chat when I returned to Ireland. At such times, the intervening years seemed to have melted away and it felt to me as though I had never left Ireland.

ELEVEN
FLYING THE NEST

I saw the danger, yet I passed along the enchanted way,
And I said, let grief be a fallen leaf at the dawning of the day.

—*On Raglan Road* by Patrick Cavanagh

After leaving school, I had a deep desire to get away and escape from all the bad things that had happened to me in Ireland. It was as if the tragic circumstances in my early life were, in some way, forcing me out of the country of my birth and urging me to start all over again.

In 1973, at the age of nineteen, I decided to answer an advertisement for an au pair position overseas. My application was successful and the employer paid my airfare to the USA, where I was to work in New York State in an area close to the Catskill Mountains. For some reason, Daddy suggested that I take Irish sausages to give as a gift to my Irish employer. I duly packed the parcel of meat in my luggage and, surprisingly, I was allowed to take the sausages through customs with me on arrival. The host family with whom I was to live consisted of Maude, from Ireland, and her husband Phil, a skipper. They had four children and were genuinely nice people. My job was to look after the young children aged four, two, and a pair of newborn twins.

Phil and Maude and their family lived in the middle of suburbia, with no shops nearby. Most of the residents in the surrounding homes were young families where the women stayed at home and cared for their children. There was nothing to do, just big house after big house, with construction going on everywhere, and it appeared to me that there must be a competition between these families to build a bigger and more exclusive home than that of their neighbours.

Then, in the process of caring for the children, something started to happen to me which I did not understand. Being around the little ones and changing their nappies triggered my own abuse memories. I was not fully conscious of what was going on for me, but I started to withdraw from everyone, including the children, and became extremely depressed. It was as if there was 'no one home' in my head. I felt empty, sad, angry, and alone, and there was nobody who could understand how I was feeling, not even myself. Incapable of articulating what was happening inside me, I became increasingly desperate, frightened, and confused. I just knew that I needed to escape and get out of this 'triggering' environment, somehow. I would find myself just standing motionless, sadly staring into space or at the ground. I didn't want to feel like this but couldn't seem to help the feelings that were overtaking me. Unable to capture my thoughts, I tried to deal with emotions and feelings that were sapping all my energy. Finding myself in a deep depression, I couldn't sleep and was constantly in a state of exhaustion, feeling that there was no way out. Being in a foreign country far away from my family filled me with grief and emptiness. I had no idea what was to become of me; at only nineteen years old, I did not want to face the future.

The host family tried to help me but, not knowing what was wrong with me, I was unable to say why I felt so unhappy and depressed. In the end, I worked long enough to repay the airfare. The remainder of my time there was exceedingly difficult for everyone in the household, as relationships became very strained. I really hadn't wanted to let such kind people down, but it was not good for either me or the children to be around each other while I was feeling like this.

Whilst still working to cover the fare, one afternoon I went to the nearest shopping centre and bought myself a Hershey's chocolate bar. This was my first experience of eating Hershey's chocolate, and I found I liked the flavour and taste. On the lonely walk home, I became a little anxious, as the distance there and back was further than I had anticipated. I still have an image of myself wearing pale green, lightweight summer bell-bottom trousers with a low waistband, walking along in the rapidly cooling evening, eating chocolate. It was getting dark by the time I began to make my way back, and the weather was cold, so it was probably late autumn.

During my stay there, I had one other outing that made a lasting impression on me. This was a weekend visit to Maude's in-laws, a Mr and Mrs Penn, who lived in a big, colonial house. Seemingly, they had offered to try to ascertain what was wrong with the family situation that was making me so depressed. During the evening, after a nice meal, Mrs Penn asked me to remove burrs from a woollen garment using a special comb. I felt safe in that house; both the bedroom and bed linen were luxurious and I, removed from the traumatic memories that were being triggered by the au pair duties of caring for the young children, was able to relax. It was as if, in my time of desperate emotional need, my inner child was being cared for and looked after by this couple.

In the years that followed, I often thought about that lovely family and the fact that I had not been able to explain or verbalise to them what was happening inside me and why I felt unable to be around their children. It had been a strange feeling for me, as I appeared to be operating on two levels, both conscious and unconscious. At the time, I felt that I was in some way being dishonest, as I was unable to reconcile the two sides. It would take me years to fully understand what had gone wrong, and why.

When I returned to Ireland, I went straight back to Baile na Ghlic, arriving just before Christmas. At this point, I was feeling incredibly angry, frustrated, and disillusioned with life. I didn't know what to do and stayed for a period with an aunt. There, the nurturing environment helped me recover from my emotional rocky patch; I got on very well with my cousins, who still consider me to be their 'other sister'.

One evening, one of these cousins and I went to a dance some miles away from where they lived. When the dance was over, most of the cars had left, so there was little or no chance of getting a ride home. Danger never entered our heads. My cousin was friendly with a couple of young men from the nearby village, who had a motorbike. One of the men first took his friend home, telling us that he would return soon and deliver us safely to our village. In the meantime, a car came down the road with three or four young men in it who noticed us and started shouting obscenities at us. My cousin and I knew that the driver would immediately turn the car around and come back to look for us again. We had just enough time to line up, one behind the other, behind a telegraph pole to hide from the men. The car sped by without the men noticing us there, leaving both of us extremely relieved at our narrow escape. Shortly afterwards, the friend with the motorbike returned with a long plank of wood, so the rider and the two of us hopped on the bike and made it home safely. I still have nightmares about that experience. Just like the time I had found myself alone in the field with Len, I realised that my cousin and I had been in a dangerous predicament, but this time my quick thinking had saved the pair of us from possible harm.

I was enormously relieved to no longer have to be around young children, as they were a trigger for my sexual abuse memories. Somehow, I recognised that I needed to avoid triggers in order to keep my traumatic memories suppressed, if I were to go on living and face the future with confidence. I had a good friend, Juliette, who had been a boarder at my school, and it was Juliette who now offered me a way out of Baile na Ghlic.

Shortly after returning from the au pair catastrophe, on New Year's Eve in 1973, I joined Juliette's dad, Mike, as he took the journey via the Holyhead ferry and then on to London by car. He was returning to live in Middlesex with Juliette and her brothers, who had also gone over to London earlier that year to work. The journey through Wales was memorable in that Mike was forced to drive with his head sticking out of the car window, because of dense fog and poor visibility. I had the princely sum of seven pounds sterling to my name when I set off for my new life in England.

By the time I arrived in London in January 1974 Juliette's family had already rented a maisonette in Middlesex, and she and I shared a double bed in a room there. Juliette used to smoke in the bedroom and put the ashtray, with the butts in it, under my side of the bed so that her father would think it was me who was smoking and not her, as he wouldn't have approved of his daughter smoking. I went along with this subterfuge in order to keep the peace between father and daughter. After work, Juliette and I would sometimes be watching a programme on television together when Mike would come home from work, walk in the door, go straight to the TV set, and turn over to the news without as much as acknowledging or consulting us. I found this behaviour very rude, though I never voiced my opinion to my friend or anyone else in the household. After a while though, Mike moved back to Ireland again, so the problem resolved itself, though Juliette and I now had to find alternative accommodation.

At first, we lived in room in a flat in a three-storey house in Shepherd's Bush. The woman who rented the flat lived there with her children and sub-let the room to us, though she did not like us using her kitchen or bathroom. She was always going into our room while we were at work, rifling through our belongings and commenting to us about the state of the room. It appeared she just wanted the money from us, without any disruption to her living environment. Not surprisingly, we felt very unwelcome there, and soon afterwards we moved to Acton to live in a bedsit that belonged to a couple, who were unofficially separated but still living under the same roof. There were weekly arguments between them, in front of Juliette and me, about which of them we should pay the rent to. This was a difficult situation to handle and eventually we left that place too.

As soon as I arrived in Middlesex, I set out to secure a job for myself. In those days, employment agencies listed their jobs in the front window of the agency, making it easy to peruse what was on offer without talking to a consultant. I landed a temp (temporary) job in a typing pool, but found the atmosphere in the office unpleasant; the other girls were generally bitchy and very unfriendly, so I didn't stay long there. I then found a job in

Shepherd's Bush with a Jewish family who were in the clothing industry. The Grainestein family were pleasant, kind, and good employers who treated me very well, and I genuinely enjoyed working for them. At lunchtime, I would sometimes go to a stall on the street and buy fruit for myself, which I found a novel experience as I had never so far in my life had to buy fruit, because fruit would be eaten straight from the trees on the farm in Ireland.

It seemed that everywhere I went, I learned surprising new things about the big city. I would observe the numerous pickpockets who operated on the underground trains and red double decker buses in central London, mainly targeting tourists. Working as a group, they would cause confusion at a bus stop when people were getting on and off the bus. First, signalling to one another, they would identify their victim or target. Then, they would surround the person, pushing and shoving, and trying to lift their wallet at that stage. However, if that didn't work, one of the group would then stand at the bottom of the stairs leading to the top deck of the bus and, as the target person went up the stairs, the wallet would then be removed from the victim's pocket, jacket, or bag. The bus conductors were well aware of the pickpockets and would sometimes warn people to look after their personal belongings. When this happened, the thieves would leave to try their luck elsewhere.

I found it difficult to cope with the unwanted attention of men at this stage. Many of them wanted to talk with me and ask me out on dates, but I was wary of them. Early on in the piece, Juliette and I met two men in Earls Court, and a date was arranged for the four of us. However, one of the men said to me, 'Next time, come out with me alone', as, apparently, he did not want Juliette around. I met up with him and was horrified by how our first date unfolded.

The man told me that he had recently split up with his girlfriend, as she had announced to him that she was pregnant. He informed me that his response to this news had been to tell his girlfriend to 'get rid of it'. I declined to see him again.

When we were living in the Acton bedsit, Juliette was going back and forth between London and Ireland at times and so, when we decided to leave the bedsit, I found myself on my own in London. I took a room that was advertised in the window of a house in Lime Grove, Shepherd's Bush. This house was owned and run by a man who lived on the premises and who did not allow visitors in the house at any time. The tenants were forbidden to close their bedroom doors at night; these had to be left slightly ajar, always. Even talking in the property was prohibited. I felt very unsafe around this distinctly odd man, whom I believed must have been in a concentration camp because of his bizarre behaviour towards the tenants, and I didn't stay long at that address.

Of course, I did also go back home on visits myself from time to time. When I returned to Ireland on holiday, I would arrive in Dublin at around 11pm and then start thumbing the hundred miles or so back to my hometown. Most of the rides I got were with farmers heading home from the pub late at night after a drinking session. One of these men who picked me up in his car said that he had a package to deliver to his brother a few miles down a side road, but I was highly distrustful of his intentions and motives. However, not intending to alert him to my suspicions, I said that I would get out of the car and try to find another lift home. In the dark, I then hid in a field on the side of the main highway, suspecting that he would return very soon to pick me up again. Sure enough, about three minutes later, the man's car reappeared, and he seemed to be frantically looking for me. I waited until he had left and then hitched another lift towards home. I must have had about five to six different rides that evening and into the early hours of the morning, finally arriving in Baile na Ghlic at around 2am. As there was no telephone in the house, to gain entrance at that time in the morning I had to throw small pebbles at one of the upstairs bedroom windows in order to wake my father up so he would come down and let me in. I was extremely relieved when I was safely inside.

On one of these trips back to Ireland from London, my friend Stacey and I decided to go to Puck Fair in Kerry. We had no accommodation booked and, as neither of us had much money, we decided to sleep in a field. Puck Fair in Killorglin, Co. Kerry is Ireland's oldest festival, a strange tradition which has its roots in 4th-century pagan Ireland. A wild goat is captured in the hills, crowned, and worshipped as King Puck for the festival, which is linked to the Celtic festival of Lughnasa, symbolising the beginning of harvest; the goat (*poc* in Gaeilge) was a pagan fertility symbol. The Queen of Puck (usually a young schoolgirl) crowns the goat, which is then placed in a small cage on a high stand where he is provided with food and water. For three days, festival-goers celebrate with markets, music, song, dance, and other entertainment, and the pubs stay open until 3am. At the end of the fair, the goat is released back into the wild.

Unfortunately for me and my friend, we didn't get to enjoy the festivities, as during the night it rained heavily, and the two of us were soaked by the morning. We abandoned the idea of going to the fair and, feeling cold, wet, tired, and miserable, embarked on the trip home. One of the rides we got was in a lorry and, as I was worn-out, I fell asleep. As I slept, the dirt from the seat transferred itself onto my saturated white jacket, which ended up filthy. Later, I struggled to clean the jacket, which never returned to its former glory.

On another occasion, I took off with my friend Kareen to see the band Thin Lizzy at a music festival in the West of Ireland. With no accommodation arranged, that night we fell in with a man who had a Mini Minor and he invited us to sleep in the car with him. I tried to sleep on the back seat of the Mini and Kareen went to sleep on the front seat. The next morning, we felt terrible as we really hadn't slept much; condensation covered the windscreen, and the smell inside the car was none too wholesome either. The noise from the festival patrons had also been very disturbing — there were people everywhere in the surrounding fields, taking drugs, drinking, and sleeping on the ground. The whole experience was a bit frightening and Kareen and I hitched back home the next day, exhausted.

Back in London again, Juliette was always the person who instigated moves and acquired the bedsits, while I just tagged along and agreed with the decisions. One of the bedsits was a room in a basement in St Stephen's Avenue, Shepherd's Bush. Again, this had only one bed in it and a couch to sleep on. The main tenant, Tuppence, occupied the other bedroom and the three of us shared an outside toilet, with no hand basin, and a small kitchenette. Often, I would be depressed and would not talk to Juliette for days over something very insignificant, probably partly because I was unhappy with our living conditions.

The only bathroom in the house where the nine residents could have a bath was on the second floor, and there was a coin-operated meter for the hot water. One extremely hot summer there was an outbreak of fleas in the bathroom, the door to which was always kept closed so that the heat and steam created a perfect breeding ground. When I entered the room to have a bath, my legs would quickly become covered with hopping fleas. The landlord, Larry Phee, eventually sorted out the problem for the tenants after giving some ridiculous excuse as to why the fleas had nothing to do with him or his property as landlord. The basement where Juliette, Tuppence, and I lived had a coin-operated meter for electricity, but little or no heating. Neighbours at the back of the house hung their washing out from the top floor windows of the apartments, and used pulleys to bring the laundry back inside once it was dry. The only good point about the place for me was the small backyard, which I was particularly happy with. This must have had something to do with the extra space and having some 'land' underfoot, having grown up in a rural setting.

There was a married couple with two small children living on the second floor. Candy was always complaining that no one cleaned the bath properly after use, saying that every time she bathed her young children, she first had to scrub the scum off the sides of the bathtub. From down in the basement, I could hear the abusive language whenever Candy went into the bathroom to wash the children. Privately, I thought that the other tenants, myself and Juliette included, probably only rinsed the bath after use and never got rid of the grime marks around the sides.

Then, Stef and Candy's marriage broke up and Stef moved back into his parents' house, which was just across the road from the tenanted house. I had never spoken to or communicated with this young man, but he started to follow me in his lorry as I was walking to the tube station on my way to work in the mornings. He would try to offer me a lift, which I always declined; I was not at all interested in him and was very embarrassed by this turn of events.

Abby, who was probably about thirty-five years older than me, lived on the ground floor. He had two separate rooms — his bedroom and a separate kitchen — which were not interlinked, so he was continually opening and closing these doors with his very noisy keys. Abby also liked to listen to classical music all the time, at maximum volume. The residents' mail was usually left on a table inside the main door in the hall, next to the coin-operated telephone box. (Everything in bedsits in those days seemed to be coin-operated.) Abby was a part-time philatelist who took a keen interest in any stamps on mail arriving for the other occupants of the house, so he always looked through the post. As he worked for the LEB (London Electricity Board) he had access to sacks of used, stamped envelopes, which he brought home daily. He worked in a customer support team area and was often rewarded by customers for helping them sort out complicated electricity bills. They would invite him to restaurants for a free meal as a way of thanking him for 'going the extra mile'.

When I was living alone in the bedsit, Abby would invite me to join him for one of his free meals if I was available; he would watch out for me as I came in and out of the house and would try and engage with me. We took turns in paying for other outings and events too, though Abby usually took me to all his 'freebies'. When it was my turn to pay, I would have to foot the bill for the two of us for whatever outing or event we had decided on, including the taxi fare home. Together we went to many productions at the Royal Shakespeare Company in London. Abby was also a member of the Anglo Portuguese Society, even though he had no connections with Portugal other than that he just liked to go there on holiday and drink port. The purpose of the society was to foster the historic relationship between the two countries by developing British people's knowledge of Portugal, its people, and culture. Abby once invited me to join him at the annual Anglo-Portuguese dinner at which HRH Princess Anne was the guest of honour. For this event, Abby and I each paid for our own tickets. On another occasion, when Abby had had too much to drink, we were waiting for a taxi when he tried to kiss me. This disgusted me and I told him to stop, which he did and never tried that again.

Later on, Abby moved to Hammersmith. He would occasionally invite me and my boyfriend, Jeffrey, to his apartment. The only piece of furniture in the living room was his chair in front of the television and a bright lamp with a magnifying glass in it. This lamp was attached to the back of the chair to help Abby see the markings on his stamps. He kept this light on even when not in use, but tilted it in a different direction so that it shone in Jeffrey's face when we were invited to dinner at Abby's. The only other seating was one small stool that I sat on, so consequently Jeffrey had to spend the whole evening standing in the living room with the light shining into his eyes.

Everywhere was blanketed in dust. The carpet had layer upon layer of very thick dust on it, despite being mostly covered in sackfuls of large plastic bags filled with used, stamped envelopes from the LEB. Sometimes, Jeffrey and I would refer to Abby as 'Abby Normal' in reference to the Mel Brooks film *Young Frankenstein*, in which Dr Frankenstein discovers that his assistant had accidentally given him an abnormal brain to implant into his monster — the brain of 'Abby Normal'. Although Abby had little or no social etiquette, he could be charming and friendly with people most of the time. He would manage to get himself invited to the homes of total strangers the next time he was 'in their neck of the woods', based on chance encounters with them.

He told me that he had worked out that the way of getting into a family for a holiday was to 'butter up' the wife, or woman of the house. Once the wife accepted him, he was in. To Abby, that meant a free holiday, and the only thing he had to do, in his mind, was to get himself to the destination. He would turn up for a two-week holiday with little or no money, taking just a bottle of wine for his hosts. He expected these kind people to provide him with food, alcohol, and entertainment, to wait upon him hand and foot, and to take him out to restaurants, with the one bottle of wine being his only contribution. Consequently, he never got invited back to anyone's home a second time, as the unsuspecting host family had felt used by him.

Abby and I would take turns at hosting meals for each other. The meal was usually chump chops and vegetables, followed by apple pie and ice cream, which Abby prepared. We ate at the kitchen table and, immediately following the meal, Abby would get up and retire to the living room, saying in a casual but serious tone, 'Which one of you is doing the washing up?' as Jeffrey and I started on it. Back in the living room, one of Abby's prized possessions would be shared before the end of the evening — each of us would have a small glass of Drambuie, which he called 'liquid gold'.

On one such occasion, on being called to the kitchen for dinner, Jeffrey pushed the bright light on Abby's armchair downwards, so that when he returned to the living room it wouldn't be glaring in his eyes. Later, when Abby re-entered the living room after the meal, he noticed that the back of his armchair was smouldering and said that he must have accidentally knocked the light; Jeffrey just kept quiet and tried not to show his guilty face.

On the second floor of the Shepherd's Bush house lived Johnny Mac, a very kind, compassionate, and generous Anglo-Indian man from Calcutta. He had been a Christian Brother in his earlier years and now had a full-time job in London. All his spare time was spent helping others in whatever way he could. Juliette and I (and later Jeffrey) trusted Johnny and would often leave the key to our basement flat with him when we went on holiday, just in case some friend or acquaintance turned up in our absence.

Tess and Mo lived on the third floor of the house. I wasn't sure what their relationship was, whether they were friends or lovers. Then Tess moved out and asked Jeffrey to assist her in taking her belongings down the stairs. Jeffrey was horrified at the state of the accommodation the ladies were living in. One of the women was a hoarder, and when Jeffrey walked on the 'floordrobe', he was ankle deep in clothes, old newspapers, pamphlets, television guides, magazines, and other items. The place looked more like a tip or a rubbish dump than a person's living room.

There were no tenancy agreements for the house and Larry Phee would come weekly with the rent book to collect the rent in cash from everyone. I became aware that, in my absence, he was coming into my room and leaving behind evidence of his visit such as a cigarette butt or a dirty teacup on the table. I was not happy with this intrusion into my privacy and got a chain lock put on my door. Phee strongly objected to my action and became hostile towards me, but I was determined that this unpleasant man should not violate my minute personal space and ignored him.

Tuppence came from the North of England. When Juliette and I first moved into the basement with her, she had her own room, and we would try and avoid her in the common areas. Tuppence worked in advertising and kept to herself, but would very occasionally have a male friend stay overnight. This then increased to a regular basis, which led me to suspect that he was probably a married man who had come to London on business and to spend the night with her. Tuppence would cook him a meal, taking over the kitchen area for hours; the couple would drink alcohol and get louder and louder as the evening progressed, creating a disturbance for me and Juliette, who were by then in bed. I did not care much for Tuppence and our relationship was very distant.

Juliette had a house rule: Both of us could meet boyfriends or friends during the weekdays, but the weekend was our time together for shopping, partying, and going to discos. We would browse the markets in Petticoat Lane and Shepherd's Bush, and every weekend we'd buy something new to wear to social functions and the discos we both loved. Juliette had a brother, a builder, who also had a part-time job as a minicab driver in the evening and late into the night on weekends. Usually, after our weekend outings, Juliette would contact him and get him to take us both home safely for free between his paid jobs. We probably never gave him any money for these trips. Once, while we were waiting for his minicab in Leicester Square, a man with a Scottish accent approached me and asked me 'How much?' I felt indignant and said to him, 'If you do that type of thing in Scotland, we certainly do not do it down here!' The man just walked away from me.

Unwelcome attention from men never seemed very far away. I went to a party with Juliette's brother, who was friends with men from a war zone area who had arrived in London as refugees. One of the men followed me when I went to the toilet and tried to force his way into the bathroom with me. I managed to close and lock the door on the man, but was very frightened by the incident and stayed close to Juliette for the remainder of the party. Perhaps one of the strangest times was when one of Juliette's married brothers and his wife were invited to a party, but the wife refused to go, so Pete then asked Juliette and me to accompany him instead. It seemed a strange sort of party to begin with, and then I realised that it was actually a wife swapping party, as car keys were being placed on the floor by the men and picked up by the women. Once the sets of keys had all found a 'match', the owner of each set and the woman who had selected them were a couple for the evening. Taken aback by this development, Juliette and I stuck close to Pete who explained to us what was going on. The three of us passed the time eating, drinking, and chatting in the kitchen area which was separate from where most of the people had gathered, before eventually going home early.

Juliette and I used to go on a Friday night to the German Bier-Keller in Trafalgar Square. Although we didn't drink alcohol, we loved the socialising and singsongs and meeting so many people from all different backgrounds and countries. On one of these evenings, I met a man who invited me to a private club called the Reinhardt Club, near Bond Street. Entry to the club was by membership, though guests could attend with a paying member, and the man and I had a nice evening, with dinner and dancing. He then invited me to join him for a weekend on his yacht, an offer which I declined. At this point, he became very annoyed with me and immediately started to insult me. I also met a few English boys and a young Jewish man named Howard, from Golders Green. Howard was very polite and pleasant and would say to me, 'You don't mind a kiss and a cuddle, but that is all you want from me'.

When I was twenty-two, I had an architect boyfriend named Breen who hailed from Portsmouth. Together we went to the now-legendary concert at Knebworth in August 1976 to see The Rolling Stones and Lynyrd Skynyrd play. Breen had organised the tickets which cost £4.25 each, and it was exceedingly difficult to find public transport to and from the venue in the Hertfordshire countryside. That summer, Britain was engulfed in a heatwave that seemed to go on for weeks, and Knebworth Fair, as it was billed, attracted a record crowd that may have been as many as 120,000 people. Everyone milled madly around the field and, as I was sitting with others on the ground, someone high on alcohol and drugs fell on top of me and nearly broke my neck. During the evening, I wandered off on my own and found myself right up at the front watching the Stones perform under the iconic massive pair of inflatable lips that formed the stage. On arriving back in

London, unable to get public transport, Breen became very angry with the situation and seeing this anger really affected my relationship with him after that.

On another occasion, when Scotland played at Wembley, buses and trains again stopped running. As I was waiting for a taxi to get home, I was approached by some Scottish supporters who had come down for the match. No taxi drivers would pick them up, so they asked if I would order a cab for them. The agreement was that I'd ask the driver to drop me off at my home first, free of charge, and then the taxi would take them on to their destination. This was the only option they had for getting around London over that match weekend, so I agreed to help them.

Around this time, I met a bald-headed artist who had an apartment near Marble Arch. Once, I invited him to the basement bedsit for dinner, but Juliette said, 'I'm not giving him dinner!' and all he was offered was sausages and baked beans. He had to wait about two hours before we served him even that. His response to the meal was, 'If I knew that was all I was going to get to eat, I would have had my dinner before I came out'. I never saw him again.

Juliette and I used to attend an alcohol-free disco in a basement somewhere in Earl's Court. Once, I danced with a man there, Rainey, who was from overseas. He invited me and Juliette to a wine and cheese evening elsewhere in London, which we attended with him. After that, he would ring me constantly on the coinbox phone in the entrance hall of the house and always wanted to know what I was doing. I was only interested in Rainey as a friend; I didn't see anything else in him. Sometime later, Juliette and I went back to the basement club and during the evening a man asked me to dance. Rainey, who was also at the disco, became jealous of this man and started a fight with him. Juliette and I left the club and never went back, but that wasn't the end of the story. After that episode, Rainey would ring me, mainly at my place of work, and shout at me on the telephone, which made me frightened. I concluded that he must have been crazy but, on reflection, there may have been a cultural element to his behaviour. Perhaps once I had spoken with him and gone with him to the wine and cheese evening — although in the company of Juliette — he believed that I was his property and belonged to him.

Juliette and I were hitch-hiking along the Goldhawk Road in Shepherd's Bush one evening when we were picked up by a man in a two-door Volkswagen. I had taught Juliette a few 'unorthodox' words in Irish for use in dangerous situations. Sitting on the back seat, I felt uncomfortable with this man, and when he stopped the car to let us out, he pushed the front seat back trying to trap me in the car. I managed to extricate myself but, in the confusion, my purse fell out of my bag and I had to leave it in the car. The purse contained my address and, not long afterwards, I received a letter from the man saying that he really would behave himself if I would go out with him on a date. He stated that he was a 'good Christian boy' and gave his telephone number so I could ring him.

When I did eventually call the number, a woman answered, asking in a panicky voice, 'What has he done now?' I explained to the woman about the purse and eventually I got it back in the post. The only thing missing from it was a photograph of me that I'd kept there.

This wasn't the only outing that resulted in a scary outcome; there was the time Juliette and I went to a house-party together in Earl's Court. During the evening, over conversation and dancing, a man told us that he was an art student and had an assignment to complete for class on Monday morning and so needed to leave the party now. He lived upstairs on the third floor of the house. He asked me if I would be his model for a quick sketch — seemingly he liked the way I wore my headscarf. Foolishly, I agreed. When I reached the flat, the first thing he said to me was, 'The shower is over there'. I turned and bolted from the apartment and made my way back downstairs to re-join the party. The lighting on the stairs was operated by a press button system and although I struggled to work it, I managed to escape unharmed. All these incidents were eye-openers for me, coming as I did from a small provincial Irish town.

Juliette's mother would often pressurise her daughter to return to Ireland. Following every telephone call from her mother, Juliette would be upset for the rest of the evening. From time to time, the pressure would be too much for her, and Juliette would pack up and take the ferry back over to Ireland for a while, leaving me alone in London.

At one point, I took an evening job in Mayfair. I would walk to Marble Arch in the evening to catch the bus or tube home to Shepherd's Bush, and on many occasions, expensive luxury cars would kerb-crawl and try to pick me up, but I just ignored them. I was targeted at bus stops too. As I was waiting to catch the bus home from Notting Hill Gate one evening, a man who had recently arrived in the country, with little or no English, approached me and I understood that he was trying to communicate with some explicit words that he wanted sex. I just indicated with my hands that he should 'go away'. At a Swiss Cottage bus stop, a lady tried to pick me up by inviting me back to her flat. She kept touching my hair, but I politely declined the invitation, behaving as courteously as I could, given the situation. Then there was the time in Shepherd's Bush when a middle-aged woman wearing a red overcoat, high heels, and bright red lipstick said something to me as I was walking home from my evening job. I didn't quite catch what had been said and asked the woman to repeat herself. It turned out she was asking, in a very vulgar manner, for sex. Unimpressed, I kept walking.

On another occasion, I observed a man who seemingly spent a great deal of his time riding up and down on the escalators in Shepherd's Bush tube station 'flashing' at women. I reported him to London Underground security, but they didn't seem too interested in his behaviour. When I worked in Chancery Lane, I used to see an older man who would travel on the bus at lunchtime every day and, when the bus stopped or braked suddenly, he would pretend that he had lost his balance. He would grab any nearby young woman around the bust, pretending that this was unintentional, which it was not. Eventually I approached him regarding his behaviour and said that I had been watching what he was doing to these young girls. He responded by giving me his telephone number so that I could contact him — which, needless to say, I did not do!

> *In this cry of pain, the inner consciousness of the people seems to lay itself bare for an instant, and to reveal the mood of beings who feel their isolation in the face of a universe that wars on them with winds and seas.*
>
> —John Millington Synge

TWELVE
FINDING LOVE

Here bring your wounded hearts, here tell your anguish;
Earth has no sorrow that Heaven cannot heal.

—Thomas Moore

Juliette and I met two Malaysian Chinese boys on one of our outings. Juliette talked to Bao, and I ended up mostly chatting with Alex during the evening and we later exchanged contact details. Ultimately however, Bao and I began a relationship. I felt comfortable in the company of Malaysian Chinese men; we would go as a group to the Playboy Club for dinner and the men would gamble. Some of these people were wealthy students, while others were from the diplomatic corps (DC) and I started to mix in a different circle, including heads of airlines and high-powered individuals. On several occasions at the Playboy Club I was given money by Bao with which to play blackjack.

Bao invited me to a Chinese wedding on a boat on the River Thames, and this was my first introduction to both Chinese food and using chopsticks — which I found so hard to handle that most of my food went under the table! Bao had also invited a Canadian girl along, and I felt that I was in some way competing with this girl, which may partly explain how I ended up dating Bao.

However, the relationship was short-lived because Bao had already planned to return to Malaysia once he had completed his accountancy studies in London, though, of course, he had not initially told me about this. I was devastated when I found out, as I knew that Bao's Chinese family would not accept me. Despite that, another Malaysian friend, Rayyan convinced me to go and visit Bao in Malaysia. Rayyan had moved to London with his wife and son, although, away from their extremely strict and structured life in Malaysia, they were now living separate lives there.

On arrival in Kuala Lumpur, I was put up in a hotel. Having seen me safely checked in, Bao then went out for the evening with another woman. After that I stayed at the home of one of his friends; Bao never introduced me to any of his family during my two-week stay there. I was extremely confused and disappointed by this, as I was mainly left alone to fend for myself in a strange country. This was the first time in my life that I had been in the tropics and it was all new and strange to me. Despite my distress about the way in which Bao was treating me now that he had clearly moved on from our relationship, I was keen to explore Kuala Lumpur. The air was filled with the wonderful aromas of Chinese, Malay, and Indian cuisine, somewhat offset by the foul smell from the open drains along the streets which one had to be careful to avoid falling into. Brightly-coloured silk and cotton batik garments crowded the small, congested little shops, while Chinese herbal hole-in-the-wall outlets offered everything from saucepans to ornaments.

In those days, a Caucasian woman walking alone attracted stares; the Malay children from the *kampung* would run away and hide when they saw me, calling out *'mat salleh'*, a Malay term used as a colloquial expression to refer to white people. Many of the people, especially Indians, wanted to touch my skin as I made my way along the streets. I still remember words, such as the *Bumiputera* (the native Malay), *gila* (crazy), *salamat pagi* (good morning), *salamat jalan* (goodbye), and the word for food, *makanan*. Kuala Lumpur city was very busy and congested; in the street markets people would wash utensils used for cooking and serving food, in basins of water on the sidewalk and dump the dirty water into the drains. The contrast between the city's rich and poor was extremely pronounced; the professional women were dressed to perfection for work, while older

Sabrina's visit to Malaysia in 1976

men and women, especially the Chinese, looked after the shops with their children and grandchildren. Construction appeared to be going on everywhere with new housing developments being built. I had come with British pounds and found my money went a long way, noticing how cheap gold, in particular, seemed to be. Climbing up to the top of the Batu Caves, around two hundred and seventy steps, was a highlight for me, as was going to Port Dickson to eat satay and to Seremban, which was especially popular for its fresh seafood caught off the western coast of peninsular Malaysia.

During my daily walks around the city, I met many friendly

Malays and Indians. One of these, a Malay-Indian man, worked at immigration and helped me to get a one-day extension on the visa in my passport before I left the country. Without the extension, I would have overstayed by a day in error, which would have caused me problems. However, the man also took me to a strip club, where the management had granted him free entry. This alarmed me, as I was extremely conscious of my safety during my time in Malaysia. Obviously, the man was a frequent visitor to the club, and, although the 'performing' ladies to whom he introduced me were all very friendly, I was not at all impressed to have been taken there.

The breakup with Bao left me feeling really unsettled for many years afterwards. I was in emotional turmoil, primarily from what had happened to me as a child, and I'd often say to myself, 'I should never have opened that emotional door, now I am unable to cope.' It probably wasn't the relationship with Bao himself that was the issue; it could have been anyone. This had been my first serious adult relationship with a man, and I found Bao's rejection difficult to cope with on an emotional level. I was dogged by fears linked to events in my past, making it very hard to handle as a grown woman. I came to the conclusion that being unable to shake off the internal upheaval, combined with my coping mechanisms as an adult, probably had nothing to do with Bao but was something deep-seated in my psyche that I could not rid myself of.

It took me a long time to recover from the heartbreak of this episode. I became withdrawn, depressed, and unable to cope with life, often staring into space and not communicating much. I just wanted to be alone. As I reflected on what had happened, I came to the realisation that there was possibly some root cause to the issue, but I had no idea what the underlying problem was or how to deal with it. I became obsessed by the relationship with Bao, to the extent that even getting through the day took all my time and energy. It was as if there was some sort of a hook, or thorn, in my emotions that I was unable to pull out. Emotions were a dangerous place for me, as I was wary of getting in touch with my inner feelings and needed to keep a lid on that part of my life at all costs. I did not want to addle my brain at that stage, as I had too many things going on and needed to remain on an even keel so that I could support myself while living in London. Despite my inner turmoil, I was still a highly-functioning person in my work environment.

Sometime later, I began dating other young Asians, mainly because I believed that this helped me to relate to men in general without it triggering unsafe memories for me. On the other hand, the face of a Caucasian man or the thought of having a relationship with one would only serve to re-victimise me or trigger me, and I had to be in control of my feelings so as not to let them get out of hand again. I craved human contact on an emotional level and found a happy medium. I could have a relationship with a man if that relationship did not remind me of someone, or something, in my past.

Whilst I was psychologically fragile, I would put on a happy outward appearance. When working in an office in Elephant and Castle I had an English colleague who was verbally abusive to me and would poke fun at me because I was Irish. Initially I did not react to him, as I had many other issues in my life to deal with. Then I made a conscious decision that, from now onwards, things were going to be different — I was going to fight back. I had had enough of this man and his abusive ways. To my surprise, one day I became angry and frustrated with his behaviour and shouted at him, giving him 'tit for tat'. From that point onwards, he never harassed me again, and I realised that he was in fact somewhat afraid of me and avoided crossing paths with me when he was alone. I would acknowledge him only with a slight smile.

All this time, Juliette was going back and forth between London and Ireland, but eventually Juliette's absence became permanent as she met and fell in love with a man who later became her husband. Alone in London without any immediate family around, I became very lonely, which fuelled my depression. I even considered suicide and had a plan. My father and I corresponded on a regular basis, and I must have told him how I was feeling and mentioned my thoughts about ending my life. Daddy encouraged me to write to him, and he promised me that after reading my letters he would burn them in the fire and that no one would know anything about the contents, only he and I.

At the time, I held a job with a firm of architects in the City of London. My boss, who was a Freemason, was an expert witness in rights of light and boundary issues and the practice was responsible for some important pieces of work. During my time with the firm, I attended the opening of Roxsonhill Music Hall, The Tiffy Street Barrier, Mark and John Lason's Special Hall, and other such projects. My boss was also responsible for some of the organisational aspects of the Lord Mayor's Ball, and I was involved in the table seating card arrangements for that function.

In addition to working during the day, I always had an evening job, as I felt that this was good for my emotional survival; I wouldn't have time to think about anything other than work. I worked from 9.30am to 5.30pm in an office and then from 6 to 10pm in an evening job. This kept me alive, fully occupied, and did not allow much time for dwelling on how I was really feeling, or allow me a chance to turn inwards on myself. Exhausted after my twelve-hour working days, I would fall into bed and sleep all night long.

At about this time, one of my weekend jobs was at a cinema in Swiss Cottage. Here, in around 1975, I got to know Messica, a Dutch girl from Amstelveen who was working as an au pair for a family in London. Sunday was Messica's day off, and I used to give her complimentary cinema tickets to attend the various shows to pass the time. This lady and I still write every Christmas, but haven't seen each other since 1975. As an usherette, part of my job was to tear patrons' tickets into two pieces, retain half the ticket and then, using a packing needle, thread these ticket halves onto a string with a knot at the end of it. This was long before computerised booking systems, and the needles and strings were handed in by the usherettes at the end of the session, probably for sales reconciliation by the management. The customers' retained portion of the ticket was their receipt for payment and would need to be produced if required by staff or management. Another cinema workmate was Chaf, who was married with two young daughters.

Chaf used to explain to me how she budgeted to make ends meet for her family, as their finances were stretched thin. Most of her grocery shopping was in the form of tinned food, and I decided then and there that I never wanted to end up in the same predicament as this woman. Once, Chaf invited me to her home, but when I got up that Sunday morning, I was finding it difficult to face the day, or life in general. I felt in no condition to socialise as I was emotionally drained and just needed to sleep, so I rang Chaf and cancelled the arrangement but felt guilty for letting my friend down — a memory I have never forgotten.

In 1977, my evening work was at the London Casino in Old Compton St, Soho. The cinema belonged to EMI and showed both movies and occasional stage productions. The last stage show was *Dean*, a musical about the life of James Dean. However, the show was not a success and the cinema was converted back to a full-time theatre and given back its original name, the Prince Edward Theatre, where *Evita* opened in June 1978. After that, I was transferred to another EMI-owned enterprise, ABC Cinemas, where I worked in the office in the evening for approximately six years. This gave me free access to most cinemas and theatres across London. Sometimes the manager would ring up and arrange for complimentary tickets for me, and, at other times, I would do it myself. Through my evening employment, I got to know and experience London's cultural side to its fullest, and all free of charge. During this period, I also paid to go to many concerts and events including Marcel Marceau (a French mime artist and actor) Rudolph Nureyev (the Soviet ballet dancer), Paul McCartney and Wings, Fleetwood Mac, Elton John, Cliff Richard, The Chieftains, Planxty, John Denver, Pink Floyd's *The Wall* at Earl's Court, and many more. In 1982, I saw Elizabeth Taylor in *The Little Foxes* in the West End.

Whilst living in London, I started to suffer from various gynaecological problems, such as pelvic inflammatory disease, endometriosis, and an infection in my fallopian tubes. I went to the emergency department at Hammersmith Hospital a number of times prior to being admitted to the gynaecological ward. On at least two occasions, I was sent home by the hospital without any treatment whatsoever. Unable even to stand up or walk, and in excruciating pain (by then I weighed about 47kg, or just over seven stone), I was told by the hospital staff that, in their professional opinion, I was constipated — which was not the case. Eventually, after returning to the hospital yet again, I was given a proper medical examination. Tests were carried out and I was found to have an infection in my fallopian tubes. I was admitted to Hammersmith Hospital's gynaecological ward, where the patients consisted of women with a variety of OBGYN issues ranging from miscarriages and abortions to problems such as mine. Hardly any sensitivity or respect was shown by hospital staff to any of the patients on an individual basis. One of the overseas attendants there was very hostile towards me; she resented getting me a bedpan or delivering my food. I noticed that the attitude of this woman was mainly negative towards Caucasian patients on the ward; she would leave food in places where they were unable to reach it because of their pain and discomfort. The whole experience in that hospital was quite an unpleasant ordeal.

On another occasion, I needed to have a breast biopsy. With no immediate family around to take care of me during my recovery, I had to catch the bus home to a cold and lonely bedsit when I was discharged from the hospital shortly after the operation. The after-effects of the anaesthetic left me feeling low and depressed in myself, and I had difficulty moving my arm, as I was in a lot of pain. I stayed home for two or three days, but eventually decided to go back to work, as the loneliness was unbearable in the bedsit and I chose to recuperate at the office instead.

After the bad experience at Hammersmith Hospital, I decided that from then onwards I would only attend private clinics and hospitals. Treatment of patients was much better in the private rather than public hospitals in London, and by then I had taken out medical insurance with BUPA, which enabled me to make the change. After that, I visited Harley Street specialists and only used facilities such as Princess Grace Private Hospital for any other medical conditions I had whilst living in London. I was treated with respect and dignity in those environments.

Between my day and evening jobs, I used to catch the tube to

Marble Arch and then walk down to the cinema to start my evening job. At that time, I carried my personal items in a willow basket. Then one day, the newspaper seller outside the Oxford Street exit at Marble Arch tube station greeted me with, 'How's Red Riding Hood today?' Although I have kept the beautiful basket, I never used it again after that.

There was an overseas student who also worked at the cinema in the evenings. He would get off the tube at the same station as me, and occasionally we would walk down to our workplace together. After this had only happened about twice, he said to me out of the blue, 'Shall we get married, then?' I was startled by the somewhat crazy suggestion, as I hardly knew the man and wasn't even in a relationship with him. However, someone mentioned to me later that he had probably wanted to stay in the country and was looking for someone to marry in order to get a permanent resident's visa.

At the architectural firm where I worked my day job, the environment was strange and dysfunctional. For a start, the strict dress code meant that I wasn't allowed to wear trousers to work. My position was designated as 'Girl Friday', and I was expected to make and serve everyone morning and afternoon tea; no employee in the office ever made themselves a drink, as they expected to be waited upon by me. I also had to do the washing up. One of the perks of the job was that I was given daily luncheon vouchers worth 15p, which — believe it or not! — helped my finances. I would buy toast with marmalade in the morning and an egg mayonnaise roll at lunchtime from a sandwich bar near my work. This was a small, family-run business owned by a husband, his wife, and her mother, whom everyone called Mum. I would sometimes treat myself to fish and chips, a cup of tea, and a slice of buttered bread from a chip shop in Theobalds Road. I went back there in the mid-1990s and found that the shop was much the same; the orders hadn't changed, and the lady who had served me in the '80s was still there working in the business.

One of the architects in the office, Art, was gay and he and I became particularly good friends. I have always got on well with gay men and have had several close gay friends throughout my life. For me, there was an element of safety in these relationships, and I often preferred the company of gay men to women as I found them to be very considerate and caring. I made many great friends in the gay communities in the UK and, later, New Zealand.

Art, like his boss, was a Freemason. He enlisted my help in learning his Masonic lines for the different degrees of progression, dressing up in his regalia and prancing around the office when the boss was out, practising his first, second and third degrees. I had to ensure that he knew his lines and was making the right movements and signals in accordance with Masonic rituals as he progressed towards becoming a member of the society. On Masonic dinner evenings, I would be Art's 'lady' as, according to him, no one there knew that he was gay. However, when we left the Masonic event, we would catch a taxi to the A and B Gay Club and, on entering the club, Art would say when referring to me, 'take no notice of her, she's in drag, tonight.' When he got drunk, which was most nights, he would often tell me that if he was straight, he would marry me. He confided many of his secrets to me and taught me all the gay terms and terminology of the time. Art and I were extremely close as a couple and remained good friends until his death. He had a permanent live-in partner in the form of a waiter from Nice who, according to Art, used to knock him about. He said Ola had refused to move out of the apartment when the relationship went cold. The locks had been changed, but Art felt overcome by fear and intimidation and eventually gave up resisting. In the end, Art and Ola made the situation work for them, and they continued living under the same roof though they were no longer in a relationship as a couple. The financial burden of running the apartment, however, fell on Art.

The boss of the architectural company was a womaniser. At the time that I worked there, he was with wife number three. I was aware that he had hidden some jewellery belonging to one of his previous wives in a drawer in his office so as to avoid passing it on to her as part of the divorce settlement. He had met his current wife at that time, a lady from Nigeria, on a train. He would sometimes send round a note to all the staff telling them to 'be gone from the office by 5.30pm sharp'. Those were the evenings when he would conduct liaisons with other women, away from his unsuspecting wife. One lady was a barrister, Ms Pettisure, who arrived at the office just after 5.30pm on numerous occasions during the working week. Sometimes in the mornings, I would find condom packages on my desk, placed there by the office cleaner, who was clearly trying to tell me something.

No female employee felt safe around this man, who would engineer things so that he could get her alone, especially near the filing cabinet section located in a corridor away from the main office. Then, he would put his arms around her and try to kiss and touch her up, while asking her to 'tell Daddy all about it.' Art believed that the man was 'all mouth and no trousers'. He said that if I saw the scrubbers he usually picked up, I would be horrified. I didn't take much notice of the boss, though I knew there was something seriously wrong with his behaviour. Then, when I was off work for a few days having had the breast biopsy, he came round to visit me at my bedsit. Initially, I thought that was a kind gesture, but the man had ulterior motives. On arrival, he tried to hug me, but I pushed him away.

'When are you going to let me introduce you to some clean, healthy sex?' he asked me.

My reply was to the point: 'If I wanted clean, healthy sex it is not from you that I would be seeking it!'

The boss wasn't impressed with that response and left shortly afterwards. I learned in later years that he had wife number four and was living with her and their son in China.

I was very conscientious, honest, diligent, and extremely good with finances and saving money. While working at the architectural practice, I applied for a Visa card and was turned down by the credit card company for no apparent reason other than what I believed to be a form of discrimination based on my country of birth, information which I had supplied on the application form. I found this situation especially infuriating, as my boss's student son, who had no income, was granted a Visa card at around the same time that I had applied and had been declined. I contacted Visa, pointing out the two situations, and they eventually issued me with a card. Over the telephone, the credit card company representative sneeringly stated that, after consultation, they had now changed their minds, 'so that you can have a meal out.'

As I was working two jobs, I rarely had time to socialise with the cinema staff. However, one evening John Koo, known as Qooie, returned to catch up with his old workmates, and I was invited to the pub for a drink with the group. The colleagues were from Indonesia, Mauritius, Sri Lanka, and England and, as all of them had bought a round of drinks, I decided to pay for a round before I went home for the night.

At this point, aged twenty-three, I thought that I was over men. I didn't know how to cope with my emotions any longer and felt it would be better to forget about romance altogether, as it might make my life much easier. Then, that evening at the Helvetia pub in Soho, I met a tall, skinny, handsome Kiwi who had arrived in London on his OE (overseas experience) the previous summer, in July 1977. This New Zealander was working behind the bar and asked Chris from Mauritius where I was from, but Chris misunderstood which young woman the barman was referring to and thought he was asking about Francesca, who was Indonesian. So, when I went up to the bar to buy my round, the Kiwi got it wrong.

'I understand you come from Indonesia', he said.

'No, I'm from Ireland,' I laughed.

'Well, at least I got the letter I right!' replied the barman, whose name was Jeffrey.

Jeffrey asked me if I would like to join him and some friends, as they were going to a concert. I agreed, though I had no real intention of ever seeing him again, or indeed returning to the Helvetia bar. However, Jeffrey now knew where I worked in the evenings and, when the opportunity arose, he would come over to the cinema and chat with me while I manned the confectionery kiosk. The manager of the cinema liked to comment on this, remarking, 'your long-legged friend is here again.'

Eventually, Jeffrey persuaded me to go on a romantic date with him and took me to see Emmylou Harris and the Hot Band at the Royal Albert Hall, where we had a 2nd Tier box, on 9 February 1978. First though, we went for dinner at Poon's, a restaurant in Soho. Over dinner, Jeffrey told me about his life. He had attended Wanganui Collegiate School, a private school in New Zealand (the school at which Prince Edward was later a house tutor and junior master). Jeffrey had gone to teacher training college, had taught at a private school, and had also been a community volunteer at an IHC[1] centre and was then a housemaster at a school for the deaf before embarking on his OE. Like most New Zealanders when they arrived in London, he had got himself a live-in job in a pub in Soho. At that stage, I did not believe one word that Jeffrey told me and suspected that he was trying to impress me with his lies! However, I later found out that he had, in fact, been telling the truth. When Jeffrey and I got together, we would often dine out. We particularly liked an Asian restaurant called Bali on Edgware Road, also a restaurant in Chinatown that had a good reputation for duck and pork, and the famous A. Cooke's Traditional Pie and Mash Shop on Goldhawk Road in Shepherd's Bush.

As our relationship developed, I made it clear to Jeffrey that he would have to make something of himself, as I did not intend to end up with a bum or a no-hoper, as I put it. It was 1978, and I thought that the computer industry looked like it would offer a promising career path for his future. I then took it upon myself to write to various computer companies listed in the Yellow Pages, giving Jeffrey's name in the contact details. Initially, he was offered a job by Boeing Computers as a trainee computer operator in Watford, just north of London. From this start at the bottom of the ladder, his career in the computer industry progressed and he went on to become a trainer, ending up as IT project manager.

My evening jobs allowed me to meet many people who went on to become lifelong friends. In particular, there was a Jewish Czech girl from Prague named Gerda, who introduced me to her friend

---

1. Society for Intellectually Handicapped Children, hence the IHC acronym. IHC advocates for the rights, inclusion, and welfare of all people with an intellectual disability and supports them to live satisfying lives in the community.

Lilting, also Jewish. Lilting's family lived in Hampstead, and her father Manie, originally from Austria, had fought alongside the Germans in the First World War before he later fled to India with his family at the time of the Holocaust. Jeffrey and I would visit Lilting's parents for afternoon tea, and Jeffrey loved to hear the stories that Manie told him about historical events that he had experienced first-hand. Lilting's mother passed on traditional cake recipes from Czechoslovakia, as her family had owned a patisserie shop there before the war. She also gave me a round kugelhupf cake tin with a hole in the centre, which she had taken with her to India when they escaped Europe during WWII.

Lilting had schizophrenia and I was one of only a few people who had any time for her, something her parents really appreciated. Lilting and I would meet once a week for lunch somewhere in London; I was emotionally supportive of Lilting and would offer her encouragement and advice. In later years, I invited her to visit New Zealand for a holiday, though, unknown to me, Lilting was very unwell at that time. I had said to her in a letter that she should never forget that she was one of the 'chosen' people. Sometime later, Lilting's mother wrote to me asking me not to mention this again, as apparently after reading that letter, Lilting had gone into St Paul's Cathedral where she stripped naked, bought all the pamphlets that were for sale, and then told people entering the cathedral that she was the Messiah. In 2010, Jeffrey and I visited Lilting at a Jewish care home in North London where the staff made us feel very welcome. We were joined by Lilting's nephew and were served a beautiful afternoon tea.

A Malaysian music teacher called Li Mei and her partner Chas, a barrister, had also become part of our circle of close friends. The only way in which Li Mei could get to sleep at night was if she drank black coffee before retiring, so when she came and stayed with us, a cup of black coffee would be carefully placed beside the bed for her. Li Mei would down this just before going to sleep—it seemed that coffee had the opposite effect on her compared with most people, who find that black coffee keeps them awake. Li Mei and Chas married in Malaysia in a traditional Chinese wedding ceremony, but unfortunately Jeffrey and I were unable to attend because of the timing. Years later, their son came to New Zealand to study and stayed with us while he attended college and university. In turn, Jeffrey and I visited Li Mei and Chas in Malaysia numerous times over the years. We found the Malaysian people very welcoming and loved the culture and cuisine of the country.

I occasionally went to church in White City, though this meant walking through council housing estates. Eventually, I decided that it wasn't safe to continue walking there by myself and stopped attending church. On one occasion, a young lady came to my door in Shepherd's Bush, told me about how God had changed her life, and invited Jeffrey and me to her church. We went along, but when Jeffrey glanced through the window as we arrived and saw the people clapping, singing, dancing, and praying in the aisles, he said there was no way he was going to go in and we left again. The same lady came back on another occasion, and I sent Jeffrey out to the door to say that I wasn't home.

My landlord, Larry Phee, didn't waste time in making it quite clear to me that he totally disapproved of the fact that Jeffrey had moved into the bedsit with me, calling me many unpleasant names. I managed to secure the lease on a renovated basement apartment in Conningham Road, Shepherd's Bush, which was part of a rehousing programme set up by the Totting Miele Housing Trust which had purchased the St Stephen's Avenue property.

The rent was £13 per week, and Jeffrey and I stayed there until eventually leaving London in 1983. During the time that we lived in the basement flat in Conningham Road, various friends and acquaintances of Jeffrey's would turn up from New Zealand. I didn't know any of them but made them welcome. When these overseas visitors arrived, they were given the living room to use as their bedroom for the duration of their stay. Jeffrey made it a house rule that visitors could stay free of charge, but they had to look after themselves regarding food. One of these visitors was a friend of Jeffrey's from his school days at Wanganui Collegiate. Manuel used to sit in the bath doing his washing. He had come over, so he said, to attend our wedding, but he took off one weekend leaving his dirty laundry in the bath and was not seen again for several months. He ended up in Austria working as a ski instructor and invited Jeffrey and me to come and stay with him. On the evening that we arrived at the house in the Alps, Manuel was nowhere to be found, though the house was unlocked and there was a semi-plucked chicken boiling in a saucepan on the stove. Apparently, he had recently been dismissed from his job at the ski resort for giving away free drinks to his friends, but the kitchen staff there were unaware that he was no longer employed and he was down at the resort having his usual free evening meal. Two more guests he'd invited showed up at the house for dinner, so then there were four people waiting for Manuel to return, but he didn't come back to his accommodation to greet his visitors for several hours. When he eventually made an appearance at the house, he had already eaten.

I had never skied before, though Jeffrey had a little experience. Manuel took us up to the slopes and, while we were talking, I moved my skis and inadvertently took off, careening into a fence. Next day, Manuel, the now-sacked ski instructor, took us up on the ski lifts. (Manuel's father, who was visiting from New Zealand, had intended to join us all on the slopes but after a few too many drinks the evening before had woken up that morning to find that he had spent the night sitting on the toilet in his accommodation and was in no fit state to take to skis.) We found ourselves disembarking at the top of a black run — the highest level of difficulty — both dressed in denim jeans and ordinary jackets, with no skiing attire whatsoever. I took one look and refused to ski down the piste; I removed my skis and plodded gingerly until the ground levelled out a bit, while Jeffrey turned his skis sideways and inched his way down the very steep slope. As we skied on flatter terrain, we built up more confidence and, despite feeling a bit sore, our technique vastly improved. Then we became enveloped in a whiteout and couldn't see a thing. Eventually, we came to a rest area where we fortified ourselves with Jägermeister shots, which warmed us up considerably, and we pressed on, back down to the resort and safely home.

THIRTEEN
MARRIAGE AND TRAVEL

What the heart knows today the head will understand tomorrow.

—James Stephens

Not long after Jeffrey and I had met, we purchased a car in the form of a brand-new, lime green Austin Mini Metro that enabled us to explore the English, Irish, and Welsh countrysides. A favourite place of mine was Bakewell, in the Derbyshire Peak District. Here we visited one of England's finest stately homes, Chatsworth House, seat of the Dukes of Devonshire, which has been used as a filming location for many period dramas over the years. The small town of Bakewell itself, with the five-arched medieval bridge spanning the River Wye, was charming; we found the locals friendly and loved the markets, where we sampled the famous Bakewell tarts. I have never lost my great love for both Bakewell and Christmas tarts, and I try to get hold of some to grace our table in New Zealand every Christmas.

Taking a trip to Wales was another wonderful experience for us as a young couple, though when Jeffrey told his English work colleagues that he intended to explore Wales, many people expressed extremely negative views. His colleagues discussed among themselves which races were their least favourite and no one could agree, but, in the end, they all agreed that every one of them disliked the Welsh the most, which surprised Jeffrey. During our trip, once the Welsh people learned that neither Jeffrey nor I was English (we were travelling in a car with English registration), there was a noticeable change in attitude for the better among those we met. For example, in petrol stations, once the attendants had spotted our number plate, they would initially converse with us in Welsh, but, having ascertained that neither occupant of the car *was* English, they would switch language and carry on the conversation in English!

Jeffrey was given tickets to the Paris Air Show, compliments of his employer at the time, Boeing Computers. The tickets included entry to the Boeing hospitality marquee that had prime views of the airshow. On the overnight train we shared a compartment, and our food, with a Swiss lady called Aatukka. As a result of that chance meeting, we became lifelong friends. Jeffrey and I visited Aatukka in Bern on numerous occasions, most recently in 2015, and she made four visits to us and our family in New Zealand.

Crossing the Atlantic, we visited Canada once and the United States twice. On one of the visits to the USA we bought a 'hop on, hop off' airline ticket with Continental Airlines that allowed us to visit many states. We had a fabulous time there, although a trip south of the border to Manzanillo in Mexico left us both with a dose of 'Montezuma's revenge', meaning we had to use our precious holiday time in San Francisco for recovery, thus missing out on many of the locations we had intended to visit. We were virtually confined to our room, which was located in the red-light district and didn't have an ensuite bathroom. When I tired of watching the Baseball World Series on TV, I would sit on the upper storey window ledge watching the operations of prostitutes and pimps below.

A 'selfie' of Sabrina and Jeffrey at Niagara Falls
during their trip to North America in 1982

I had cousins in two areas in the United States, so Jeffrey and I went to visit both families, who made us feel very welcome. My grandmother's sister, Nuala, had left Rimelow in 1920, and my grandmother, Wilma, used to write to her in America. Wilma would ask if Nuala ever considered coming back home to Ireland, as many of the emigrants had returned when things had not worked out for them in America. Wilma would tell her sister about the neighbours, who owed her money, and other local news. By sad coincidence, Nuala's husband was accidentally killed, leaving her with three young children who were subsequently put in state care for a while in America, continuing a theme. The American branch of the family is still in possession of the bible that Nuala was given as a present when she left Ireland, and I have a letter that my grandmother Wilma wrote shortly after Nuala arrived in the USA.

Jeffrey and I had become engaged in 1980, while on a big trip to the United States. However, Jeffrey made it clear that there would be two conditions to our getting married: Firstly, he would eventually be returning home to New Zealand, and I should keep that in mind, and, secondly, he would only get married in an Anglican church. (His mother was Presbyterian, while his father was Anglican.) I readily agreed to these conditions, perhaps not giving as much thought at the time to the 'moving to New Zealand' part as I might have done.

The two of us went to the annual Harrods January sale together in 1981. Five minutes before closing time, I had a quick look around the women's department where a beautiful cream dress immediately caught my eye. I bought the gown, priced at £75, but left it at the store and returned later to have it altered and fitted, at a further cost of £15. I treasured it for years and when in 2019 Moira, our only daughter, asked if she could incorporate it into her own wedding dress for her marriage to an English police officer in Cornwall, I readily agreed.

I arranged my Irish wedding whilst living in London and applied to be married in the Church of Ireland (Anglican Church), which was accepted. I had to spend the two weeks prior to my marriage living in Ireland, during which time the banns were displayed. The only May date that was available for the nuptials fell on the twenty-second, a Friday, which was neither the custom nor the tradition in Ireland, but that was the day that was decided upon. The ceremony was to be held at 4pm to allow the mainly farming guests time to complete their tasks for the day so that they would be able to enjoy the wedding celebrations uninterrupted.

A few days prior to the wedding, there was a loud knock on my father's front door. I was informed that Canon Koleraine, a member of the chapter of the local Catholic cathedral, had asked to talk with me. Immediately, there was a scurry, as my father disappeared out the back door of the house. I walked to the front door and invited my visitor in. Without beating about the bush, Canon Koleraine announced to me that he had been informed that I intended to marry soon in the Church of Ireland, and it was his duty to tell me that if I went ahead with the marriage as arranged, I would not be officially married and that any future children I may have would be bastards. Outraged, I told him that his teaching was totally out of order and that his doctrine was incorrect. I also made it clear that I would be going ahead with my wedding in the next few days and that it was none of his business whom I married, or where the wedding was held. After a twenty-minute argument, Canon Koleraine gave up and left. Shortly after that, Jeffrey arrived at the house, having travelled from London. My immediate greeting to him was, 'Your timing is perfect as you've just missed Canon Koleraine's verbal abuse.' Daddy then reappeared in the living room and enquired as to what had gone on, but I went about my business and didn't allow myself to be daunted or derailed by some religious ignoramus prior to my wedding day. I paid little or no attention to what Canon Koleraine had said to me, though I did wonder privately how the man had dared to talk to me in such a manner.

A few years later, when I was married and a mother living in New Zealand, I found myself chatting after a funeral service at Whenuatapu with Fr Leon, an Irish priest from the local St Mary's church. I told him that I lived in Bayview and mentioned that my father had spent many years in a seminary. A few months later, I heard that Fr Leon had recruited some of his congregation to make enquiries to find out whether there were any unbaptised children of Catholic parents living in the community. He considered that such children should be baptised into the Catholic Church, and, soon enough, he paid a visit to our house. I invited him into my home and for the next half hour or so the priest argued with me, trying to convince me to have the children baptised in the Catholic faith. He said that he was not bothered about the adults, only the children. This gave me something of a sense of déjà vu, as it took me right back to the days preceding my wedding in 1981 when I'd had the argument with Canon Koleraine in Baile na Ghlic. There was no way Fr Leon was going to convince me that he was right, and he got so upset with me at one stage that his teeth were chattering. However, when he finally left, my parting words were that he was more than welcome to come back anytime and visit our home. Jeffrey made the comment that there was 'probably nothing worse than two strong-willed Irish people arguing!' Months later, I ran into Fr Leon again, and I greeted him with a hug. He was obviously somewhat embarrassed by the friendly encounter; he just smiled at me and said nothing.

Some three decades on from my wedding, while I was back in Ireland on holiday, Jeffrey met an Irish girl and her boyfriend who were travelling around New Zealand together. Jeffrey mentioned to the young woman that his wife was from Baile na Ghlic, whereupon the Irish lady pondered aloud whether Jeffrey's wife knew her uncle, Canon Koleraine. When Jeffrey next spoke with me, he asked me if I knew this Canon Koleraine. I laughed at his question and asked did he not remember him, before reminding my husband rather sharply about the event just before our wedding.

'Of course, I bloody remember Canon Koleraine!' I said.

It did cross my mind to wonder what the Canon might have said all those years later about his niece and her boyfriend travelling around the world together, unmarried, after his unfounded judgement of me back in 1981.

In those days, guests gave wedding presents — there was no 'gift register' and the bride and groom just accepted what was given to them. Our presents were deposited in a corner of my father's living room and included kettles, toasters, sheets, towels, and ornaments. The donors of the gifts were mostly identified, but I never discovered who had given a few of the ornaments. As is the custom in Ireland to this day, some people gave money, the cash being enclosed in an envelope with a card. Because Jeffrey and I already had a fully furnished flat in London, many of the items were duplicates that we left in Ireland for others to use.

Our wedding day dawned fair; the sun shone and the rain stayed away for outside photographs. I had chosen to carry two stems of pale purple silk sweet peas as my bridal flowers. However, the wire stalks were partly exposed, so just before the wedding, I called in at the local drapery shop, Dobinson's, and bought some lilac velvet ribbon to wrap around the stems. The shop assistant asked me if I was going to a wedding, and I replied that indeed I would be, that afternoon. Still curious, the attendant then asked who was getting married and was very shocked to learn that it was the bride in the shop, doing the purchasing on the morning of her wedding! (Dobinson's store had the old-fashioned Lamson

Jeffrey and Sabrina on their wedding day in 1981 in Baile Na Ghlic

rapid spring cash carrier, or rapid wire carrier system, whereby the sales docket and money were put into a wooden carrier by the sales assistant and sent to the shop's central accounts office. The change was then returned to the customer within a minute or so.) I still have the arrangement of sweet peas, some forty years later, which I treasure as a reminder of our wedding day.

Daddy walked me down the aisle of the little church and gave me away; I had a bridesmaid and a flower girl as my attendants and Jeffrey's best man was one of his childhood friends. Among the guests was my friend Lilting. Forming the centrepiece at the reception was a beautiful, three-tiered traditional iced fruit cake which I had asked a neighbour from my old home across the street in Baile na Ghlic to bake for me; in the end, it was a gift, because Helena refused to take any money for it.

Tea, coffee, and sandwiches were served as the wedding party arrived at the hotel, prior to the main meal which was at around 6pm. The three-course wedding breakfast had a starter, a main of either chicken or turkey, followed by dessert. Two choices were offered for each course and, later in the evening, more tea, coffee, and sandwiches were served with the wedding cake — all of this for the princely sum of £5 a head plus wines! After the wedding, the remainder of the cake was cut up, and anyone who had sent a present, but had not been able to attend the wedding, was posted a small piece of cake in a specially designed box with a liner, accompanied by a 'Thank You' card for the gift.

A band had been arranged to provide the music, but, at the last minute, I discovered that the musicians had somehow booked themselves for two functions on the same day and would have needed to leave the wedding by 8pm. Feeling somewhat let down, I hastily recruited another, local Irish showband who played music, with one aim — to get people dancing. And dance they did; it was a wonderful evening, with the music finishing up at around midnight. It was customary for the bride and groom to change into casual clothes once the wedding party was well underway and depart for their honeymoon, leaving the guests to continue the celebrations, which, in this case, carried on till around 2am. After the festivities, Jeffrey and I spent the night at the Lakeview Hotel in An Clár.

Then, on the day following my wedding, I did something strange that I did not really understand at the time. Back in Baile na Ghlic, I took a stroll down East Street with my new husband, Jeffrey, feeling that I needed to pass by the shop belonging to the cobbler, Jimmy Deviouss. Subconsciously, perhaps I wanted him to know that I was now married and that he had not destroyed my life. Later, I discovered that the photographer who had been commissioned to take our wedding photos had displayed a bridal portrait of me in his shop window, without my permission. This picture became part of his advertising campaign in Baile na Ghlic for several years afterwards, which upset me, as I was uncomfortable with the idea that Deviouss may have seen a picture of me on my wedding day.

After our wedding, Jeffrey and I drove up to Killibegs in Donegal and then over the border into Northern Ireland for our honeymoon. This was the first time I had been in the North. We drove around the outskirts of the cities and smaller towns, and, when we came back across the border to the Republic of Ireland, (Éire), a British Army officer told us that we were fortunate that we had not been stoned because we were driving a GB (Great Britain)-registered car. One thing that really struck me about that trip to Northern Ireland was the number of unemployed people just standing around on street corners without any hope for the future. What neither Jeffrey nor I had realised was that it was the English Spring Bank Holiday weekend in Northern Ireland.

Bobby Sands[1] had died in HM Prison Maze two weeks earlier as a result of his hunger strike; other prisoners were refusing food. That weekend, numerous busloads of supporters had come over the border from the Republic in support of the hunger strikers, which further added to the tense atmosphere. Between March and June of that year, ten IRA/INLA[2] prisoners starved themselves to death.

On a trip across the Channel, Jeffrey and I enjoyed a weekend in Brussels. When returning on the ferry, the usual formalities involved going through passport control aboard ship, and we proceeded to do this. When I handed my passport across the desk for processing, additional questions were asked by the immigration officer who ended up consulting with what appeared to be a plain clothes police officer. It was only when we got back to London that evening that we heard the news that, at the same time as we had been in Brussels, the IRA had assassinated Lord Mountbatten off

---

1. Robert Gerard (Bobby) Sands, (9 March 1954 – 5 May 1981) was the leader of a 1981 hunger strike in which Irish Republican prisoners protested against the removal of Special Category Status, which differentiated between political prisoners and criminals. Sands was a member of the Provisional Irish Republican Army (IRA) and had helped to plan the 1976 bombing of a furniture company in Dunmurry, which was followed by a gun battle with the Royal Ulster Constabulary (RUC). He was arrested while trying to escape and sentenced to fourteen years imprisonment for possession of firearms. While serving his sentence, Sands was elected to the British Parliament as an Anti H-Block candidate. He died in the Maze Prison's hospital at the age of twenty-seven, after sixty-six days on hunger strike, and his funeral was attended by 100,000 mourners.
2. The Irish Republican Army (IRA) was formed in 1919 as a successor to the Irish Volunteers and is a paramilitary organisation seeking an end to British Rule in Northern Ireland and the establishment of a republic. The Irish National Liberation Army (INLA) was formed in 1974 and is a republican socialist paramilitary organisation originally known as the People's Liberation Army. It is the paramilitary wing of the Irish Republican Socialist Party (IRSP).

the coast of Sligo in Ireland, as well as carrying out the Warrenpoint ambush (the deadliest attack on the British Army in Northern Ireland during the Troubles) and setting off a bomb in the Grand Place, the central square in Brussels.

In those days, people travelling on an Irish passport were often harassed by British immigration officers; it was as if the presence of an Irish passport automatically indicated that the owner must be an IRA terrorist. It was a form of discrimination on the part of those immigration officers against the general Irish population. On one occasion, a Northern Irish immigration officer at Heathrow Airport wanted to know why my friend had a different hairstyle from the one she had in her passport photograph. I thought this was a ridiculous statement to make to a fashion-conscious young woman.

'I am sick and tired of your stupidity! Do you really think that the IRA, who you are looking for, will be travelling on Irish passports? No, they will probably be travelling on British passports and, because of your stupidity, YOU JUST KEEP MISSING THEM,' I said to the officer.

Surprisingly, he then apologised to me for his discriminatory behaviour and said that he would not harass me ever again, though he would certainly remember me!

Bitten by the travel bug, in the early years of our relationship and marriage Jeffrey and I were always on the go. Together, we travelled around Europe visiting France, Switzerland, Holland, Luxemburg, Liechtenstein, Denmark, and Germany. On a trip to West Germany, we took the transit road to Berlin[3]. Unfortunately, we overshot a turn-off on the transit road and were then stopped

---

3. During the Cold War, visitors from Western Allies countries were allowed to visit West Berlin, although the city was in East Germany. There were designated road routes through East Germany, and the journey was slow because of border formalities and inspections.

by the waiting East German police, who wanted money from us. After hiding my cash in the car, I produced travellers' cheques, but the officers then took our passports and returned shortly afterwards saying, 'Souvenirs, New Zealand'. I gave them coins totalling about eighty pence in Sterling, which they appeared to be happy with, as they then directed the car across the road and waved goodbye. When we left West Berlin to travel to Hamburg, we reached the East German border crossing where the underneath of the car was checked with mirrors. Jeffrey's passport photo was scrutinised, section by section, to ensure he really was the person in the photograph. He was asked if we were carrying any televisions, and whether anyone was hidden underneath the car.

Not only was this trip our first glimpse of the stark reality of Communist East Germany, it was also our first experience of steak tartare; we were horrified that anyone would eat what we considered to be raw mince with a raw egg on the top of it! (It was actually marinated minced beef.)

Further adventures took us to Scandinavia, where we drove around staying in hostels and sometimes sleeping in our car, as we found travelling expensive in that part of the world. However, this was more than compensated for by the stunning landscapes and interesting towns and cities, which were quite different in character to those in Britain and Ireland. In Stockholm, we stayed on the *af Chapman*, a full-rigged steel sailing ship — one of the city's most famous landmarks — overlooking the Gamla Stan (Old Town) and the Royal Palace. In Stockholm, we hired a car and travelled south to Helsingborg, then north up to Oslo in Norway and on to the Arctic Circle. We then drove across to Finland and down to the capital, Helsinki. Then, leaving Helsinki — one of our favourite places because of the marinated raw fish and the delicious breads we ate there — we caught a ferry back to Stockholm.

On another occasion, we had a two-week holiday in Tunisia, which included a trip into the Sahara Desert, a visit to Carthage, the amphitheatre of El Jem, and to the troglodyte village of Matmata (used in *Star Wars IV – A New Hope*). We had travelled with Freddie Laker Airways, an airline that pioneered the 'no-frills' model, and only got back to London two weeks before the company was liquidated, leaving thousands of holidaymakers stranded overseas.

Sabrina on the edge of the Sahara Desert in Tunisia, 1982

A long weekend on Guernsey in the Channel Islands was also a memorable break. We stayed in bed and breakfast accommodation, and I really liked the place with its French influence — I remember that we had to register our presence on the island on arrival. (Although citizens of Britain and the

Republic of Ireland didn't need passports to enter the Channel Islands at that time, they did need to show ID, as the islands are what is known as the Bailiwicks of Jersey and Guernsey.)

FOURTEEN
A NEW LIFE IN AOTEAROA NEW ZEALAND

An té a bhíonn siúlach, bíonn scéalach
(He who travels has stories to tell)

—Irish saying

I would have been happy to stay permanently in London, but, of course, Jeffrey had told me that one of the conditions of our marriage was that I had to agree to return to New Zealand with him to live. I had wanted to buy a flat in London, but Jeffrey felt that if that happened, we would probably never return to New Zealand. So it was that after having lived in London for ten years, I arrived in New Zealand in June 1983 with my husband. We planned to settle initially in the city of Wanganui, in the North Island, where Jeffrey's family lived.

The journey from Auckland to Wanganui involved driving down SH4 through the Paraparas, a notoriously long, hilly road, which was a little overwhelming for me. I had a feeling of having been kidnapped and wondered where on earth Jeffrey was taking me. The native forests, tree ferns, and unusual birdcalls and the small towns that we passed through with their wooden buildings seemed very alien to me after the rolling fields, hedgerows, stone walls, and solid houses that I'd been used to in Ireland and England. Travelling to exotic places on holiday was one thing, but it felt to me that I'd exchanged everything that was familiar for a totally different environment, despite the fact that English was the predominant language spoken in my new homeland. At first, I felt terribly isolated and could not bring myself to look at a map of the world, as I became overwhelmed with distress at seeing where I had ended up, so far away from family. However, that feeling began to subside relatively quickly as I settled into life in my adopted homeland. After all, I had my husband, who was employed at the Wanganui Police Computer Centre (a job he had secured prior to arriving back in New Zealand after having spent six years overseas) by my side.

My in-laws had an elderly gardener named Alf, who was in his nineties and who had, years earlier, worked for Jeffrey's grandfather on his farm. Alf would come to the house once or twice a week and do the weeding of the flower beds for them. Jeffrey's parents said he really didn't do much, but they hadn't the heart to say that they no longer wanted him, so he just kept turning up. I used to make Alf a cup of tea each morning, and we would spend time chatting over our cuppas. As time went on, we built a great rapport, and Alf would refer to me as 'my girl'. His wife, Helen was even older than Alf. In April 1920, King George V's elder son, Edward, Prince of Wales, who later reigned briefly as King Edward VIII before abdicating, had visited New Zealand to thank the Dominion for its contribution to the Empire's war effort. Arriving in Auckland on 24 April, he spent four weeks travelling the country aboard a lavishly appointed royal train and a motor coach. Helen had been one of the waitressing staff on the train, and after the tour she was presented with the embossed silver teapot that was used on board during the prince's visit.

In later years, Jeffrey and I and our children would always make time to visit Uncle Alf when we were in Wanganui. If Alf heard that I had been in town and had not visited him, he would be upset, so I would always try and pop in for a short while. The skin around Uncle Alf's eyes was very loose; his eyes were often weeping, and he usually had a runny nose, but I tolerated being given a kiss by him on arrival. When he was about ninety-eight years old, he asked me one day, in a profoundly serious manner, how Joan Bloggs could have had a baby when she was not married? Alf was extremely puzzled by this, and I ended up changing the subject, as he was unable to understand the concept of pregnancy without marriage. Alf and Helen's house was incredibly old and everything in it was either antique or just plain ancient; they were still using an old wringer washing machine in the 1990s. On one occasion, I admired a painting of deer by a fountain, and Alf said to me, 'That is going to be yours one day.'

Sabrina visiting Waitangi, New Zealand, in 1984, where the Treaty was signed in 1840

Alf once told me that when he had asked Helen to marry him, she had enquired how much money he had, and, when he told her, she'd replied that when he had a very specific amount, then he should come back and ask her again. This he did, and they were married for over sixty-five years. Even after they were married, they kept their finances separate. They had no children, and each had their own belongings; it was his money and his belongings and her money and her belongings. To supplement their income, they grew flowers and made jams and marmalades and sold their produce at the local market. Presumably, they each kept the money accrued from their own labours!

Helen and Alf would never roast or fry meat; it all had to be boiled, and visitors were always likely to find a chook boiling in a pot on the stove. That would mean soup for lunch and a main meal of chicken, all in one pot, with leftovers that would last the old couple a week. Our children in particular loved Alf and Helen's home, as there were many places to explore and hide in. Their favourite hiding place was behind Alf's big, old, heavy coats that hung on a stand in the hall. The smell in the house was not too wholesome, and I would tell the children that they must wait until they got home to use the bathroom. I was always a bit worried about being offered a cup of tea in the house in case I picked up unwanted germs.

Helen died when she was in her late nineties, and Alf decided that all her money and belongings should be given immediately to her family. When it came to his turn, he said, the same would happen for him, and everything of his would be given to his side of the family. However, Jeffrey's mother was given a silver hand mirror from Helen's estate. Alf had a good friend, a Hungarian man who, after Helen's death, used to visit him every day, take him shopping, and make sure he was keeping well. The two men appeared to have a sort of love-hate relationship and were continually arguing about everything.

Eventually Alf had to go into a rest home for a short time, as he had fallen out of his bed and got stuck between the bed and the wall. He was in respite care when our family visited him for the last time. When we arrived at the rest home, Alf said sternly to me, 'nearly time you arrived, I've been waiting for you!' What I did not notice at the time was that he was sitting on a commode, as Jeffrey later told me. Alf and I spent time together, and the old man really enjoyed chatting with 'my girl', just like old times when I had first arrived in New Zealand. Alf would always refer to England as 'the mother country'. A few days later, Alf passed away; it was as if he had just waited to see me for one last time.

Sometime later, the deer painting was given to me, as well as a gift from Alf's family of an old willow pattern teapot that the couple had received as a wedding present, probably in the 1920s. I also bought Alf's cane-sided couches, which I use to this day, still with their original coverings.

I tried hard to get a job in Wanganui, but, despite my best efforts, finding employment was difficult. I had various interviews and at one of these, a partner in a firm of architects said that if they were to employ me, they would be concerned about what people might think of my accent, and no offer of employment was ever received. After being turned down for a few positions, I became frustrated and decided to seek employment further afield, in Wellington.

I travelled up and down between Wanganui and the capital by bus, a journey of about three hours, and, from Monday to Friday, would stay in various places that offered cheap accommodation in Wellington. On one of these bus journeys, I met a kind Māori gentleman called Huirangi whose whānau (family) came from

Taranaki. Huirangi and I would spend the journey talking about the similarities between the Māori and Irish cultures and the importance of indigenous languages. Huirangi told me that he was involved in a programme to encourage the resurgence of te reo, the Māori language, and with the founding of Māori television. I looked forward to the conversations that I had with him on the bus trip home to Wanganui on Friday evenings. Huirangi would always keep a seat for me, and we would sit together for the duration of the journey. That was my first introduction to Māori culture, and I treasured that encounter with Huirangi when I was a newcomer in Aotearoa New Zealand.

Eventually, Jeffrey got a transfer to the Ministry of Defence, where he was one of the first civilians to work in their computer centre. Initially, he was given a Housing Corporation house as part of the transfer, and we lived in Cannons Creek for about six months until we purchased our first home further north in 1985, using money that I had come into through my father's sale of the farm in Ireland. (He distributed some of the funds to me.) In addition, I also received an inheritance from my Uncle Sett, who had died in 1985. This enabled Jeffrey and me to purchase our first home in Bayview, which put us on the 'property ladder'. The three-bedroom house, with a beautiful view of Kapiti Island, cost $69,000 in 1985. The home was located north of Wellington, where our family lived for sixteen years.

In September 1985, I packed some necessary things into the Renault 12TL, drove thirty kilometres to meet Jeffrey, and together we made our way across the city to Wellington Hospital to welcome our first baby. On arriving at the hospital at around 5.30pm, I ate some yoghurt, and we went for a walk in the hospital grounds. At approximately 7pm, we returned to the labour ward together. With the assistance of Jeffrey, I made myself comfortable; my husband was an excellent help and a great support, which meant that very little intervention by hospital staff was needed. There was a fan in the room, and I found a focal spot on the wall that became the centre of my attention throughout the short labour. At eleven minutes to ten, I gave birth to a son, naturally, without any medication.

Jeffrey and I named our baby Jack and were as delighted with him as any new parents can be. Jack developed jaundice soon after his birth, which is not uncommon. On one particular day, I was holding him in my arms trying to breastfeed him when the sister, or nurse in charge of the maternity ward, came over and plucked the baby from my arms.

'Put him down, you're not going to have time for that nonsense when you get home!' she said, in a nasty tone of voice.

In common with many new mothers in the days following childbirth, I was feeling very vulnerable, and the nurse's unnecessarily harsh manner made an unforgettable impression on me.

As Jack grew from a baby into toddlerhood, I was perhaps overprotective of my son. I decided that Playcentre[1] would be the most suitable form of early childhood education for him. Taking him to Playcentre meant that I was able to stay with him while he was very young and, later, when he reached the age of four, I could leave him alone on some of the days when he attended the sessions

---

1. Playcentre started in New Zealand in 1941 as a more structured form of playgroup run by parents, and quickly grew to become a nationwide early childhood education and parenting organisation. Operating on the philosophy that parents are first teachers, and encouraging child-led play and learning through discovery of the environment around them, it also offers parents the opportunity to gain a qualification in Early Childhood and Adult Education. Playcentre states its mission as *Whānau tupu ngātahi — Families growing together*. Although indigenous to New Zealand, it is now also established in Japan.

without my being present. I embraced the Playcentre philosophy and then embarked on Playcentre training myself, as well as taking papers at the College of Education in Wellington. I earned a Higher Diploma in Early Childhood Teaching in addition to taking recognised papers in what was known then as special education — early childhood, working with children with disabilities or special needs. I became a registered early childhood teacher and continued my involvement in Playcentre long after my children had started school. Playcentre gave me a sense of community; it was as if I had rediscovered childhood again myself in that environment, and this helped with my own healing process.

In a way, my adult self and my inner child, with my own children alongside me, could feel safe and enjoy everything that Playcentre offered. I kept to myself and did not connect very deeply with the other adults there, but was particularly good at initiating conversation on a general level. Children seemed drawn to me and, since having my own babies, I had overcome the earlier feelings that had challenged me during my stay as an au pair in the USA. I had a natural rapport with children, something I believed could not be achieved simply through study. One woman appeared to be jealous of how the children related so well to me.

In late 1985, Abby, now retired, embarked on a trip to New Zealand. My heart sank when he told me that he was coming to visit for six weeks. Jack was about six weeks old at the time — Abby would refer to the baby as 'Young Hopeful'. The last thing any new mother really wants is a demanding visitor arriving for an extended stay. En route to New Zealand, Abby stopped off in Malaysia and stayed with our friends, who said afterwards that he had been demanding, expected to be waited upon all the time, and contributed nothing during his stay, as he had little or no money. I was embarrassed for having introduced him to our friends, as he appeared to have abused their hospitality as he had done with others in the past. He never took any spending money with him when he went on these holidays and behaved like a spoilt little child.

Soon after Abby arrived at our home, Jeffrey and I were working through a schedule for his holiday and telling him about all the places he should visit in New Zealand, which sights to see, and so on, when he dropped a bombshell. He told us that he only had three pounds left for his holiday and that he would not be going anywhere. Naturally, my first thought was, 'What on earth am I going to do with this man for six weeks? I'm already trying to cope with being a new mother — I really don't need this!'

My solution was to take Abby fishing to local rivers in Lower Hutt and Waikanae. According to Abby, he had been advised by staff at New Zealand House in London to purchase a particular model of fishing rod which would net him a great profit, if he were to sell it in New Zealand before he left the country to return home. So, I would sit in the car with Jack, or put the baby on a blanket on the grass to sleep while Abby spent most of the time fishing — or what he termed 'fishing' anyway. In reality, his time was mainly spent trying to retrieve his spinners from the bushes on the opposite bank of the river; he did not catch a single fish during his entire six weeks in New Zealand. I would always bring a picnic for the two of us in an effort to turn these trips into social occasions. Abby expected to be provided with three substantial meals a day and would just sit at the table and wait to be served his food. He didn't even offer to help with any of the washing-up or other housework. Both Jeffrey and I were relieved when the time finally came for his departure — and we were not entirely surprised when no local retailers were interested in purchasing the 'special' fishing rod, which is still stored somewhere in our attic almost forty years later.

Just over two years after Jack's birth, Jeffrey and I welcomed our daughter, Moira. We arrived at the hospital at 3.40am after having dropped off Jack with friends of ours, a Malaysian family in Tawa, who had offered to care for him while I was in hospital. On entering the labour ward, a staff member tried to encourage me to get into the spa bath, but I declined. 'Suit yourself then, but you will be here all night,' said the nurse.

Then, at 3.57am, some seventeen minutes after arriving at the hospital entrance door, I gave birth to Moira naturally in the labour ward, without having needed any medication. The baby and I were in hospital over Christmas, though I was allowed home for a few hours on Christmas Day to have lunch with my family. We went home together about five days later.

When Moira was about nine months old, she started to suffer from bad ear infections. First, I took the baby to the Himana Medical Centre, but the doctor there told me that there was no ear infection; however, later the same evening, Moira was admitted to hospital from the emergency department, accompanied by me. The baby had an exceedingly high temperature, and then her eardrums ruptured, which brought both me and her some relief. I was up all night in the children's ward, as it was virtually impossible to get any rest or sleep with the various crying, sick children and all the activity on the ward. I thought that the best place for me and my baby was at home. Moira was more settled at this stage once the eardrums had burst, so I checked her out of the hospital and took her home.

A few days later, I went back to the GP for a referral to a specialist because of Moira's ruptured eardrums, which had come about because he had missed the infection. However, the doctor was unwilling to help me. 'You had a bite at the cherry and there is no more help for you', he said, presumably because I had checked the baby out of hospital having been admitted from the Emergency Department. I considered his behaviour to be extremely unprofessional and self-referred to an ear, nose and throat (ENT) specialist. On examining Moira, the specialist informed me that the GP didn't have the sophisticated equipment or the general expertise to see that the infection was located *behind* the child's eardrum. From that time onwards, I made sure that my children only saw an ENT specialist for problems of that nature.

When Moira was about two years old, she fell down the fireman's pole at Playcentre. I immediately took her to the same local GP and expressed concern that my daughter had possibly broken her nose in the fall; however, the doctor insisted that this was not the case. The accident and my concern were registered on Moira's medical file and an ACC[2] form was generated documenting the event. Some twenty years later, Moira discovered that she had, in fact, broken her nose all those years earlier at Playcentre just as I had suspected. As an adult, Moira had nasal reconstructive surgery to rectify the childhood accident, paid for by ACC and performed by the ENT specialist she had been seeing since she was very young. Although it was not a pleasant experience, she was glad when she had healed from the surgery. She had gone through her teenage years with low self-esteem from feeling ashamed about how her nose had looked, often being teased and called names at school.

. . .

---

2. The Accident Compensation Corporation (ACC) (Māori: *Te Kaporeihana Āwhina Hunga Whara*) is the New Zealand Crown entity responsible for administering the country's no-fault accidental injury compensation scheme, commonly referred to as ACC. It provides financial compensation and support to citizens, residents, and temporary visitors who have suffered personal injuries.

When Jack was three-and-a-half and Moira about eighteen months old, I was invited to attend a ladies' prayer group in a local community. There, I had a conversation with an older woman called Hasthma about her children and family. Hasthma told me that her own children were now all grown up and that she also had grandchildren. A week or so later, I was talking to Keta, another young mother with children in the group, about a passage in the Old Testament that referred to women who were barren and unable to bear children, quite unaware that Hasthma was listening to our conversation. Hasthma immediately started screaming and shouting at me, though I did not know what the problem was and responded to the woman's attack, which did not help matters. Immediately, I got up and took my baby into the bathroom, pretending Moira needed a nappy change, all the while crying from the shock of the verbal abuse I had received from Hasthma. I left the meeting and never returned to that women's group. No one from the group rang me later, or encouraged me to come back.

A long time afterwards, I met Hasthma and apologised for perhaps having caused an offence to her all those years earlier. Hasthma said that she had often thought about ringing or visiting me to say sorry for her angry outburst, but could never bring herself to do so. She then went on to tell me about her life and background, saying that she was extremely embarrassed by her behaviour that day but had been unable to talk about what had upset her. She said that as a child in England, during the Second World War, before being shipped out to New Zealand she had been told that both her parents were dead. She had a very unhappy childhood in New Zealand, which had scarred her. However, what upset her the most was when she discovered that her father was, in fact, still alive and now remarried and living in New Zealand as well. When she contacted him, he had no interest in her whatsoever, which had devastated her.

Later, each time she became pregnant, she miscarried. The hospital's suggested remedy was to 'go home, get over it and get pregnant again,' which had left her extremely wounded and traumatised from the repeated experiences of loss. She never carried a child to full term herself. Her children were all adopted and throughout her adult life she bore both the grief of not being able to bear children and of her father's rejection. It was the full force of that grief that had been dumped on me at the women's meeting years earlier. However, I had no ill feelings towards this woman, although emotionally I had — unknown to Hasthma — also struggled with things in my own life and was in no position to make any judgement on her.

As a mother, my focus was on my children, and I would dedicate all my time to them, giving my son and daughter my undivided attention. I would take them for walks each day, bringing a picnic to enjoy as part of the outing. Sometimes we would sit on a bench in the park, and I would read books to them; at other times, I would drive to Aotea Lagoon to let the children feed the ducks, burn off energy in the playground, and run around exploring. Much of my childhood on the farm had been spent outdoors in the natural environment, and I felt this was important for my own children.

Without any relatives nearby to lend a hand with the children, I also leaned heavily on Jeffrey, who helped with caring for Jack and Moira in the evenings. He would read them books, such as *The Chronicles of Narnia, Robin Hood, Treasure Island, The Hobbit, The Lord of the Rings* trilogy and the Bible. Storytime before they went to sleep was a nightly ritual, and the bedtime routine would take up to half-an-hour. 'Catch foot day' was a game made up by Jeffrey; he sat in the corridor while the children tried to run past him without his catching one of their bare feet. Jeffrey was only allowed to catch them by a foot, which led to much shrieking and excitement prior to bedtime which the children loved and which gave me some child-free time to myself.

I used to reflect on my life experiences and the uncaring nature of many human beings. I didn't always find it easy bringing up young children without any emotional help or encouragement from close family. Overseas communication at that time was by letter or telephone, though international calls were expensive and charged by the minute. There was no internet, no Viber, Skype, Zoom, or WhatsApp, and I had little or no support from my relatives in Ireland. Had my mother not died so tragically young, I felt she would have been a loving and supportive grandmother, even from a distance, and missed not being able to write to her about the children's progress and achievements and even their routine childhood illnesses and accidents.

FIFTEEN
CHURCH AND COMMUNITY LIFE

I am the way and *the truth and the life. No one comes to the Father except through me.*

—John 14:6

In 1984, before I became a mother, I had gone into the Abundant Life Centre in Wellington to find out more about the beliefs of their particular church. There, I met a woman who later turned out to be the pastor's wife, and she impressed me by not criticising any other churches. She said that their church's beliefs were much the same as those held by other churches, except that they did things a little differently at Abundant Life. I was pleased to hear this statement, and Jeffrey and I started to attend the weekly home church in Paparangi.

The Abundant Life Centre turned out to be a Pentecostal church, with a cosmopolitan congregation. Members of the congregation talked with us and said that we should ask if there was anything we did not understand so that it could be explained to us. If we found ourselves feeling overwhelmed, it would be better for us to sit down, relax, and take time out. The pastor was a Fijian Indian, while the welcoming host family was Malaysian Chinese. Jeffrey and I felt entirely at home among the Chinese, Malaysian, Fijian-Indian, Filipino, and other ethnicities represented in the group. I had spent many years in church before the age of eighteen, but now, for the first time, I made a short declaration based on biblical scriptures (Romans 3:23, Romans 5:8, Romans 10:9, Isaiah 64:6).

Scripture says, 'In the hope of eternal life' God has chosen us, accepted us before the beginning of time, or before the foundations of the World. Even if we feel unworthy, are on the outside, have been abused, rejected, and have been cast out by society, this is the good news for us.

God the Father sent His son, Jesus Christ, God the Son, the Word of God, who is in essence of the Heart of God or the Love, Grá (Irish for love), Aroha (Māori for love), who was born into this world to bring humanity back to God the Father. Jesus bridges the gap between God and us. God the Holy Spirit, the Holy Spirit of God, the very essence or the Spirit or Life Force of the Living God, the Enabler, Helper, or Paraclete, is instrumental in the work of the Father and the Son, Jesus Christ, on earth in drawing us back to the Father; three persons, all individual in One God.

Titus 1:1-2 tells us:

> *Paul, a servant of God and an apostle of Jesus Christ for the faith of God's elect and their knowledge of truth that leads to Godliness in hope of eternal life, which God, who does not lie, promised before the beginning of time.*

And in Ephesians 1:4 we read that:

> *For He chose us in Him before the creation of the world to be holy and blameless in His sight.*

Ephesians 1:6 also says:

> *To the praise of His glorious grace, wherein He hath made us accepted in the Beloved.*

The Bible appears to be telling us that the order is hope of eternal life, chosen and accepted in Jesus Christ since the foundation of the world, followed then by repentance. It is as if there has been an airline ticket purchased for each of us with our name on it, a seat number, date, flight time, and destination. Our part is to decide whether we want to turn up and get on that flight to the destination printed on the ticket. This is an individual choice each of us must make: We have free will, and that decision has nothing to do with belonging to, or being born into, a particular church heritage or a denomination. Some of us will, of course, miss that flight to eternity.

The breaking of the Ten Commandments is sin and ultimately separation from God, doing things our own way and turning our backs on Almighty God. Repentance is a change of heart and life, to turn 180 degrees and begin to travel in the opposite direction, the right direction. Acts 2:38 says, 'Repent and be baptised, every one of you, in the name of Jesus Christ for the forgiveness of your sins'. According to John 1:9, 'If we confess our sins, He is faithful and just and will forgive us our sins and cleanse us from all unrighteousness.' The Bible states in John 3:1-21 that a person cannot enter God's presence, unless he or she is 'clothed' in the righteousness of Jesus Christ or, in other words, born again, or has accepted Jesus Christ as their Lord and Saviour, the only way to God.

Who can be forgiven? Everyone who turns to the Lord. In 2 Chronicles 33:1-20, King Manasseh did evil in the eyes of the Lord; he practised every conceivable evil and perversion, devoted himself to witchcraft, and was a murderer, even sacrificing his sons to a pagan god. But when he was taken into captivity, he earnestly cried out to God and repented. King Amon, his son, was worse than his own father, King Manasseh. After King Manasseh repented, he had the kindergarten-aged Josiah, his grandson, sit on his knee and be taught the ways of God by him. Josiah would only have known his grandfather during the years that King Manasseh had faithfully served the Lord and not during the years that King Manasseh had done evil in the eyes of the Lord, before he had repented. If Manasseh can be forgiven and be changed, so can each one of us.

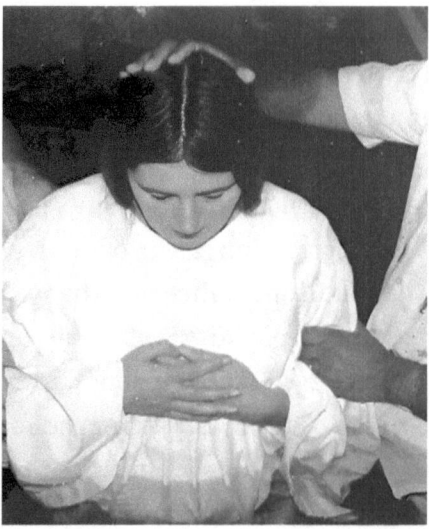

Sabrina at six months pregnant getting water baptism in Wellington, New Zealand, in 1985

The prayer, or declaration, that I made went something like this:

Lord Jesus, I know I am a sinner, but You died on the cross and shed Your blood for every sin I have ever committed. I am sorry for that sin and I turn from it now. I ask You to come into my life and be my Saviour, my Lord, my God, and my Friend. I choose to follow You from this moment forward. Thank You for calling me, accepting me, and forgiving me. In Jesus' name I pray, amen.

Baptism is an important event in the believer's walk with Jesus Christ. The Bible talks about water immersion baptism, in which a believer makes a public confession of their faith. Jesus led the way by example of water baptism:

And Peter said to them, 'Repent and be baptised every one of you in the name of Jesus Christ for the forgiveness of your sins, and you will receive the gift of the Holy Spirit'. —Acts 2:38

Baptism, which corresponds to this, now saves you, not as a removal of dirt from the body but as an appeal to God for a good conscience, through the resurrection of Jesus Christ. — 1 Peter 3:21

Numerous Biblical references to baptism can be found in the Scriptures — just a few examples being Romans 6: 1 -18, 1 Corinthians 12:13, Acts 2:41, Colossians 2:12, Galatians 3:27, John 1:33; 3:5, and Luke 3:16.

I had never spoken to Alan of the Abundant Life Centre in Wellington, and he knew nothing about me, but in June 1985 he stated in a prophesy about me:

Thou hast a heart even to seek after the deep things of God. For as the Lord had sought thee out from across many waters, He has answered the searching of thy heart and has revealed Himself unto thee.

Yea! The Lord would cause thee to continue to walk in that path, for He would reveal more of Himself unto thee and He will cause thee to walk in a closer way unto Himself, so that He can reveal in a greater way Himself unto thee.

Yea! Hunger and thirst after the things of God. For the Lord would cause this to come upon thee; this hunger and thirst and this dissatisfaction of things that have gone. Yea! and He will plant in thee, even a joy to seek the things of the new.

Yea! For the things you hunger and thirst after now, are the things of God and thou shall be as a fragrance in His presence; for He desires thy fellowship. He desires thee to sit before Him and wait upon Him and seek things of many, who run this way and that way and do not have time to seek after but yea! the Lord would cause this to come upon thee, even that desire to wait upon Him and even that desire to know the deep things in Him. For it is the Lord who has placed this hunger upon thee but oh!

Wait upon the Lord, look not unto distractions, look not unto things that might call thee, but set thy heart to wait upon the Lord and He shall speak to thee, even in the quiet places, even in the secret places.

He shall cause His voice to be heard by thee, yea! For He has called thee over many waters and has caused thee to seek Him and has drawn thee unto Himself, so that thou may be a fragrance, in the presence of the Lord, thy God.

Over the years as I raised my family, I would listen to *Today* with Derek Prince, an international Bible teacher, theologian, and pastor, on Radio Rhema. I found the teachings of Derek Prince to be Bible-based and very sound for my Christian walk. Born in Bangalore, India to a British military family, Prince had been educated as a scholar of Greek and Latin at Eton College and Cambridge University and held a Fellowship in Ancient and Modern Philosophy at King's College. He also studied several modern languages including Hebrew and Aramaic at Cambridge University and the Hebrew University in Jerusalem.

I often took the children to spend the school holidays at El Rancho Christian camp in Waikanae, which offered a cheap and enjoyable holiday for the family. We would rent a cabin, and the children could enjoy the freedom of exploring the well-kept grounds with me. There were many different birds, including peacocks, that the children looked forward to seeing. In August 1988, Jeffrey and I went to hear pastor Peter Morrow from the New Life Centre, Christchurch speak at an event at El Rancho. As we were listening to him talk, Peter Morrow's lecture turned to the subject of the things people had gone through in their lives. The pastor said, 'Some of you have gone through things I have never ever experienced. I have never touched what some of you have been through. Oh! How I love hearing of experiences that people have gone through and being able to minister unto, but I know some of you have touched things that I have never ever touched and you are in a unique position that I am not in today....'

Then this man whom I had never met before, and about whom I knew nothing at all, approached me.

'You are in a position where I believe, sister, you can be a wealth to some people who have not the same insight, the same understanding that you have. For God is going to pull forth the scales from your eyes, and you are going to see further into the human heart, and you are going to see that heart open, and you are going to be a caring person that is going to put your arms around ones who have known what it is in their despair and hopelessness to feel that all was folly; and you are going to come with a word of comfort and a word of strength. God has not left you. His heart is towards you and He is going to cause you to gather up others, until you have a group of people around about you who will have the same heartbeat as you have, and you will be able to minister unto others and you are going to bring them into that place, as the gifting of God operates through you,' he said to me.

In the Bayview community, I was one of those people that everyone felt they could drop in on anytime. However, in most cases, this was not reciprocated. I longed for care and nurture from others, but God impressed upon my heart that 'the very thing you want, I want you to give it away, for in so doing, you will receive healing'. I realised that all young mothers need a bolt-hole where they can relax and be mothered themselves, and my home appeared to offer the perfect place for that. Like me, these women often had no family or local support networks. They would expect to be given tea as they relaxed and socialised, allowing the children to play together in my home. At the end of the day, these young mothers would just pack up their children and walk out, leaving me to clean up the mess and embark on preparing the evening meal for my own family.

As a caring person, I would also often cook a meal for those in the community whom I considered to be in need. One such person was Poppy, whom I decided to visit after the birth of her second baby, taking a home-baked fruit cake for her. Poppy, like me, had had a traumatic childhood and had shared this with me on one occasion. Poppy told me that when she was aged about four, she and her sister had been found locked in a vegetable cupboard in the house, having been there for about three days. The little girls were in a severely distressed state and had been placed in foster care. Poppy insisted to me that this incident had had no effect on her life, but I thought otherwise. When I arrived at Poppy's house with the cake, Poppy immediately said to me, 'I was praying that God would send me someone who would understand how I am feeling right now, and then you turned up.' Although I made no comment, I felt that the trauma in Poppy's early life had probably resurfaced when she found herself having to cope with two young children.

There was a woman in her sixties called Ursula who gave me the impression that she understood my plight in having no female relatives nearby. Ursula would often talk with me on the telephone, offering moral support. However, when the two of us were chatting like this, Ursula's husband, Don, had an annoying habit of continually clicking the phone extension in an effort to stop the conversation, as he probably wanted to use the line himself. No-one would ever cross Ursula, as those around her found her an austere and frightening character, and it wasn't unknown for her to tear women apart with her words. One Sunday night, seeking a bit of time out from the children, I went alone to the local school hall prayer group gathering. At that time, Jeffrey and I were having some alterations done to our house by a building contractor, and I was finding the whole business chaotic and disruptive. I expressed to Ursula how difficult I was finding things with the combination of building work and young children and mentioned to the older woman that she was fortunate to be retired and to have a less stressful lifestyle. Ursula immediately flew off the handle, shocking and deeply wounding me with her response. 'If you think I'm going to help you, you have another think coming to you!' she shouted.

In the group, there was a woman called Audrey, a divorcée in her late fifties, who lived in the same community. The very next day, Audrey turned up at my home and offered to take the children out for a walk to give me a half-hour respite, which helped enormously. The outburst by Ursula was never resolved, and when I met her in the supermarket, Ursula's words to me were along the lines of 'I can say anything to you, you're just like a daughter.' I later wrote a letter to the couple and apologised for any offence I might have caused them; I never got a reply. From that day onwards, I protected myself from being abused or dumped on by other women and never again reached out for help.

Between the late 1980s and early 1990s, Jeffrey and I held a house group in our home. This continued for many years and gave me the opportunity to ensure that my children were safe, without having to get in a babysitter to whom I would have had difficulty entrusting their care. However, I noticed that when the adults left in the evening, no one ever offered to help with the dishes or tidying up. I had opened my home to others, prepared home baking and provided nice food for those who attended, and yet, the other women — and, in particular the older women who had been mothers themselves— did not see that I had small children and no family around. They didn't offer any assistance. I was not going to spell it out to them; if that was the way they were, then so be it — but it was disappointing. I decided that once my children had grown up, I would never forget how hard it had been, with no support network. I made the decision that I would not fall into the trap of 'older woman syndrome' that some of these women now seemed to have developed. That is, they appeared to have totally forgotten what it was like to be a young mother and had become almost hostile and intolerant towards other mothers and their small children, with the possible exception of their own offspring and their grandchildren.

I met a lifelong friend, Kris, through this house group. Kris had just married her second husband and was now stepmother to his two boys. The two of us had much in common, and, although we came from different parts of the world, we got on very well together. One of the tips that I gave Kris was that it was acceptable (and much cheaper!) to hang laundry outside on the clothesline to dry. Prior to that, Kris had only ever put the damp washing directly from the machine into the dryer.

I encouraged my friend to have compassion toward her two stepsons and to work towards a positive outcome for everyone in her household. Kris said that I was the first person she had met who had challenged her negative thinking about the problems of having two stepchildren. She found that, as she changed her attitude, with my encouragement she began to find her situation more tolerable, and her home environment settled down pleasantly. Then, at the age of thirty-eight, Kris had her own baby and went into a complete and utter spin as her life was turned upside down. Kris and I are still close friends some thirty-six years later, though Kris has had some serious psychological issues and has been through ECT for depression. I have always been there for her. I never wanted to know the cause of my friend's distress, but was always ready to lend support when needed. Kris came and stayed with Jeffrey and me during some of her depressive episodes, and I had to enlist the help of mental health services several times. One such occasion was when Kris saw my wedding dress hanging up in the wardrobe and could not stop crying; perhaps it triggered some memories for her. Nowadays, when we get together, we often laugh about those times, though they were profoundly serious.

During the years that Jeffrey and I held the house group,

various people would come and go. Most of the people that came were initially unknown to us and were, as such, friends of a friend. When I was heavily pregnant with Moira, a couple called Di and her husband, Ludwig, from Rekie, showed up. Ludwig was some twenty years Di's junior, and he wanted to lay hands on my pregnant belly and pray for the unborn baby during our prayer group meeting. This request was unacceptable to me, and I refused, saying somewhat sharply that no person was going to touch me in that way unless I had invited them to do so. Years later, I learned that Ludwig, who continued to live with his wife Di, had undergone a sex change and was by that time a woman.

A close friendship similar to a mother-daughter relationship developed between me and Audrey. Audrey lived alone, as her grown-up children were settled overseas, so Jeffrey and I would invite her for dinner and, over the years, included her in family functions. I was fully aware that more of Audrey's needs than mine were being met by this arrangement. When Audrey turned sixty, I hosted a birthday party for her and encouraged her to invite whoever she wanted to celebrate the occasion with her.

Audrey's life story was a sad one. Things had started to go wrong in her marriage after the miscarriage of her fourth child. Her husband was unsupportive, and Audrey ended up in a psychiatric hospital, undergoing numerous ECT sessions for depression and attempted suicide. Following the breakdown of the family, the children remained with their father, who eventually remarried. Audrey was upset about the fact that she had been unable to retrieve any of her personal belongings from the family home when the marriage ended and that she had received no financial compensation. She said that at that time, she believed the law in New Zealand stated that the person who left the marriage was not entitled to anything, though this piece of legislation was changed shortly afterwards.

An obsession with her ex-husband appeared to consume most of Audrey's energy. She had built a life for herself, working long hours as a secretary in various (according to her) dysfunctional government departments and had managed to get enough money together to buy a small property in Bayview. She was pleased with her success, following her earlier health problems. Audrey confided to me and Jeffrey that her father had sexually abused her, but said that this had happened only once, when she was twelve years old, and that it had had little or no effect on her. She appeared to idolise her father and thought that he had been a wonderful man. One day, Jeffrey said to Audrey that her father could not have been a particularly good man, considering what he'd done to her, and encouraged her to acknowledge that. He suggested that she go and sit by her father's grave and tell him exactly what the effects of his behaviour had been on her life. Jeffrey felt that Audrey was putting the blame for her mental health on her husband, when, in fact, in his opinion, the blame rested fairly and squarely on the serious behaviour of her father.

Audrey and I had a type of mother-daughter relationship, but when one of Audrey's adult daughters came back to live in New Zealand, she pushed me out of the relationship and drove a wedge between me and Audrey. I felt displaced and sad that the friendship ended like this, but I also acknowledged that Audrey needed to try and repair the damaged relationship she had with her own family and, in particular, with her daughters. Audrey and this particular daughter would have horrific, abusive arguments about the effects of Audrey's behaviour when her children were young and what it had done to them. Sometimes, this information was too distressing for me to hear. Audrey shared with me the difficulties she was having with this now forty-year-old daughter saying she would, at times, have preferred it if she had stayed overseas. It appeared to Audrey that whatever she said or did was wrong; she was continually being verbally abused by her daughter, despite trying her best to avoid the endless conflict.

Then, Audrey's mother died, and she sold up in Bayview and moved back to her childhood home. She subdivided the property, spending what remained of her savings on surveyors' fees, although she never did sell the subdivided portion of land. At this point, Audrey's second daughter returned from overseas, and it turned out that she did not get on with her sister. The two adult daughters were competing for their mother's sole attention, meaning that Audrey had to arrange her life to accommodate matters and to diffuse the sibling rivalry. She could only have one daughter in her company at any one time, as she tried valiantly to avoid stressful situations.

The third child in the story was Audrey's son, Freddy. While still in his teens, he had fathered a son with a woman who was now in a lesbian relationship and had more children in that relationship. Freddy was married to a woman who was about twenty years his senior. Audrey and her family were fond of this woman, but the couple went to live in Britain (perhaps to be further away from any distraction of family, both hers and his). According to Audrey, Freddy and his wife were very much in love and were always nurturing that love over in London. However, to the shock and horror of Audrey and her daughters, Freddy then left his wife for a younger woman. He reconnected with an exchange student whom he had met in New Zealand years earlier, when she was a teenager, and moved overseas to be with this recently-divorced lady.

After Freddy remarried, there was a complete and utter breakdown in the family between Audrey, her son, and his two sisters. Prior to his second marriage, Freddy used to communicate with his mother and was generally a good son, helping her out with money. But, according to Audrey, his new wife 'put an immediate stop to all that.' The two daughters would argue with their brother whenever he briefly visited their mother. They expected him to support her financially, and relationships became strained all round. Freddy would turn up in New Zealand out of the blue to see his father and son, and would announce, without any prior notice, that he had half-an-hour to spare in which to squeeze in a quick visit to his mother. Audrey was not happy with that arrangement.

Always simmering in the background was Audrey's hate of her ex-husband. She blamed him for all her woes and, after various discussions, Audrey encouraged the younger daughter to lodge a claim against her father for abuse — or so the elder sister told me. When this daughter confronted her father, he was extremely distressed that she would ever make such an allegation against him, according to Audrey. Audrey and her younger daughter said that they would both celebrate the day he died. All things considered, I was glad not to be closely involved in Audrey's life any longer by this stage, though I would occasionally ring her and send cards and gifts.

For me, the end of the relationship came when I called Audrey one day and, playing a little guessing game on the telephone, asked, 'Guess who this is?' Audrey became incredibly angry with me and said, furiously, 'Don't you ever play that game with me again!' I had meant no offence and was upset at the way I had been spoken to. After that, I stopped calling Audrey and was no longer involved in the ongoing family dramas.

For eight years, I took a visually impaired lady named Lotty out shopping once a week, on a voluntary basis. Lotty was in her late seventies and her GP, Sienna, who also lived in the same community, and I worked together to ensure Lotty's medical needs were met when her health started to go downhill. She was admitted to the geriatric ward of a local hospital for assessment and, as part of this medical process, I was asked to be Lotty's support person, which meant that I sat in on the medical assessment. I then discovered for the first time that Lotty already had a diagnosis of schizophrenia and had attempted suicide many times in the past. Sadly, Lotty's behaviour started to deteriorate and my children began to be afraid of her, to the extent that it was no longer appropriate to bring them with me on my visits.

One thing that greatly upset Lotty was that the Dally Foundation (which provided support for people with impaired vision) told her that she was not allowed to come back to their social gatherings until she had completed additional training, even though she had been attending the meetings for years. This new requirement appeared to be as a result of complaints from the volunteer drivers after she had damaged their car and the cars of others whilst getting out. Lotty would open the passenger door to exit the vehicle and then use her foot to kick it wide open, sometimes banging the door into another car parked next to it. By anticipating this behaviour and running around to the passenger side to open the door myself so that Lotty only had to climb out, I managed to avoid any damage occurring to my own and surrounding cars.

The decision by the Dally Foundation had a devastating effect on Lotty's already fragile wellbeing, as she considered the Foundation to be her 'family', and, according to her, they had now rejected her. One Christmas, the Foundation put on a Christmas function for their members at St Bede's Church, but Lotty was excluded from the invitations. I had discovered that the function was on and rang the Foundation to ask why Lotty hadn't been invited. The person who answered the telephone was somewhat annoyed by the question and replied that the only way that Lotty would be allowed to attend would be if I were to bring her and stay with her for the duration of the party to meet all her physical and emotional needs, as the Foundation was not responsible for looking after Lotty in that way. Neither was I, but in order to prevent the old lady's feelings from being further hurt, I agreed to this arrangement and Lotty had a wonderful time with her so-called 'friends'.

I was inspecting rest homes on the coast one day so that I could make a recommendation for Lotty's long-term care when, sadly, I received a telephone call from the police in Porirua advising me that Lotty had taken her own life whilst in the geriatric ward of the local hospital. On arrival home, I found Victim Support were already at the house. The incident was reported in the newspaper as having happened at Porirua Psychiatric Hospital instead of the actual location, which was at the local general hospital.

Sienna did not charge for Lotty's medical care, and she helped me plan the funeral arrangements. I chose the clothes in which Lotty should be laid to rest and I went and sat at the funeral home with the body in the casket. I told Lotty how I was disappointed in what she had done, as I really had cared about her wellbeing and had been trying to help her. After Lotty's death, I talked with the Dally Foundation, and they denied that she had ever been deliberately left off the guest list for the Christmas function. The Foundation seemed embarrassed that, having benefitted greatly from her estate, the behaviour of some of its staff could possibly have in some way contributed, among other major factors, to Lotty's demise.

The funeral home gave Lotty's ashes to me to dispose of, and, after about a year of being kept in the garage while Jeffrey and I decided what should be done with them, they were eventually scattered at sea from a boat that belonged to a family friend of ours.

I also became an accredited visitor for Age Concern and made weekly visits to a woman named Bridie, who lived in a nearby rest home and was assigned to me. Then, when this lady became very unwell, she was removed to the local hospital where Lotty had taken her life. I continued to visit and care for her while she was there. I would meet Jeffrey on his way home from work and hand the two children over to him to care for until I got home later in the evening. For several weeks, I went up to the hospital to feed Bridie her dinner. I discovered that the hospital staff would put the food in the patient's room but did not stay to assist her with feeding. Then they would return sometime later and, if the meal was uneaten, they would remove the tray of untouched food. No one apart from me appeared to care that Bridie was unable to eat by herself. I didn't know what Bridie was dying from, but one thing was certain — I wasn't going to let her die of hunger. I would feed her the meal and I brought along a plastic baby cup with a spout so I could give her drinks each evening. I also made sure that Bridie had clean, dry nightdresses.

When Bridie eventually died, I went to the funeral, which was conducted by the Salvation Army in Lower Hutt. The officer talked about Bridie's life and how she had been 'saved' during one of their visits to the pub where she drank and how she, in turn, had become a salvationist. During conversation after the service, a Salvation Army officer said to me, 'I was wondering to myself, what would you know about a hard life?' I was taken aback by his comment and, in response, said that I was familiar with human suffering.

. . .

Over the years, when I had noticed my father praying, I had asked him what he was praying about. I was surprised by his answer, which was 'a happy death'. Daddy passed away in his sleep in 1994; he was found lying on his back, resting on a pillow with his two hands behind his head. His prayers had been answered. I managed to get a 'compassionate' seat on a flight to London in order to attend my father's funeral. The whole process of getting over to Ireland from New Zealand was incredibly stressful; all the people on compassionate seats were put together, and I found myself sitting next to a man who was returning to attend the funeral of his brother who had committed suicide. I was glad to have made it back, despite only arriving in my hometown, Baile na Ghlic, about a half hour before the start of the funeral service. I was pleased to learn that my father had read my last letter I had sent to him and hoped that perhaps he had taken my advice and forgiven himself before his passing. After the funeral, I met up with his solicitor, Mr Relish, to whom my father used to refer as 'Daddy D'. Mr Relish said to me, when making a reference to The Valley of Kidron, 'Sure, no one wanted you, and it was the best we could do at the time.'

In conversation, Mr Relish also told me that my father had had 'nothing'. However, unknown to the solicitor, I had received a lump sum in February 1985 from the sale of my father's family farm, and this had helped me and Jeffrey purchase our first house in the Bay. There were no comforting words expressed at the time of the bereavement by Mr Relish. At the time, I described him as being 'as ignorant as a pig', with no finesse, no matter how well-educated he may have been. Years after the sale of the farm, my father had applied for the state pension, or what was commonly known in Ireland as the old-age pension. On numerous occasions, he would get someone to drive him to the offices to enquire about his entitlement to the pension, only to be rejected time and time again. The authorities told him that, as he had sold the farm rather than giving it away free of charge to a family member, he was not entitled to a pension. He died, aged 82, never having received a pension from the Irish State.

I had expected the process of grieving for my father to be as severe as that which I had experienced when my mother had died, some twenty-eight years earlier. However, as an adult, I grieved differently compared with how I had done when I was a child, though I missed Daddy tremendously. The loss of his frequent letters and our shared conversations left a big gap in my life at a time when I was going through a period of great emotional turmoil. I often thought about my father's life and believed that, ultimately, the shame he felt he'd brought on his family by being rejected for the priesthood as a young man, and the depression that later overshadowed him, could have largely been avoided had he not been promised to God from the cradle. The tragic loss of his wife would have been easier to bear if he had had the support of academic colleagues and sporting friends that he might have had in a different version of his life.

> Thanks for your very interesting last letter. I have a few questions for you. (1) What were the reasons "the Fathers" said you were an unsuitable candidate (2) Have you ever forgiven your mother and father (in the name of Jesus) for their reactions to what happened — consequently you felt rejected by them (3) Have you ever forgiven yourself and stopped blaming yourself for it all — it was perhaps outside your control, you did your best. Perhaps the prayers at the time of your illness as a child would have been better served if they had prayed for you to be do its "Will of God" rather than specifying how you they (Holy Bros etc) would like you to turn out, God's will and man's will often differ, you can still serve God without being in 'Robes'. Perhaps 'Robes' were not Gods will for your life

Sabrina's last letter to her father in 1994

SIXTEEN
BIRTH OF A MONSTER

To everything there is a season, and a time to every purpose under heaven: a time to be born and a time to die.
—Ecclesiastes 3:1.

Therefore do not worry about tomorrow, for tomorrow will worry about itself. Each day has enough trouble of its own.
—Matthew 6:34

In the early 1990s, I responded to an advertisement in the local newspaper seeking participants for a research project that was being conducted by an employee of Child Youth and Family Services (CYFS) who was completing a master's degree. The topic was resilience, and the researcher was looking for adults who had had traumatic early childhood experiences but had become successful adults who generally led normal, healthy lives without having been incarcerated or had resorted to drugs, alcohol, and other addictions. The two main factors that appeared to have dictated success for these adults were that, firstly, each of them had had at least one important person in their life who had believed in them as a child; secondly, that the individual had a belief in a higher being — not necessarily a churchgoer, but a person who held a belief in God.

The primary school in Baile Na Ghlic where Sabrina was beaten in 1958 by Sr Cuffer

I only had brief memory glimpses of what had happened to me as a young child. However, when I touched my head, it sometimes seemed to me as if it was in a partially frozen state. At other times, I felt like part of my head had 'pins and needles' in it. When Moira reached the age of about four, this appeared to trigger memories of the sexual abuse that I had experienced at the same age. Once, when I was in Taupo on a weekend break, I woke up in the middle of the night feeling as though my head was about to explode, and I thought I was going mad. I prayed, saying, 'Please God, you talk about peace in the Bible; can I have it now, or otherwise I will go mad', and to my surprise, the peace of God appeared to come over me, and I was able to have a peaceful night's sleep. Psalm 142:3-7 'When my spirit grows faint within me, it is You who watch over my way. In the path where I walk people have hidden a snare for me. Look and see, there is no one at my right hand; no one is concerned for me. I have no refuge; no one cares for my life. I cry to You, Lord; I say, "You are my refuge, my portion in the land of the living." Listen to my cry, for I am in desperate need; rescue me from those who pursue me, for they are too strong for me. Set me free from my prison, that I may praise Your name. Then the righteous will gather about me.'

Every morning at around 3am, I would wake up — it was usually the same time each morning — and find myself turning things over in my head. I would stay awake for hours, ruminating, and then would struggle to get up, as I was exhausted. I tried to believe in God, but always had trouble with such concepts as 'God is love, He is a God of compassion and a caring God,' as none of these things had been evident in my experience of life. Like Habakkuk (a Biblical prophet thought to have lived in the seventh century BC) who lamented to God the suffering and injustice in Israel and asked God what He intended to do about this, I would question God, asking, 'Where were You, when I was raped; where were You when I felt so alone and unloved; where were Your hands and feet, the people who represent You?' I would have question after question for God and was often also incredibly angry with Him.

When I struggled like this, I would sometimes seek help by ringing a free radio telephone counselling service. On one particular day, a man I had spoken with a few times before said, 'You have two things that you are struggling with: one is guilt, and the other is condemnation.' He asked me, 'which one is it for you?', which I found very unhelpful, and I no longer wanted to communicate with him after that.

One consolation for me at this point was that I had a beautiful view from my kitchen table. I would sit there in the morning, cradling a mug of tea, and I reflected on life as I gazed out over Kapiti Island. I needed this time to be alone with myself and my thoughts. I also loved flowers, the colours and the scents, and when I was feeling sad or depressed, I would go into the garden and walk around contemplating the flowers, appreciating the beauty in them. As I wandered in my garden, some of the darkness would lift from me, in the same way that a change of scenery often helped the depression to lift. I would go away for a weekend every six weeks or so, which also appeared to shift the dark feelings for a while.

I knew that, deep within my psyche, there was something seriously wrong, and I began to have difficulty relating to Jeffrey. I investigated options for help, and the two of us decided to attend six free couples' sessions of counselling. However, during what was only the second session, I began repeating, 'There is a man, there is a man', and the counsellor appeared to recognise what was going on. According to him, I was starting to remember my sexual abuse and was trying to disclose this. He immediately put a stop to the session and tried to refer me to another male counsellor who dealt with sexual abuse, but I was reluctant to go and see him. I didn't know what was happening to me, or what the words 'There is a man, there is a man,' really meant. What I did feel was rejection at my time of great need. The need to disclose my trauma was once again put on hold.

Sometime later, I sought counselling myself at an ecumenical centre in Lower Hutt, where I met a pleasant English woman, Stella. I paid for the weekly sessions myself, and my first communication with Stella was, 'I haven't come here for you to sort me out.' The counsellor responded by saying that she was pleased that I had said that, because she was 'not in the business of sorting people out'. This immediately put me at ease, and a good rapport was subsequently built between us. I had several weekly sessions with Stella, but began to experience some horrific nightmares in between my appointments. I would write down the content and then talk about the dreams with my counsellor. The main images in these dreams were of stallions and bulls, which I found strange and frightening in nature. Stella allowed me to talk about my life and never made too many comments or passed any judgements on the events that I described. However, nearing the end of my time with her, Stella said, 'In conclusion, all I want to say to you, Sabrina, is that the hand of God has been on your life.'

Feeling strong enough to carry on again, I moved forward with my life and did not go back to see Stella. I still had no real concrete memories of what had happened to me as a young child, but the 'pins and needles' sensation in my head was still there, and it felt like that part of my brain was somehow on hold. Then I had a dream in which I was frantically trying to mend, or fix, a broken vessel, part of which had been broken off near the rim. A voice in the dream said to me, 'I want you to stop trying to mend this broken vessel yourself, for I am the potter and you are the clay, so stop trying to do this work yourself. I have made this vessel and it is I who will restore it.' I was astonished by the dream and just pondered on it at times. Then I read Isaiah 64:8 *'Yet You, LORD, are our Father. We are the clay; You are the potter; we are all the work of Your hand'*, and, immediately, the dream made more sense to me.

In a subsequent dream, I heard the voice say that my life was 'like a young tree that has been vandalised and slashed, and has now matured and had moss growing over the injuries on the trunk and bark.' The voice in the dream again spoke to me, saying, 'When I remove the moss from the bark, look underneath, there are many slashes and wounds to the trunk. With time, the moss has hidden these wounds and slashes, but I am about to do a work and heal this tree.' In yet another dream, the voice said to me that my life was like a pressurised barrel with a lid tightly sealed, but very soon that lid would be blown off and the pressure would be released. I understood that the barrel probably represented my life and the suppressed events in my early childhood, which were about to come to the surface. I neither knew when this would happen, nor what the barrel contained.

Shortly after that, I took a trip up to Wanganui alone in the car and, as I drove, I listened repeatedly to a favourite Irish ballad. Then these words and imagery came to me: *Gazing through the windscreen pane, I see a rainbow in the distance smiling through the rain and I hear the whispering raindrops dancing on the pane. My memories rush me and take me back to childhood, dare I look back again? To get to the other side of the 'Jordan', it will be a bumpy ride, with cascading waters, terror and letting go of pride. Battered, bruised and stronger, I know that I will get safely to the other side.*

The words and imagery seemed to have opened a door into my unconscious memories of my early childhood, though at that stage, I still had little or no idea of what lay below the surface in my subconscious. I continued to have increasingly weird dreams and, one evening, I was explaining a dream or nightmare over the phone to my friend, Kris. In this dream, I was sitting in the driver's seat of a car when someone came up to the driver's door and said to me, 'See, I can open that door, if I want to.' I replied, 'No, don't do that! When I am ready, I will open that door myself.' Then I glanced over my shoulder into the back seat of the car, and there I saw my abuser, dressed in a dark suit, smirking at me. I recognised those teeth as belonging to the man who had raped me when I was almost four years old. I knew instantly who that man was: Jimmy Deviouss, the Baile na Ghlic town cobbler, 'the cripple'.

'Do you know what the car represents?' Kris asked.

I replied that I didn't, and then Kris explained that the car probably represented my body. When I heard those words I sat down, very slowly, on the edge of a couch. It was as if my life were moving in slow motion, and I was no longer able to stand upright; I fell silent as I realised that the car did, indeed, represent my body. Kris, on the other end of the phone, was totally unaware of what was happening to me. I made my excuses and ended the call shortly after that. Psalm 119:50 *'My comfort in my suffering is this: Your promise preserves my life.'*

That evening, and over subsequent days, I was flooded with graphic memories of my childhood abuse. At that stage, I was no longer able to keep the recollections under control. As more and more horrific memories emerged, the voice in a dream said to me, 'I want you to put your hand in my wounded hand, and we will walk through this together.'

This gave me encouragement, for although I knew it was going to be a rough road to recovery, I had the conviction that, with God's help, I would make it through the darkness and come out stronger in the end. My metaphorical labour had started, and I was about to give birth to a monster from the past; for me, that monster was well overdue and needed to be expelled. Over the years, I had had to continually put the birth of this monster on hold until the time seemed right — but then, no time was ever going to be right to deal with such a delivery. I had been searching for the right time and place, when I was surrounded by caring, supportive people, in order to give birth to the monster, but sadly, so far in my life I had found almost nothing but rejection and more abuse.

All the signs were now present that the symbolic birth was imminent, and I knew that I needed to be able to cope with a deeply traumatic event. I could no longer ignore that nesting instinct; regardless of my circumstances, the monster was on its way. My whole life passed before my eyes as if on a conveyor belt; I was acutely distressed and felt completely out of control. I could identify all the people, relationships, and events that were before me on that conveyor belt and, in many cases, sought forgiveness, where appropriate, for my own wrongdoing, even at this confronting time.

My neck went out of alignment, my head hurt, I bled, I felt as if I was being choked and suffocated; I felt the tightness and pain around my wrists and thought I was going to die from the heavy weight I felt on my body and that my life was about to end. When Jeffrey came into the kitchen after work, I was terrified of him. I was in a catatonic state, unable to move from the position in which I found myself. Filled with fear of my husband, it was as if he now represented the abuser of the almost four-year-old child. I was now at the emergency, or crisis, stage of remembering the abuse.

My children did not know what was wrong with their mother; I could not stop crying, or even stand upright. When I did try to stand up, wave after wave of grief would force me to collapse onto the bed again as I experienced uncontrollable sobbing, wondering if it would ever end. I was re-experiencing the foul smell of the man's body; I saw his face clearly; his ugly teeth had made a lasting impression on me as a vulnerable child. Detail by detail, all the traumatic memories of my rape returned and hit me like a ton of bricks. I suffered an overwhelming sense of terror and dread and wondered to myself how any man could do this to a defenceless little girl.

I felt utterly alone in my experience; Jeffrey was also helpless, and the children were very distressed to see their mother in such a state of emotional turmoil. As well as giving birth to a monster, I felt that the ordeal was perhaps similar to what happens to an individual who is near death and is being shown everything they have done throughout their life. It felt at the time like a 'near death experience'.

During the emergency stage of remembering, my family and I went up to our beach house for some respite. I spent most of the time we were there lying on the bed, crying uncontrollably. As the memories came flooding back, I felt I needed to be able to identify with my four-year-old self, and it seemed to me that the best way for me to do this was to find a little girl who appeared to represent myself at the age of four. By this time, my own daughter was aged seven-and-a-half, so I went down to the local store and restaurant and sat outside on a bench until I saw such a girl at the shop. I approached the child and asked how old she was. When the little girl replied, 'I am four,' that was all it took for me to have a visual picture of what I may have looked like. That settled the matter and, fortunately, the parents didn't ask why I was enquiring about the age of their daughter.

Sometime later, I came across an old bible in my home which had been in my possession since 1973 when I first left Ireland. In it, there was a photograph of Jimmy Deviouss, the cobbler, with me sitting beside him on a blanket in the backyard of my home in Baile na Ghlic[1]. It had been taken some time in the mid 1950s. 'The cripple' had a cigarette hanging out of the corner of his mouth. Finding the old photo was almost as terrifying an experience for me as it had been for me all those years earlier when Deviouss had raped me.

Jeffrey tried valiantly to help me, but at times his mere presence would trigger more of the abuse memories. It was as if, to me, my husband had become the paedophile. I struggled to get through daily life with Jeffrey and the children under these circumstances, feeling at times that I was Sabrina the little girl

---

1. This photograph is reproduced in Chapter 3.

trying to cope and, at other times, that I was Sabrina the adult, the wife and mother, doing her best to muddle her way through. Eventually, I sought the assistance of a sexual abuse healing centre, Whare Mahana. A counsellor there encouraged me to get the handbook *The Courage to Heal* by Ellen Bass and Laura Davis, which I found extremely enlightening. I discovered that reading and absorbing the book gave me a sense of control over the current events in my life, as it offered me some insight into what might happen next in the process of healing. The tumult of reliving the abuse was like a terrifying nightmare, and I decided that I needed to manage the situation myself and not risk getting hurt by the ignorance of others. I was unable to trust anyone except my husband with the sacred place in which I had now found myself.

One of the things that I noticed about the women whom I was mixing with at the Whare was that most of them were very hostile towards men, and towards God; I did not feel the same way. I had a loving husband who supported and cared for me, especially with the events around my now-emerging traumatic past. I believed that I had only survived thus far in life because of my belief in God, without which I would probably have taken my own life as planned earlier, especially during those late teenage years in London. I continued to trust in God to get me through the process of dealing with the childhood abuse. I had never come across someone who had spoken about such a traumatic life experience before; nor had I ever heard of anyone else who had experienced supressed childhood memories and had had to deal with that early trauma as an adult. Perhaps it was just not something that people talked about.

It was terrifying, as an adult, to feel the physical pain as the anguish of the violated little girl emerged. The discovery had sent me into a state of shock; it was incredibly hard for the adult self to comprehend what the child had been through. Other than Jeffrey, there were no family or friends with whom I could share my burden. My life had been upended, and this had an effect not only on me, but also on my husband and our children. There wasn't much assistance or support for us as I tried privately to navigate the seemingly insurmountable obstacle of dealing with the horror of childhood rape. I remained a part of the Whare Mahana centre for several years and, as time went by, I became stronger and stronger. Eventually, I was able to stop going to the centre, but have always carried a debt of gratitude for the assistance I received from those very understanding and caring women who came to my rescue in my time of need.

One side-effect of the remembering process was that I had numerous panic attacks; many were triggered by the cold air from freezers in the supermarket. I would suddenly have to run out of the store as though there were an emergency; I never knew when the next attack might strike. After doing some research, I learned how to handle these episodes and used breathing techniques to control them. I had a heightened self-awareness and a good idea of what was happening to me, so was also able to help Jeffrey gain an understanding as to what was occurring, so that he did not become too distressed by the new situation that now dominated our lives.

On top of the almost unendurable grief, I also realised for the first time in my life that my mother's death had not been my fault after all. Another realisation that I made at this time was that I was not, and never had been, stupid. In fact, I was astounded by how well I had survived all those years, carrying the heavy burden of the rape and violence. It began to dawn on me just how brave, adaptive, protective, and resilient I had been throughout my teenage years and adulthood. My adult self was proud of my young self, acknowledging how well I had managed alone throughout my life; I started to honour and cherish my inner child.

The paedophile in Baile na Ghlic had threatened me not to tell my mother, or anyone else, what he had done to me. This had scared me into silence for decades. Since the death of my mother when I was eleven years old, I had believed that this was in some way related to the fact that I had betrayed the paedophile and thus brought about my mother's passing. I unconsciously carried the burden of my mother's death, feeling that it was my fault, for nearly thirty years.

Once the memories had fully emerged and begun to subside, I felt as though a psychological cleansing had taken place in my mind, body, soul, and spirit. I felt very much better after my menstrual cycle at that time; for me, it represented a symbolic cleansing of my body. It was as if I was getting rid of that foul, filthy, violent, and sexually deviant man, the cobbler, Jimmy Deviouss, 'the cripple', from my life once and for all, and I began to feel clean again. Over the next month, the crying stopped and the grief abated, and I finally felt that I was regaining some control of my life. I was astonished that I had lived with this horrific abuse since early childhood and that I had carefully managed to keep it at bay for so long. When I cast my mind back, I could now see avoidance stimuli and, in particular, of the triggering television programmes that I used to walk out on. I had sometimes said to Jeffrey, in rather a panicked state, 'Turn it off!' when anything I didn't like came on the TV, and now I finally understood why.

During my short time as an au pair, changing the nappies of the young children I was caring for must have impacted on my suppressed memories, sending me into a seemingly unexplained deep depression. It all made sense now, as did the boyfriends that I had unconsciously chosen because they were not likely to trigger my hidden earlier memories. As an adult woman, fully aware of what had happened to me, I was now in awe of my younger self and fully embraced her.

The most traumatic, or crisis, stage lasted for days rather than weeks. Afterwards, I was no longer the same person. Things had changed, and I became emotionally stronger as time went by. However, I still felt very much alone as I navigated the processes of discovery, processing, and acceptance, as the women that I knew were neither supportive nor interested in any way in what I had just been through. When I mentioned the shock I experienced at remembering my abuse, no one was in the least bit curious about what I had to say. It seemed to me that most of the women I thought of as friends were, in fact, a bunch of uncaring, so-called 'Christian' women. I received far greater understanding from the non-Christian women at the Whare Mahana than I did from those in my immediate circle. James 2:26: *'For as the body without the spirit is dead, so faith without works is dead also.'*

I did not really feel drawn to talk much with other survivors about my own childhood abuse, as I wasn't concerned with feeling sorry for myself or being trapped in the past. I needed to acknowledge it and then move on with my life. I no longer wanted to be a slave to memories of abuse, or to give the rapist any further power; he had already robbed me of so much, but now that I no longer feared him, he had no influence over me anymore. I was careful to write down and document all the recollections as they emerged, as I needed to get the facts straight in my mind and piece everything together to solve the puzzle, once and for all. I was methodical in conducting my own research and made the effort to find out where the cobbler, Jimmy Deviouss, had lived at the time I was sexually abused.

It turned out that the man I had christened 'the cripple' was living in our family home during the electoral registered years of 1953 and 1954, which covered the period during which I had been born. Then, in 1961, the electoral roll showed him living diagonally across the street from our home in Drury Lane. I managed to ascertain that I had first entered school at the convent in Baile na Ghlic in September 1958, when I was four years and two months old. I then received a letter from the retired principal, Mr Jones of Asher National School, confirming that I had started school in the countryside on 3 March 1959, when I was four years and eight months old, which was when I moved with my parents to live on the farm. I left the rural primary school on 15 October 1966, four months after the death of my mother, when my father and I returned to live in the same house in which I had been raped in 1958, some eight years earlier.

SEVENTEEN
THE JOURNEY TOWARDS HEALING

A highway shall be there, and a road and it shall be called the Highway of Holiness. The unclean shall not pass over it, but it shall be for others. Whoever walks the road, although a fool, shall not go astray.

—Isaiah 35:8

As my healing journey progressed, I had another dream, in which I was in a car travelling on a big highway. The voice in the dream said to me, 'In the past when your car broke down, it was left unprotected on the side of the road. Then the highway thief robbed and helped himself to the parts of your car, unhindered. Now look, I have erected a sign on the highway for you, which says NO STOPPING and you will therefore feel safe travelling on this highway from now on, under my protection'.

I recognised that in order to complete the healing process, I needed to obtain formal recognition of what had happened to me and that this would require input from a medical practitioner. I consulted my GP who, in both April and May 1995, registered the disclosure of historical sexual abuse. The doctor wrote a letter following the consultation:

> *I saw this lady in my clinic on 19 April 1995 and again on 9 May 1995. She had no specific stress symptoms at the time and as the consultation evolved, it appeared that these were precipitated by her attempting to confront her sexual abuse as a child, committed allegedly by Jimmy Deviouss in Baile na Ghlic.*
>
> *The feelings described at the time were that she was overcome with grief, so she could not stand up, she had uncontrollable crying, sobbing, shaking, feeling nauseated. She also had a fear of dying and death. She had a fear of enclosed spaces and an invasion of space, a feeling of suffocation, panic, shock, terror, and fear of the dark and even of her husband, becoming agitated in his presence. The latter, lasting about three days. Body symptoms that she exhibited and mentioned were stiff neck, right leg shaking uncontrollably, sore stomach, back pain, pains in her side, sore vagina, wetting herself when coughing and crying, mucous in her mouth, occasional vaginal spotting and intermittent vaginal discharge and itch. Baseline time blood tests were done including hormonal status assay which showed that she was not perimenopausal. Ms Sabrina had organised herself counselling for this problem with an accredited counsellor, Mr Gar and has been to a sexual clinic. I understand the symptoms are now in control and that she is, with co-operation of people in New Zealand, including the Police, trying to press charges for the alleged childhood offence with the Irish Police.*

Sometime later, I decided to write to my abuser and, after locating his current address and discussing my intention with the Whare Mahana counsellor, I sent a short letter dated 30 June 1995, by registered mail for the attention of Jimmy Deviouss:

The time has now come to break the silence.

I no longer fear the threats you made over my life, should I break the silence.

What you did to me then was a criminal act and still is — punishable under the law of the land.

I want you to know I have clear recollection about your sexual violation of me, as a young child and can never forget the devastation this sexual violation/abuse has caused me.

How dare you have sexually violated me in such a way and abused the position of trust you so carefully had built with me.

You may be an old man now but that does not excuse you from the criminal act of child sexual abuse you committed on me in Baile na Ghlic.

I expect you to reply within four weeks of receipt of this letter.

Having made this brave move, I further took the decision that I would inform An Garda Síochána (the Irish police force) about Jimmy Deviouss and the historical offences he had committed against me. I felt that it was important to have the details of my sexual abuse documented in Ireland for posterity and contacted the Porirua police station to ask for advice about the correct format for filing such a report. In due course, I received a call from Det. Pete, who offered to help me carry out the process. This compassionate and professional detective interviewed me, by now aged forty-one, and a decision was made that a report should be sent, via Interpol, to An Garda Síochána in Baile na Ghlic. Pete and I built a good rapport, and I put my trust in Pete, who I felt was a credit to the New Zealand police force.

When Jimmy Deviouss was first interviewed and questioned by An Garda Síochána, he said that no child had been living in the Dowling household when he was there. However, I was born there in 1954, while the cobbler was residing at the house prior to 1959 and before he moved across the road from our family home. Obviously, Deviouss was lying, and Irish census records contradicted his assertions.

Sgt Burelly of An Garda Síochána prepared a statement on 20 April 1996, and this was received by Det. Pete at the Porirua police station in New Zealand on 12 August 1996. Sgt Burelly was fully aware that Jimmy Deviouss was a paedophile operating in the town of Baile na Ghlic and concluded, after having interviewed him twice, that Deviouss was almost certainly guilty of the alleged crime committed against me all those years ago. However, due to the lack of further complaints against him, An Garda Síochána were unable to formally charge him over the matter.

In my report, I had mentioned that Jimmy Deviouss was known to both my father and my Uncle Bart. Sgt Burelly made comment on the fact that Bart Laughton was known in the vicinity as a very respectable man and that he doubted that he had had any association with Jimmy Deviouss, the paedophile. However, I knew that Uncle Bart used to visit Deviouss whenever he was in town, both socially and for his shoe repairs. I also knew that, years later, whilst he was living alone as an old man in Baile na Ghlic, my father had developed a habit of visiting Deviouss for an hour or so on a Wednesday night for a chat about 'old times'. On one occasion during a visit back to Ireland, I had needed to locate my father and had knocked on the door of Deviouss' house. The cobbler had just stared through me, saying nothing, before going to fetch my father for me. This had left me feeling extremely uncomfortable.

While I was still recovering, I attended a prayer meeting at a large gathering of Christians on the Kapiti Coast. A time of prayer was offered to the congregation, so I decided to go up for prayer. When I told the prayer leader why I had approached the altar, he said, 'Do you know what your problem is?' I carefully listened for the answer, but what came next upset me deeply. He said, 'You just want to punish.' I was devastated by this and sat down quietly in a state of shock, wondering who, or what, I supposedly wanted to punish. Surely, I was the one who had been punished for more than thirty years. Confused, I asked myself angrily, 'How did the prayer leader dare speak to me like that, having no idea of what I have been through, or how I have had to cope, over the past three decades?' Having finally arrived at the point of healing, I felt that the way he had treated me was appalling, probably driven by sheer ignorance on his part. I resolved that from then on, I would be on my guard to protect myself from the ignorance of people who had little or no understanding of trauma.

Shortly after this incident, I went to another Christian gathering on the Kapiti Coast and, again, I went up for prayer. This time two women prayed for me, and, as they prayed, I had the feeling that warm oil was being poured down my chest, and I experienced tremendous healing. In the Bible, there are more than forty verses about anointing oil. James 5:15-16 states: 'If anyone among you is sick, let them call the elders of the church to pray over them and anoint them with oil in the name of the Lord. And the prayer offered in faith will make the sick person well; the Lord will raise them up. If they have sinned, they will be forgiven. Therefore, confess your sins to each other and pray for each other so that you may be healed. The prayer of a righteous person is powerful and effective'.

On another occasion, while I was alone at the beach house, I was feeling very distressed and called out to the Lord. Immediately, I was enveloped in the presence and power of God. This was an incredible experience for me, as I immediately felt overcome with God's love and never wanted to let that feeling of love and security go. This love was also healing for me.

When I became upset about something minor, such as the way Jeffrey had spoken to me or glanced at me, I would withdraw into myself. It would take me some time to come out of myself again, or to return to the present. I was dealing with reactive or situational depression. Most of the time, Jeffrey didn't know what he had said or done to cause this reaction, and usually I didn't know why I had reacted in that manner either. In addition, I was also dealing with transference, which refers to the redirection of a person's feelings for a significant person onto another person. I would spend the ensuing days trying to work things out in my head. In the end, I usually came up with the answer after lying awake for hours at night, which was an extremely exhausting process, but I had great reserves of determination and did not give up easily. I was a fighter.

Throughout my life, I had always been particularly good at escaping emotionally, as I was able to make my mind leave my body. When this happened, I would find myself in a beautiful, elegantly furnished room that had a piano in it; it was a tranquil, safe haven. Soothing chamber music played, and I could listen to it in comfort and security. To this day music, especially chamber music, has the ability to transport me away from myself to a place of refuge. I found myself able to look down at any situation or event and feel removed from it, as if I were not part of it. I could see everything that was taking place and, at that stage, I did not understand how I was able to do this. No one had ever talked to me about such a strange experience.

Later, I learned that my escape mechanism had a name — it is known as dissociation, or being in a dissociative state. I sought professional help and practised techniques for being 'present', learning to remind myself that I was no longer that small, abused, and violated four-year-old girl. Now, as an adult woman, I learned how to bring myself back into the present. When I reverted to the four-year-old state of trauma, crying and sobbing uncontrollably, Jeffrey would call my name. My husband would remind me of where I was, who I was with, and that I was safe right now with him. This was not an easy task for either of us to master, but we succeeded.

There seemed to be no support available at that time for the partner of a person with emerging sexual abuse trauma. Jeffrey had no one to turn to; it was not a subject that he could talk to another man about over a pint in the pub. In 1995, there were support groups for men and women affected by sexual abuse but no support for the partner of the abused person or the affected children in dealing with the effects of the disclosure. This has changed today with support available. Everything appeared to be very victim-focussed, and women have always been much better than their male counterparts at seeking help. I tried to reach out to my mother-in-law, Jenny, who did not understand my plight. When I attempted to tell her about my life in the residential school, Jenny's response was to dismiss what I described.

'That did not happen to you,' she said.

This seemed bizarre at the time, but the reasons behind Jenny's reaction were eventually revealed. During the mid-1990s, Jeffrey and I usually took the children to see their grandparents in

Wanganui every six weeks or so. I had a tendency to be overprotective of the children and would never trust anyone, except my husband, to oversee them. This meant that Jeffrey and I had little time away from the children, as I felt I had to ensure that they were being safely taken care of at all times. Jeffrey's parents, Jenny and Kev, would occasionally babysit for us; this would happen once Moira and Jack had been put to bed. While allowing them to babysit required a great deal of trust on my part, it did enable me and Jeffrey a small amount of desperately needed, child-free time.

Sabrina with Jack and Moira in 1993 in Wanganui feeding the stock on Jeffrey's parents' farm

Then, on one occasion after Jenny was widowed, we arrived at her house to find her visibly upset. After dinner, with her nose bleeding and in a state of extreme distress, she blurted out to me and Jeffrey, 'When I was eighteen, I had a baby and now he has turned up!' She then lapsed into silence. The child, named Euan, was now in his fifties. He had been adopted as an infant by a family living about three hours' drive away. That day, he had visited Jenny's house prior to the arrival of our family and had left a box of chocolates for his half-brother Jeffrey and me, by way of his introduction to us. For some unknown reason, Moira and Jack, who were about eight and ten years old at the time, thought that their Nana was telling their parents that she was in fact a man, something that necessitated further explanation!

Following my mother-in-law's dramatic disclosure, I realised it was little wonder that Jenny had shown no sympathy for my sad story, as she herself was carrying around her own deep grief and burden of unresolved issues. Perhaps Jenny was unable to empathise with the plight of someone close to her because of her own sense of loss. I felt some compassion for her, but, over the next few years, the relationship between the two of us became something of a rollercoaster ride. Jenny attempted to have two separate family relationships, one with Jeffrey and his sister and the other one with Euan, trying to keep them compartmentalised.

Jeffrey and his sister had only been told about ten years earlier (when they were both in their thirties) that their own father, Kev, was himself adopted. Kev had worried about telling his children about his adoption for fear of being rejected by them. On the contrary, the news didn't alter Jeffrey's relationship with his father at all, though it partly explained the feelings Jeffrey always had regarding not really 'fitting in' with Kev's side of the family. When Jeffrey had a conversation with his mother after her disclosure about Euan, he suggested that she had had the perfect opportunity, when their father had told Jeffrey and his sister about his own adoption, to make her own admission regarding the baby she'd had adopted. He felt that instead of keeping it secret for all those years, it would have been somewhat better for his mother to have made the disclosure when he and his sister were growing up, as it might have been easier for them to accept their half-brother when he did eventually enter their lives. Privately, I felt that no time was really the right time in such circumstances, when a person had become used to carrying profound hurt and guilt. Little did I know it at the time, but a similar situation had occurred in my own mother's life, though that was not to be discovered until much later. Now, I wonder about the grief my mother may have carried with her to the grave.

I loved my family and they came first, no matter what. When we were living in London, I used to say to Jeffrey that he must have been sent to me by God. As a young woman, I had often feared the idea of having children, because I never wanted them to have to go through what I suffered as a child and would not have wished my life experience on anyone else, let alone my own offspring. At the same time, I also recognised that my personal challenges were unique to me; Jack and Moira were individual beings with their own life experiences, which were not the same as mine. I doted on the children; they were the best thing that had ever happened to me, and I made a conscious effort not to transfer my fear and anxiety onto them.

As the children got older, we would go to stay in a friend's holiday home at Riversdale in the Wairarapa. Then, in 1994, Jeffrey and I purchased our own holiday home in the Horowhenua area, a house that still holds many happy memories for the whole family, as there were always visitors, celebrations, gatherings of friends and family there. I used to call that house my 'Elim'[1] as it was a place of rest and peace for me, where I could relax and

---

1. Elim means 'a place where in God's presence, at His provided oasis, no-one will be left out from his provision and blessedness'.

recharge my batteries with my family. (Jeffrey and I were not afraid of financial risk-taking and, after purchasing the beach house, we invested in a rental property in Wellington South a few years later.)

At times when I needed to work through an emotion, I would head for the beach, sit down on a large trunk of washed-up driftwood, and write in the sand with a stick, listening to the pounding of the waves on the shoreline. If I found that sleep eluded me at night, I would focus on the waves crashing and the wind blowing, finding the wild sounds of nature at the beach house very therapeutic.

EIGHTEEN
STUDYING TRAUMA AND THE RYAN REPORT

There is risk and truth to yourselves and the world before you.

—Seamus Heaney

In 1998, as part of my studies, I completed a mini thesis on understanding, surviving and overcoming childhood trauma. The following is an excerpt from that presentation:

> 'Prior to 1976, childhood trauma was not recognised. Shortly after that, researchers and other medical professionals began to understand that children could be emotionally wounded by severe trauma and that they needed help just as much as adults.
>
> Prior to 1976 also, mental health professionals believed that children were too young to be affected by trauma. It was believed that children who were hurt, sexually molested or witnessed a tragedy, would forget about it, if the parents did not talk about the event. Society may be still

struggling with this legacy today. It was believed that once the trauma was erased from memory, by not talking about the event, the child would have no lasting emotional scars.

It was only after the 1966, Aberfan, Wales disaster when a slag heap and a huge pile of rock had slipped down the side of a mountain, killing one hundred and sixteen children, that the National Health Service and mental health professionals in Britain, for the first time began to take the effects of trauma on children seriously.

Psychiatrist, Gaynor Lacey noted that the play of the fifty-six surviving children had become "grim and serious" and she "observed personality changes in the children." This was the first-time children had been studied directly rather than relying on what their parents had to say." [1]

In 1976, twenty-six children from Chowchilla, California were kidnapped on their way home from school. After the children were all safely returned, it was announced by officials that the ordeal had had no effect on them. However, five months later, parents complained that their children were suffering from horrible nightmares and intense fears.

Psychiatrist Lenore Terr spent time with these children and their parents. The first results of Terr's Landmark Study of Children and Trauma was published in 1979. The research by other Mental Health Professionals that followed confirmed her suspicions that PTSD (Post Traumatic Stress Disorder) was widespread. [2]

---

1. Portfield, Kay Marie. *Straight Talk About Post Traumatic Stress Disorder*. New York: Library of Congress Cataloguing in Publication Data, 1996. Chapter 4, p. 79.
2. Terr, Lenore. *Too Scared to Cry: Psychic Trauma in Childhood*. New York: Harper and Row Publishers, 1990. Chapter 5, p. 100.

It was by now becoming apparent that children were also affected by horrible life experiences and had been living for years with unrecognised and untreated trauma.

Being unable to put feelings and experiences into words does not mean that children have been unmarked by trauma.

At the Centre for International Peace Studies at McMaster University in Ontario, Canada, a group of Mental Health Professionals recognised the symptoms of PTSD in children and set in place programmes to treat them.

The four stages of bereavement, as outlined by John Bowlby, Theorist, are the same for children as for adults. These are: (1) denial, (2) protest, (3) despair and (4) resolution or detachment, including finding new relationships to substitute for the lost ones.

Bereavement is more difficult for children than it is for adults. Adults mourn for about a year, children on the other hand may become stuck for years in just one phase of the mourning process.

Next to the traumatic event itself, a parent's reaction was crucial and had the most powerful influence on how the child would deal with the trauma. "The way children see and understand their parents' response is very important."[3] *A panicking parent may increase the child's distress and the child's shame associated with the trauma will increase, if the parent remains silent and pretends the trauma never happened.*

---

3. Portfield, Kay Marie. *Straight Talk About Post Traumatic Stress Disorder.* New York: Library of Congress Cataloguing in Publication Data. 1966, Chapter 4, p. 79.

The symptoms of trauma will differ depending on the age and stage of development of the child and when the trauma occurred. Many symptoms, in addition to the absence of flashbacks, are quite different from those of adults.

Children will often deliberately rid their minds of all thoughts of the traumatic event and of the feelings that arise when they have these thoughts, to heal themselves and make everything appear fine. This conscious pushing aside of thoughts and feelings is different from denial, disassociation or emotional numbing because it is a conscious decision.

Changes in behaviour may appear soon after the event or months or years later, according to the American Academy of Child and Adolescent Psychiatry. Behavioural changes may include clinging to adults; persistent phobias or fears; sleep problems; physical problems; withdrawal and preoccupation with the trauma, repeated re-enactment, regression, foreshortened future and the desire not to grow up.

Displacement is a very potent, unconscious mental mechanism for moving anger onto others. Rage, which is anger out of control, is a barrier to getting close to others.[4] *Angry children, when grown up, often turn to alcohol, street drugs and psychoactive medication to dampen the rage.*

Trauma sets up four kinds of repeated dreams, exact repetitions, modified repetitions, deeply disguised dreams, and terror dreams that cannot be remembered upon awaking. All of these dreams leave the dreamer with an uncomfortable nervous feeling. Traumatised children do

---

4. Catherall, D.R. *Back from the Brink: A Family Guide to Overcoming Traumatic Stress.* New York: Bantam Books, 1992. Chapter 9, p. 192.

not usually recognise that they are dreaming their old traumas.'[5]

Two years after completing my thesis, in about 2000, I made a visit back to Ireland. There, I had a discussion with a lawyer regarding information that had been advertised in the newspaper, referring to the Commission to Inquire into Child Abuse in Ireland (CICA),[6] as it was finally coming to light that generations of children in that country had been subjected to the most appalling abuse while living in the very institutions that were supposed to be caring for them. I agreed to having my name registered concerning my time of residence at The Valley of Kidron residential institution. This was a general registration with a solicitor who had advertised such services.

Over time, busy with my life in New Zealand, it slipped my mind that I had filed the registration, and I relied on the internet for finding out what was going on with CICA. Then the Irish government decided that it would proceed with the establishment of the Redress Board. Legislation was published in mid-2001 and, in March 2002, the Residential Institutions Redress Act passed all

---

5. Terr, Lenore. *Too Scared to Cry: Psychic Trauma in Childhood*. New York: Harper and Row Publishers, 1990. Chapter 11, p. 210 and Portfield, Kay Marie. *Straight Talk About Post Traumatic Stress Disorder*. New York: Library of Congress Cataloguing in Publication Data, 1997. Chapter 4, pp. 74-76.
6. The Commission to Inquire into Child Abuse (CICA) was one of a range of measures introduced by the Irish Government to investigate the extent and effects of abuse on children from 1936 onwards. It was commonly known in Ireland as the Ryan Commission, after its chair, Justice Seàn Ryan. The commission's work started in 1999 and it published its public report, commonly referred to as The Ryan Report, on 20 May 2009. The Commission investigated all forms of child abuse in Irish institutions for children. The majority of allegations it investigated related to the system of sixty residential reformatory and industrial schools operated by Catholic Church orders that had been funded and supervised by Ireland's Department of Education.

stages in the Oireachtas (Ireland's national Parliament, comprising a Lower House, the Dáil and an Upper House, the Seanad Éireann and the Oireachtas Committees). The Bill was signed into law by the President of Ireland on 10 April 2002 and became known as the Residential Institutions Redress Act 2002.

In 2005, I submitted a summary of the childhood abuse I had experienced in Ireland, as requested by CICA (Amended) 2005. The institutions covered by the inquiry included schools, industrial schools, reformatory schools, orphanages, hospitals, and children's homes. For the purposes of the inquiry, a 'child' was deemed to be a person who had not attained the age of eighteen years at the relevant time.

As part of the submission process, I outlined the abuse I had suffered in The Valley of Kidron and the beating I had received at the age of four at the hands of Sr Cuffer when I first started school. In October 2006, I decided, after reading more information on the Residential Institutions Redress Board, that it was time that I submitted an official application from New Zealand, as I had forgotten about the application completed six years earlier. My application was submitted on 28 October 2006 and was received by the Residential Institutions Redress Board in Dublin on 9 November 2006. It was then returned to me, stamped in bold, red lettering with the words LATE APPLICATION FORM.

Undeterred, I sat down and wrote again:

Late Application Form — dated 28 October 2006

Dear Sir/Madam
I first made a submission to the Commission to Inquire into Child Abuse in approximately 2002. In July 2005, I attended an interview in Dublin. It was my understanding that my submission to the Commission was one and the

same as the Residential Institution Redress Board and that my application was covered by my submission to the Commission to Inquire into Child Abuse.
Furthermore, I am unaware of any advertising in New Zealand by the Residential Institutions Redress Board informing "survivors" of Residential Institutions on making an application to the Board within 3 years of the establishment day, when I am unaware of the establishment day of such a Board.
Please find enclosed information related to my late application.

On 19 December 2006, the Redress Board replied:

The Board has considered the request of the applicant for an extension of the application period in respect of this application.
The Board has considered the request and decided:
The Board does not consider that there are exceptional circumstances (within the meaning of the S.8(2) of the Residential Institution Redress Act (herein after 'The Act') such as to allow the Board to exercise its discretion under the Act
And/or
The Board is not satisfied that the applicant was under a legal disability by reason of unsound mind at the time the application should have been made and therefore the provisions of S.8(3) of the same Act do not apply.
In reaching the above decision the Board has considered
The application received from the applicant
All accompanying documentation
All explanations tendered by or on behalf of the applicant

together with any submissions made on the applicant's behalf

The application is therefore not validly received within the statutory period provided in the Act and will not be further considered.

This letter of decline was signed by three different individuals. I was astonished to receive such a reply from the Redress Board. After some investigation, I informed the Board that my original application had been made in 2000, through an Irish solicitor and, with the help of the solicitor who had lodged the original document, my application was subsequently progressed. An assessment was arranged for me and, as a result, the Redress Board awarded me in the region of NZ$65,000. This sum was by way of compensation for the abuse I had suffered as a child under the age of eighteen years. It included a contribution to a funeral fund, among other things.

On 20 May 2009, almost nine years after I had first responded to the request for submissions via the Irish lawyer, the Report of the Commission to Inquire into Child Abuse, known as the Ryan Report, was published in Dublin. Shock and horror were expressed in Ireland, and all over the world, when the Ryan Report came out. How could such things have happened in Ireland without anyone being aware of them?

The blame was put on the religious institutions who cared for these children, and rightly so. However, in my view, there is a second part to this story that needs to be mentioned: Families in Ireland showed little or no concern or compassion towards the children who were institutionalised. My own experience in The Valley of Kidron residential school showed that the day pupils who attended An Scoil Ghlantacháin did not want to be associated with the so-called house children. These students were looked down upon and despised by the day pupils and their families. Little or no understanding was shown for the plight of these children. The day pupils were often advised by their parents to keep away from the house children, who were treated as if they were the 'scum of the earth' by such families. Yes, the rest of Ireland was very much aware of the situation in which many of these children found themselves, through no fault of their own. Make no mistake about this, Irish people are very class conscious and many of them are snobs in their own right.

Well, the Irish are no different; it is merely their accent and cultural values that make them different from others — but this is the same for every nation. I believe that you get 'the good, the bad, and the ugly' in every race.

Pride and snobbery have nothing to do with race, culture, what a person owns, or how they speak. One might ask the question: Why did this widespread child abuse happen? It happened because people are proud, self-centred, and only concerned about themselves and their offspring, their own status, their own self-worth, and their own self-importance. Nothing much matters beyond that, and this attitude still exists today throughout most of the world. Therefore, 'When you point your finger at others, remember that the other three fingers are facing back towards yourself!'

The general Irish population knew what was going on behind closed doors and is as much to blame as the religious orders themselves. Those in authority knew that paedophilia was rife in the country but did nothing about it. Shame on you, Ireland! In other words, at that time in Irish history, many people did not give a damn about others; it was every man or woman for him or herself. That is how atrocities have been fostered and allowed to prevail in the world. I only need to look back at how the neighbouring farmers treated my father when my mother died for proof of this: They were greedy and out to take advantage for themselves, a fat bunch of unscrupulous landgrabbers!

From published literature and online research, I gleaned this information:

> *The Redress Board was set up in 2002 in order to make awards to people, who as children, were abused while resident in industrial schools, reformatories and other institutions subject to State regulation or inspection.*
>
> *During its 16 years in operation, the Board has processed 16,650 applications for awards worth almost €970 million.*
>
> *However, the total of the Board's work, including when legal fees are considered, as well as the pay-outs, comes to €1.1 billion.*
>
> *The average value of award was €62,250, with the largest being €300,500.*
>
> *Of the 16,650 applications which the Board processed – 12,016 awards were made following settlement; 2,994 awards were made following hearings; 571 awards following review; and 1,069 applications were withdrawn, refused or resulted in a nil or no award.*
>
> *There were 2,211 late applications, received from 2005 to 2011, which were processed.*
>
> *It is understood that no claims are outstanding to date. 20 November 2018.*[7]

Religious Orders Contribution

The State has reached a milestone in securing church

---

7. TheJournal.ie dated November 20 2018. (TheJournal.ie is an internet publication in Ireland. It was a mixture of original and aggregated content, before moving to entirely original content. The website was founded in early 2010).

assets to cover the cost of abuse redress after the Christian Brothers fulfilled its pledge to complete its contribution of €30 million.

This largely completes cash pledges worth €110 million from religious organisations who offered in the aftermath of the publication of the Ryan Report to part-fund redress and support for 15,000 former pupils.

However, religious congregations have yet to transfer more than twice this amount in the form of property which they pledged to hand over to the State about a decade ago.

In all, the total cost of the State's contribution to redress for survivors of residential institutions is likely to be in the region of €1.5 billion.

Some 18 religious congregations involved in the management of most of the residential institutions in which child abuse took place have made contributions toward costs incurred by the State.

To date, they have contributed more than €235 million of the €480 million which they have offered to contribute.

They have made these payments under two rounds; a legally binding indemnity agreement in 2002, and "voluntary offers" made in 2009 following the aftermath of the Ryan Report.

The bulk of money they agreed to pay under the 2002 indemnity deal – €128 million – has been paid. The transfer of two out of 60 properties remains to be fully completed.

The 2009 Ryan Report, which found there had been endemic abuse and neglect in the institutions run by religious congregations, led to calls for these organisations to contribute about half of the cost of the €1.5 billion redress costs.

> *While a total contribution of some €725 million was sought by the government at the time, the congregations offered €480 million.*
>
> *This included money paid under the 2002 indemnity deal, plus further cash and properties valued by the congregations at just over €352 million.*

The year after the Ryan Report was published, in 2010, I found myself in casual conversation with Clodagh, a neighbour from my old street in Baile na Ghlic, who was now working as a housekeeper at the local convent. I started telling her about the abuse I had experienced from Sr Cuffer all those years ago and, to my surprise, Clodagh informed me that Sr Cuffer, now known as Sheila, was retired and living in the Baile na Ghlic convent. Apparently, Sheila often paid visits to the residents at a local rest home. My first reaction on hearing that news was not particularly charitable; however, Clodagh asked if I would like to meet up with Sheila, and an appointment was duly made.

When I arrived at the convent for the meeting, I waited in a room for the woman I remembered as Sr Cuffer, wondering what it would be like to see her again after all this time. Sheila, clad in very ordinary clothes and looking a great deal less intimidating than I remembered, came in, and we greeted each other. It was clear that neither of us knew what to expect, but the timing of the reunion felt right. After initial pleasantries, I brought up the subject of the information I had submitted to the Redress Board regarding the beating I had experienced as a very young child at the hands of this nun. I continued by explaining to Sheila what I remembered about it, not really concerned whether Sheila could recall it or not. That was not why I was there that day; it was much more important that I had full recollection of it and of how it had traumatised and affected me over the years. Sheila listened quietly to me.

'When you first put in your complaint about me with the Redress Board, I thought that you might have been a monster, but here you are now, and you have proved me wrong,' she said.

She went on to explain that, back in 1958, she was in her early twenties and had recently completed training college when the event took place. Due to the whooping cough outbreak in the country, she was responsible for an unusually large class and also oversaw the singing lessons for the whole school. At the same time, she was being assessed by an inspector from the Department of Education for her teaching practice skills following graduation, all of which had put her under extreme pressure. In addition, she said that her father had died at around that time and the Mother Superior of the convent had not allowed her to attend his funeral. Her mother was left to care for the younger siblings and to manage the farm, which the Irish Tax Department then forced her to sell in order to pay death duties.

> May God's peace be with you & forgiveness for anything in the past.

A note from Sr Cuffer to Sabrina after they met in Baile Na Ghlic in 2010

To understand this, it's important to explain here that in Ireland in the 1950s, a man was not required to pay death duties on the value of the farm when his wife died, but the wife was expected to pay such death duties if her husband died. This often resulted in women being forced to sell the family farm during their time of bereavement, the farm being the only source of income for the surviving family members. The price was often reduced, or lowered, to achieve a quick sale to pay the enormous death duties required by the Irish government within a specific timeframe.

Many an opportunistic, greedy local farmer got wind of the circumstances of such women and ended up getting a bargain for himself at the expense of the poor, unfortunate widow left trying to provide for her young children on her own. Often, her only options other than selling the farm were to remarry quickly or emigrate.

According to Sheila, she had, perhaps understandably, become very depressed after the death of her father and was unable to cope with life. It was probably during this depressive episode that she had lashed out and struck me for being 'disobedient'. She was of course unaware that I had, just four months earlier, been physically assaulted and violently raped. Notwithstanding that, I heard that Sr Cuffer had a reputation over the years at other schools of being physically abusive towards her students. As the saying goes, 'The Devil can quote scripture for his own purpose'.

Sheila admitted that whilst she did not remember the incident in detail, she believed my claim and that she had, indeed, committed the crime as reported to the Redress Board. There in that private room, we put our arms around each other, and I forgave Sheila for what she had done to me. Whether or not Sheila could recall it was of no consequence to me. Sheila then told me that she had been diagnosed with breast cancer and did not know how long she had to live, so my visit was very timely for her. She asked that I not mention the report that was made to the Redress Board to anyone else in the convent, and I readily agreed, as I believed it to be a private matter.

NINETEEN
UP AGAINST THE BATTERING RAM

A battering ram is a siege engine originating in ancient times and designed to break open the masonry walls of fortifications or splinter their wooden gates. In modern times, the term battering ram has come to represent heavy-handed polemics.

> When people don't believe in you,
> you have to believe in yourself.
> —Pierce Brosnan

In the early 2000s, when Jack and Moira were in their teenage years, I operated a preschool near our home. The school was in a low decile area, and I had to fund many of the teaching resources at my own expense, because there was a chronic shortage of money in that community.

After about two years in the job, I decided that I wanted to complete further studies in a different field. While my children were still attending school, I studied full-time at a church-based learning institution located about thirty miles north of Wellington.

There was a clause that stipulated that once a student had signed a contract for the two-year study course, they would not be allowed to cancel after the first week of attendance at the facility without forfeiting the whole year's tuition fee. The first week or so was orientation-based, meaning students did not go straight into their studies. I went into a panic, feeling trapped in this archaic, institutionalised system. The feeling I had was similar to being back in The Valley of Kidron all over again, but I had no way out, except by forfeiting the year's tuition, so I decided to give it a go.

I found studying while caring for my family difficult, and, most of the time, I felt stretched. However, I was very disciplined and at around eight o'clock every evening, I would remove myself from the main family living area without too much disturbance or distraction and go and study in the basement office. Jeffrey took over most of the domestic duties in the evening, and we worked well as a team. On top of studying and running our home, I was expected to provide free domestic services to the college, even though I was a day student. I later learned that the institution was in financial difficulty; the tuition fees were higher than Victoria University's yearly tuition fees at the time. I found myself wondering what on earth I had got myself into. However, I persevered, and, after about two years, I qualified in my field. Later, I became a member of the professional association related to my qualification.

During my training programme, I spent around six months helping with the rehabilitation of inmates at a women's prison. Some of the young inmates were in jail for corrective training, though according to the female prisoners their hourly appointments with me were the only corrective training they received. Shortly after that, I set up a small private practice in the vicinity and operated my own business.

A local acquaintance suggested that, now in my fifties, I

should apply for part-time work with an organisation called the Accident Compensation Corporation (ACC) Sensitive Claims Unit (SCU), a Crown entity with a no-fault criterion. The Sensitive Claims Unit had been set up to help people who had been sexually abused. My job was initially administrative in nature, and I was responsible for the allocation of reports submitted by counsellors or psychologists to individual staff members for their action. Later, a senior position became available in the SCU, and I was encouraged to apply for the role by one of the team leaders in my department, which I duly did. My application was successful and, being more than capable of doing the job, I was happy with the promotion and my new, well-paid position.

However, almost immediately, I found myself swamped with work. No matter how hard I worked eight hours a day plus late into the evenings and on weekends, more and more work piled up for me to action. The situation became totally unrealistic and would have been unmanageable for any one person. Most of the work at that stage was accepting or declining SCU claims in respect of sexual abuse, based on the Crimes Act. No overtime was paid, and neither was there any acknowledgement of the extra work required to complete the tasks. I undertook all the extra work free of charge in order to stay on top of my workload and not let the claimants down, in accordance with the Crimes Act.

I would often arrive at the office on a Monday morning to find that hundreds of additional files had been electronically transferred into my name over the weekend, without any prior consultation. When a claimant rang the SCU, the caller would be informed that I was now in charge of their case, as the files had been allocated to my name by the team leader, Linda, whom I came to think of as 'The Liar' because of the lies she would tell. Most staff knew that this team leader could not be trusted to tell the truth; some played the game with her in order to get what they wanted. I had never come across such a liar before; the woman would continually contradict herself because of her lying. She would often boast about how she had been taught to get the fingerprints of any person in the office who came near her desk or filing cabinet in her absence.

No regard was shown for my workload; I knew that my colleagues in the department were also in similar situations. Each person working at the SCU had a totally unrealistic caseload that was completely unmanageable within the timeframe of the working week. The SCU showed no regard for the wellbeing, health, and safety of its employees. Staff could only manage to do so much work in a day and morale was at an all-time low. This had nothing to do with a person's ability or mental capacity; it was a simple workload problem — nothing more, nothing less. Taking annual leave was often extremely stressful for an employee. While they were on holiday their caseload would just pile up, unactioned, and when they returned after their break, they would feel overwhelmed by the amount of work that awaited them. Only the odd file would have been actioned, usually because a lawyer had become involved.

At around that time, Jeffrey and I had overseas visitors who were shocked that I was having to work evenings and weekends just to keep up with the sheer volume of work that was being given to me. They wondered aloud what sort of a country New Zealand was, treating its workers this way. They were horrified by the way in which I, as an employee of a Crown entity, was being exploited. Not long after that, I moved on to dealing with the SCU after claims had been accepted, which required more in-depth, detailed work in managing fewer claims.

Every decision that the SCU staff made regarding the claimant in relation to the Crimes Act was open to review. The review process was a long-drawn-out affair which entailed, in most cases, the case manager going head-to-head with lawyers. Many of these lawyers had been appointed through legal aid to assist the claimants, and some of them reviewed every decision, repeatedly. For the staff, this review process was laborious and required complete research and documentation of the claimant's file. One review alone was time-consuming in itself, not to mention all the other work that was required to manage the files of other individuals on a day-to-day basis.

The team leader whom I had privately christened 'The Liar' had her favourite people in the office, namely Larodo, Vitun, and Develesh. She went out of her way to protect these three employees from becoming overwhelmed and from being abused by the system, which was what happened to the rest of the staff in our department. This protection entailed the team leader's passing on her favoured staff members' most difficult claimants to me and others. In addition, Linda worked behind the scenes to secure transfers for Larodo and then Vitun to head office and, later, a promotion for Develesh as a reward for lying for the ACC SCU during an Employment Court hearing against me.

There was an atmosphere of fear and intimidation in the SCU office. Bullying by management was rife; one could only suppose that the managers themselves were under tremendous pressure from their immediate superiors. Some staff could only cope by switching off and doing the minimum amount of work within the hours allocated, with the result that many of the claimant files were left unactioned. Most of the files at that time were still paper based, with some of the transactional information such as telephone calls being entered on an electronic log in a computer system. In order to cope with the demands of her job, one colleague used to hide claimants' folders allocated to her behind filing cabinets and take no action on them. When the management enquired regarding inaction on a particular file, no such file could be located. The situation only came to light after the staff member had left her job, and the hidden folders were eventually discovered behind the filing cabinets.

When referring to my workload, a colleague remarked that the SCU was 'good at flogging a willing horse.' SCU management would abuse employees who showed commitment and were willing to work hard in their roles, never acknowledging a job well done. The only reward was more and more work. This had been the case for me during the first few years of my employment with the organisation. My work ethic throughout life has always been 'If something is worth doing, then it is worth doing well', and I never made a complaint to anyone. Meeting after meeting was called by ACC head office and SCU to try and resolve workloads; internal and external reviews were carried out, but nothing ever changed, because basically there was not enough manpower to do the work required. I believed that the SCU was offering a service to the public that it could not afford to administer. Staff felt trapped and often tried to move to other departments within ACC, though only one or two employees succeeded in escaping. It appeared that once a staff member was in this toxic department, there was little or no way out other than by leaving the SCU. Many of the SCU employees suffered from vicarious trauma, which is an occupational challenge for people working and volunteering in the fields of victim services, law enforcement and emergency medical services. Additionally, most staff in the department suffered from burnout.

External supervision by an ACC-approved supervisor was offered to the SCU employees on a regular basis, but this had no effect on the case workloads. In reality, it was more of a PR exercise by the ACC head office, so that it would be seen as a caring employer. Other departments within ACC did not appear to be as abusive as the one in which I worked, which attracted mainly female management, people that I considered to be nasty in nature. Strangely, considering that it is a caring profession, most of them had been nurses in a former life. Unfortunately, the SCU appeared to provide the perfect environment in which these bullies could thrive. I noticed that power went to the heads of many of the women in the organisation, making them unkind, especially to other female employees; male staff members were treated in a better manner.

ACC had many ex-police officers working for it in the investigation department. Both the public and staff were constantly under various forms of surveillance. The modus operandi for the SCU was that the mainly female management would hone in on a particular staff member to whom they may have taken a dislike to or, perhaps, they wanted to get rid of. Then management would absolutely hound the employee, first by trying to force him/her out of the SCU through their own choice. Redundancy was rarely paid: bullying an employee out of the organisation was the SCU's redundancy strategy. (I was aware of at least one person that this happened to during the time of my employment; her name was Mary-Kate and she was driven out of the SCU in that manner.) When this approach failed to work, reinforcements would be enlisted from the ACC's head office to put further pressure on the employee in an effort to get rid of her through harassment. On one occasion, there was a great upheaval in the office when some of the staff in our department received what was considered to be an inappropriate email showing a cartoon of a whale with an erect penis. Any staff member who had read this email and then sent it on to another colleague was immediately dismissed, without any warning or notice. This directive had come from ACC's head office.

As part of the dismissal procedure, management quoted the

terms of employment to the person being dismissed. No warnings were ever given to an employee and dismissal was immediate. A diligent and conscientious young man named Milo, who apparently did not forward the email but had received it, looked at it, and read the caption, was also dismissed. Milo was distraught over losing his job, but as the manager, Mrs Hawes (nicknamed 'Horse Face'), both liked and valued him, she explained that the directive had come from ACC's head office, saying it had not been her decision to fire him. (ACC later paid this sacked employee in the region of $5000 as compensation for his dismissal, instead of the larger amount he was claiming via his lawyer.) Mrs Hawes of SCU apologised to Milo and said that she would be more than willing to give him an excellent work reference without making any comment to the fact that the SCU had, in fact, sacked him for what was considered serious misconduct. She told him that his dismissal would not be recorded by the ACC HR department, thus allowing him the freedom to seek employment elsewhere, unimpeded. Perhaps ironically, he eventually ended up working in the area of mental health. The main reason for the dismissals was that ACC as a corporation was overly concerned about its public image and would go to great lengths to avoid negative press.

Because I was methodical in my work, I got great results for the SCU. That meant I always 'dotted the I's and crossed the T's' and was successful in lowering the amount of money that ACC's SCU had to pay out to the public, as well as meeting the needs of the claimants as they related to the Crimes Act. My superiors found no fault with my results or with my work ethic. In fact, a visiting manager once commented to the SCU management team, 'You seem to ignore Sabrina, who sits there working hard in that corner of the office.' This was the only person who had ever acknowledged how hard I was working as an employee. My colleagues and I at the SCU had good relationships, despite my reputation for calling a spade a spade.

There was a strong push within the organisation to get claimants off the system, as they were costing ACC and the government, and ultimately the taxpayer too much money. It was only a matter of time before I was asked to take a different direction with my work. I was assigned an exceedingly difficult task that no one else in the SCU wanted to touch. The job in question was exiting what were considered to be long-term claimants, or the 'tail', out of the SCU system by careful management of that process. The SCU took the view that these long-term claimants were using up a large portion of resources and needed to be carefully managed off their dependency on ACC payments. The work would entail constantly going head-to-head with the lawyers appointed by the claimants to oppose the SCU's every decision, a task that would probably require legal knowledge and expertise. This unenviable job did not appeal to me or to any of my fellow employees and, when I was asked to take it on, I indicated to my team leader, Linda, that I was unwilling to do so.

Apart from anything else, I feared for my safety and wellbeing because of the difficulty in working with such claimants (many of whom had numerous and varied diagnoses) in the unsupportive environment provided by the SCU. I had already been threatened by a claimant and had lodged a complaint with the police. Although I made the decision to turn down the new job requested by my superior, I continued to complete my work to my usual high standards. Almost immediately, there was a systematic approach by the SCU management to get rid of me by turning my life into a hellish experience in the work environment. The relationship between me and Linda deteriorated, and we did not acknowledge one another's presence because of my refusal to work on the 'tail' claims.

Once the management's approach had failed in trying to force me out of my job, they enlisted the assistance of a person from head office known informally as 'Gary the Hit Man' to do the job for them. Without any prior discussion, Gary started by manipulating my entry swipe card so that it would only allow me access to the building between 8am and 5pm. The card would no longer work outside these hours. In conjunction with Linda, Gary next instigated a system of micromanaging me whereby I was now required to write down everything I did throughout the day, in intervals of minutes, and I had to meet with Linda to go over the weekly log of my work schedule.

Surprisingly, I did not receive any negative feedback from Linda to indicate that I was doing anything wrong in my work. In fact, these meetings turned out to be a relatively pleasant experience between us. However, I felt that my team leader had made the bullets and was now getting Gary to fire them. Linda was still involved, alongside my own SCU manager, Mrs Hawes, in the implementation of the strategy to drive me out. Occasionally, I would sense, from the way she was breathing, that Linda was feeling stressed by the process.

My business telephone calls with claimants and contractors were now being monitored and listened in on. My work emails were remotely interfered with, and some were removed and shifted elsewhere by ACC technical support, based at head office, who had been instructed to do this by Gary (also situated at head office). Suddenly, I found myself in a very unsafe environment at the SCU because of the all-out, targeted assault on me and my employment. Next, the SCU, under the direction of ACC head office, tried to force me to have a psychiatric assessment, which I refused to comply with, as I believed that the problem, rather than being psychologically based, was one of workload, bullying, harassment, intimidation, and a toxic working environment.

What had I done to cause the suggestion that I needed psychiatric help? I had decided that I would call a halt to the abusive employment conditions which I had been subjected to by the SCU for the past three years or so. As far as I was concerned, a line had been drawn in the sand. I was no longer going to allow the SCU to abuse me by moving hundreds of files into my name without prior consultation. Nor were they going to force me to perform an extremely difficult new task that no one else would take on and which required, in my opinion, legal knowledge.

Of course, the SCU did not accept any responsibility for its own abusive behaviour or actions, and showed little or no duty of care for the wellbeing of its staff in our department. It appeared that the ACC management believed the fault for enormous case workloads, burnout, and low staff morale rested with the employees. As such, anyone who had a problem with workload or coping in that hostile environment was considered to have psychological problems, and needed to have a psychiatric assessment.

When a staff member refused to be psychiatrically assessed, such refusal appeared to work in favour of the ACC if the case came before the Employment Court. A psychiatric assessment was not used as a remedy or a way to help an employee, but could be seen as having been weaponised by this appalling Crown entity. Such assessments were being used as a tool by the ACC as part of its process of forcing unwanted employees out of the corporation.

Larodo and others were never offered psychiatric assessments, despite wanting to escape the abuse in the SCU for a safer environment within the ACC organisation. Some employees did undergo assessments, at the request of management, who were clearly targeting staff that they wanted to hone in on. One such individual was Teara, who had a beautiful, gentle spirit and only saw good in everyone until she joined the SCU. She ended up in a chronic depressive state as a result of the workload and abusive environment in which she found herself. The SCU then moved her sideways, mainly to avoid a backlash from senior Māori advisers at the ACC's head office who were aware of the situation for staff in our department. Eventually, Teara left the ACC's employment, but she is still traumatised some twenty years later by the treatment she received whilst working there and, in particular, from Linda in SCU. Teara now lives with nightmares about the abusive work environment and the bullying management who ran the department. Most of the employees who ended up being driven into the ground by this employer were highly qualified individuals in their fields of expertise.

I am aware of individuals still working for SCU in that same department where I once worked all those years ago. I have been told recently that nothing has changed in the past two decades. Work morale is still low, workloads are still unmanageable, and the employees still work in an atmosphere of fear, intimidation, and bullying. I come back to the statement I made all those years ago, that the ACC's SCU was offering a service to the public that it could not afford to administer; nothing about that has changed either.

My own employment with the ACC's SCU ended at the Employment Court. I spent approximately $20,000 of my own money on legal fees in my dealings with ACC, while ACC management enlisted the help of its top-heavy legal team in the fight against me, so both parties at the hearing had their own lawyers. When my lawyer and union delegate left the room for a short break at one stage during the hearing, the officiating

Employment Court officer, in front of everyone present, went into an all-out attack on the role of the union within ACC's SCU. When I told my lawyer about this behaviour, the Employment Court officer denied it all; he too was just another liar. I now found myself in the midst of an entire 'Den of Liars'. This action by the court officer was embarrassing, disgusting, and totally unprofessional; here was another example of abuse of power by a Crown court in New Zealand. Far from acting in a proper manner, their modus operandi at times seemed more like thuggery.

Part way through the hearing, the ACC's SCU further enlisted Develesh, a case manager and one of my colleagues, to lie to the court on its behalf. Prior to this, Develesh and I had had a good working relationship and got on well; we'd often gone out for morning coffee breaks together. On one of the last morning teatime outings, I was aware that Develesh appeared, in her friendly manner, to be fishing for information. On behalf of the ACC, Develesh lied to the Employment Court regarding the working conditions in the SCU. In return for giving misleading information, she was promised a promotion to the position of team leader within the SCU following the hearing. Whilst I can only comment on my own workload and the abuse I experienced at the SCU at that time, I am also fully aware that no one in that department dared to speak out about what was going on for fear of losing their job. In effect, Develesh could be said to have 'sold her soul to the Devil' by lying on the promise of a promotion.

Naturally, the Employment Court had no knowledge that Develesh was there for the sole purpose of giving an inaccurate description of working conditions in our department within the ACC. As a result of her statements, the Employment Court decided that ACC's SCU was, in fact, a caring employer in that it looked after its staff by offering them a psychiatric assessment when apparent problems arose in the working environment.

According to Develesh, there was no concern about workloads, bullying, intimidation, or fear in the department. She stated that she was there on behalf of our department in her capacity as representative of SCU case managers. Afterwards, I told Develesh that I would never be able to look her in the eye again after the lies she had told. Then ACC issued me with a letter advising me that I was not to make further contact with Develesh whilst in the employment of the corporation. I heard that my former colleague and friend was indeed elevated to the promised position of team leader. However, this promotion turned out to be short-lived, as Develesh ended up leaving ACC sometime later, for reasons unknown, and moved to another government agency dealing with vulnerable children and families.

I have an extraordinarily strong sense of justice. In my view, the only way in which the SCU will ever be held to account for the abuse of its employees, both now and in the past, is if the government of the day conducts an official inquiry, spanning many decades, into the historical abusive working conditions there. In order to get a true and accurate account of the abuse in the department, such an inquiry should include talking to former employees whose employment covered any period of time during the past twenty to thirty years. It would need to be conducted by an independent organisation that is not sympathetic to the behaviour of SCU management or by ACC's lawyers. It should be a thorough, independent inquiry, not an internal review, not another whitewash; there have been too many of those in the past. Perhaps it should be similar to the Ryan Report, published in Ireland in 2009.

Like most survivors of abuse, I believe that there comes a time to pronounce the truth, no matter what the price. The role of the

Employment Court in ascertaining how employees are treated by the SCU would require talking to a cross-section of the employees in the department in which I worked, in confidence, rather than relying on the evidence of a person put forward by ACC to lie on the promise of a promotion for doing so.

The parameters of such an investigation should not be determined by a need primarily to protect those government departments and Crown entities on the world stage. In my opinion, there were underhand dealings going on between the Employment Court and the ACC. Obviously, the Employment Court was not impartial and certainly did not conduct a fair hearing for me. I believe that the Employment Court and ACC were in collusion, their principal aim being to avoid negative press at all costs.

In the end, my lawyer was given two options by the Employment Court. Either I could continue to work for the SCU, but I must reimburse ACC for its full legal expenses and costs, which the Employment Court ruled should be paid because ACC's SCU was shown to be a 'good employer' (based on the untrue picture painted by Develesh) and, therefore, the case before the court was null and void. Alternatively, I could resign, effective immediately, and walk away from the SCU empty-handed. Team leader Linda, in conjunction with the manager, Mrs Hawes, decided that I would receive no references for a future employer; the SCU would merely refer to the start and finish dates of my employment with the SCU. I chose the second option, as I had already spent enough of my own money on legal fees and had no intention of paying for the ACC's legal expenses and costs in addition to my own. A return to the toxic and hostile environment of the SCU would have had an extremely negative effect on my wellbeing, as well as on the wellbeing of the colleagues I worked with, particularly bearing in mind the lies that

Develesh had told the court in order to get the organisation off the hook. There was so much institutional abuse and disrespect for the wellbeing, health, and safety of its employees going on in the SCU that its core values of 'Prevention, Care and Recovery' could certainly not have been said to extend as far as its own employees. I and others have been left with long-term memories of a bullying, abusive, and intimidating employer.

As part of the employment process in New Zealand, potential employers may ask interviewees the question, 'Have you ever had a case heard at the Employment Court?' How an individual answers this question can determine their employment prospects. It appears to me that bad employers such as ACC's SCU are never brought to justice. Rather, the employee in cases such as the one in question is ultimately penalised. Generally, the ACC reports to the government, and one thing that neither of them wants is to garner negative press. The ACC would go to any length to ensure this does not happen, no matter what the cost, lies or no lies. Employees were warned not to talk to media and, if they did, there would be serious consequences for their actions. Once I left the organisation, I had difficulty in getting it to refund my pension contribution. Eventually, I did receive my money, but not before contacting the corporation on numerous occasions.

As a curious postscript to this distressing period, some months after the Employment Court hearing, a person representing the Ministry of Justice — the government department in charge of the Employment Court — rang me and suggested that I might possibly like to apply for a position that had become available in the department for a case manager. I declined the invitation. After my horrific experience at the hands of the SCU, I resolved that I would never again be an employee, only an employer. I fulfilled that promise to myself to the end of my working life.

· · ·

The Irish expression *Fuair sé a raibh tuillte aige sa deireadh*, 'He finally got his comeuppance,' sprang to my mind when I heard, on the so-called 'kumara vine', that 'Gary the Hit Man' had been dismissed from his position at the ACC's head office for inappropriate sexual behaviour, or serious misconduct as it was known. However, his dismissal was conducted by the ACC HR department and senior management in such a way that the reason for his dismissal would not be recorded on his employment record. At that time, under the leadership of the CEO, the HR department ensured that no reference would be made to potential future employers regarding Gary's inappropriate sexual behaviour. Thus, he was guaranteed that his employment prospects would not be jeopardised. But what about his victim or victims, or indeed possible future victims? What about the ACC's slogan of Prevention, Care and Recovery?

I believe that Gary was privy to too much inside information concerning the corrupt workings and dealings of the ACC, meaning it would have been too damaging to both the corporation and the government should he have chosen to go to the media when the situation went sour on him. The best possible outcome for all concerned was to pretend that the inappropriate sexual behaviour had never happened. Gary apparently *resigned* from ACC and quietly left, without too much fuss. Following his dismissal, Gary's initial employment was with yet another government department. His new employer was never told by the ACC of his previous sexual misconduct, or that he had, in fact, been dismissed because of it. This was a blatant cover-up by ACC to protect both the man and the organisation itself from any negative media coverage. This is an appalling situation, especially when one considers that the corporation is in the business of rehabilitating victims of sexual abuse under the New Zealand Crimes Act.

In an article that appeared in the *Dominion Post* on 2 October 2008, this Crown entity came under further investigation for having a bullying culture and massive workloads that still remained, despite having been the subject of investigations by the Labour Department four years earlier, in 2004.

After these events, Linda got her own comeuppance, so to speak. Mrs Hawes went on to be involved in yet another Crown entity, dealing with claims in relation to a tragedy in Christchurch. It would appear from media reports that she was later investigated for nepotism. When the media started to investigate Mrs Hawes, she left — or was forced out of — her job. However, she continued to gain senior employment opportunities, unhindered, in similar environments. Her track record was one of bullying and intimidation of those around her and yet she appeared to just slot in, unchecked, to similar organisations.

I was aware that other SCU employees were treated differently from me. Milo had been (somewhat unfairly) dismissed for reading an inappropriate email, but no reference to that was put on his employment file by HR and he was given a glowing reference. Gary was fired for inappropriate sexual behaviour but, again, nothing about the real reason for his employment being terminated was recorded on his file. He was given good references even though ACC, as a corporation, was potentially putting more people at risk because of his sexual tendencies.

Thankfully, I never needed to refer to the SCU in my future business dealings. When this episode in my life was finally behind me, I purchased a business and went on to become a successful property owner and developer later in my life. However, I still reflect on the personal price of standing up against institutional abuse within New Zealand, and I have never regretted taking a stance against the bullies. Hiding institutional and organisational abuse in New Zealand is still rife; Kiwis have a tendency to look at everyone else in the world and point the finger, but New Zealand is not without fault, despite what some may believe. A serious conversation needs to take place around abuse in the workplace; that affects many adults, especially those who are employed by the various government departments and Crown entities. My ordeal at the Employment Court and the behaviour of those involved remain with me as a permanent reminder of that abusive era in my life at the SCU. My view is *'I don't give a damn what you think! I know the truth.'*

TWENTY
'AMAZING' GRACE AND OTHER FRIENDS

Old friends pass away, new friends appear. It is just like the days. An old day passes, a new day arrives. The important thing is to make it meaningful: a meaningful friend — or a meaningful day.

—Dalai Lama

In July 2004, after the difficult period in which I had been employed by the ACC Sensitive Claims Unit, I met Grace, a woman who was to figure prominently in my life for a number of years.

Grace had recently returned from living overseas, where she had been since 1954. Her late husband had made provision in his will that she would receive money from his Trust account towards the construction of a house in New Zealand, should she decide to return there after his death in the late 1980s. On Grace's own death, this Trust money was then to be gifted to a prestigious school. Grace had been born in 1924 and was in her late 70s when she commissioned the building of a new house in Whakatū. About two-thirds of the money for the construction came from her late husband's estate. She spoke with a perfect, upper-crust English accent and had very sophisticated tastes when it came to jewellery, hairstyle, clothing, and appearance — only the best was good enough for her. In winter, she wore a handmade, reversible mink coat (which I eventually inherited after the named recipient in Grace's will declined to accept it). She was somewhat pretentious, which appeared to impress people of a similar nature and ilk.

Those in the town who knew Grace thought that perhaps she was a member of the British aristocracy or maybe one of the English gentry, as she seemed so posh. In fact, she had taken elocution lessons during her years in England, with the aim of improving her status. She purchased a new car and had many extra luxuries included in the layout of the house. Early in 2005, she moved into her very well-appointed and comfortable home, to which she continued to add ever more features for her convenience. Grace started visiting me regularly on Thursdays and would stay for a couple of hours. She would occasionally turn up on Sundays too, sometimes bringing a handful of vegetables from her extensive garden.

She and I would chat over tea; we enjoyed one another's company and quickly built up a great rapport. Jeffrey, however, was less impressed — he would often go out shortly after Grace's arrival, leaving the two of us to talk. He would say at times to me that he didn't know how I could tolerate Grace's snobbery and that ten minutes was enough for him. I could see past Grace's façade though, and, as time went by, I got to know the other woman very well. I shared much about my own life with this new confidante, and Grace appeared to be extremely interested in my life story. We would go out to functions together and always had a good time socialising.

Grace was a keen artist who painted in watercolours and, as such, she joined the local branch of the Decorative Fine Arts Society, the Art Society, and other such organisations. Throughout her life she had been on many art destination holidays all over Europe and Ireland, organised by the fine arts societies of which she had been a member at one time or another. She said that following her marriage, she and husband Brian, an antiques dealer, had lived in Kensington and Knightsbridge when they first arrived in London. Grace also told me that Brian was gay and that the marriage had been one of convenience so as not to embarrass his well-known, upper-class family at a time when being openly gay was not an option in New Zealand. Grace and Brian never divorced, and she kept his surname throughout her lifetime.

From the time they settled in London, Grace would frequently shack up, as she put it, with wealthy men and had resided in various European countries. She told me that she and Amos, one of her partners, had become very wealthy working in the black market money exchange business in Cyprus during the 1970s, when the well-off residents of the island needed to get their money out of the country. Grace and Amos would drive around Europe with vast amounts of cash in the back of their van to be deposited in countries that were tax havens. Hence, she was always moving from country to country.

Sometimes I would receive little gifts from Grace, who once took off the necklace she was wearing when I admired the moonstone in it, and gave it to me. She would offer me garments that she no longer wanted, all of which were of particularly good quality, reflecting Grace's impeccable style. After about seven years or so, it seemed that Grace began to feel that she could now fully trust me with some of her secrets, and she started to open up about her early years in New Zealand. I was the only person that knew who Grace really was. An only child, she had grown up with her mother and father in Onehunga, Auckland. Her childhood was not a happy one, as Grace said that her mother had been very strict with her and that she had often been physically disciplined. She had numerous first cousins with whom she had played as a young girl but, since leaving New Zealand in 1954, she had had little or no contact with them. When she turned eighteen, she decided on a career in nursing and, as part of the application process, she needed to submit her original birth certificate along with the completed application form. When her birth certificate eventually arrived in the post, to Grace's amazement and horror, it had a line across the front bearing the word ILLEGITIMATE.

Utterly shocked and distressed, Grace could not believe what she saw and confronted her parents immediately. It was only then that they told her the truth, which was that they were, in fact, her foster parents. At that point, they decided to adopt Grace as their own daughter, and, shortly afterwards, the three of them attended a court session in order to finalise the adoption. A new birth certificate was duly issued which did not have the word 'illegitimate' on it, and Grace applied for her nursing course using this certificate, secure in the knowledge that, from then on, no one would ever know that she had been born out of wedlock. The trauma of her devastating discovery had remained with her throughout her adult life, however.

Grace often wondered about the dressmaker that they would sometimes visit on Onehunga High Street. She thought that perhaps the woman had been her birth mother; Grace believed that she had possibly inherited her sewing skills from the dressmaker. She also knew that she had Jewish ancestry. She recalled an elderly couple who had come several times to visit her at her parents' house. She had cried each time they turned up and had refused to go with them, so, eventually, they gave up trying to build a relationship with her and never returned to see her again.

She thought it likely that they could have been her maternal grandparents. Grace found it extremely difficult to forgive her adoptive parents, as she firmly believed that the only reason they had not adopted her earlier was because they would have lost the weekly fostering allowance that they received from social welfare. Only when she was eighteen years old and there was no more money to be had through that channel and Grace was about to embark on a career, did they finally adopt her. From then on Grace preferred to use her birth mother's maiden name which she thought sounded more posh than plain old Jones, the name of her adoptive parents. Then, she married into what could be considered high society, never revealing who she really was, and shortly afterwards the couple left New Zealand. On the other side of the world, Grace proceeded to reinvent herself as someone of great importance.

For many years, Grace helped Brian, who had a keen eye for perfection, in the antique business and together they acquired many pieces of fine art and jewellery. When anyone asked her where in Auckland she had lived, she would always say St Mary's Bay. Perhaps she had rented a house there for some time after her marriage — who knows. After several years of marriage, Grace discovered that Brian was having relationships with other men, and she decided that it was time for her to sort out her own life. They parted company, but never divorced. I understood from her that Brian had eventually died of an AIDS-related illness.

At one stage in our friendship, Grace informed me that she had given me power of attorney in respect of her wellbeing. She had a small, cancerous spot on an external part of her body, and I would, at that time, take her to medical appointments, after which we would always go out for coffee. The receptionist at the doctor's practice was unfriendly towards me, and, on one occasion, I overheard the woman referring to me as being 'the caregiver'. I corrected the receptionist, and told her that I was, in fact, a friend of Grace's and not her caregiver.

By 2012, Grace was seriously unwell and called for me to be with her. I spent the night with Grace at her house, looking after her and getting little or no sleep in the process. The following morning, Grace was unable to attend to her own toileting needs, so I took care of things. As it happened, I had planned on going away for that weekend, and it was difficult to find anyone at short notice who could take care of my friend in my absence. Eventually, I managed to have Grace admitted to a rest home for a few days until I returned. I helped Grace, still in her nightwear, from the house to the car — a process that took about thirty minutes. Grace had to lean heavily on me for support, but was still chatting away normally. En route to the rest home, we waved to a mutual friend, Kaleo, whom we spotted on his way to the Saturday market. Over the weekend, I telephoned the rest home to enquire about Grace's wellbeing and was told that she was being assessed, so I sent my regards via the staff member. When I came back after my short absence, I was told that Grace had been assessed in the rest home by her own doctor, and it had been determined that she had suffered a stroke. She was now in the process of being transferred to the local hospital for further assessment. On the evening of my return, I was with Grace, now in a room in the hospital's Accident and Emergency department, until two o'clock in the morning. Grace seemed in good form and, following further assessment, was moved onto the general ward.

I went up and down to the hospital and ran errands for Grace over the next few days. Then Grace developed a lung infection which made her uncomfortable. As often as not, as soon as I arrived home the nurses would ring to say that Grace was asking for me, so I'd have to drop everything and go back up to the hospital again. The deterioration in my friend was becoming very marked. On one of my visits, Grace said to me as I held her hand, 'You know, everyone should have a daughter'. It then appeared that the hospital had contacted Grace's lawyer with the assistance of some extended family members and discovered that Grace had a living will and, in accordance with her wishes outlined in this, there would be no further medical intervention. The decision was made that the only treatment that Grace would receive from that point on was morphine from a pump, in order to make her comfortable.

On the Thursday night before her passing, I spent the night with Grace in her hospital room, talking and praying, during which time Grace would put pressure on my hand in recognition of my presence. As part of this time together, I talked to the now semi-conscious Grace about forgiving her adoptive parents, asking for forgiveness for herself, and renewing her relationship with her Maker. I went up again on the Friday afternoon and spent time with Grace, but there were several visitors there, and extended family were soon due to arrive. I decided that this was the stage at which I would bow out and leave Grace to have her final hours with her extended family.

Before leaving the ward, I collected Grace's personal belongings, and I decided to deposit these items with her lawyer before close of day. (I had earlier suggested that my friend keep only a credit card, keys, and a few items of clothing at the hospital.) I kissed Grace and said my goodbyes to my friend, whom I never saw again. When I met with the lawyer, he dropped a bombshell, saying, 'You do know that you and I are her executors?' I had never been informed that this was the case. If I *had* known that, I may have been more assertive regarding Grace's wellbeing at the hospital. I was left feeling frustrated and angry, because, prior to this, neither Grace nor the lawyer had mentioned anything about my being appointed as one of the executors. Perhaps understandably, when some members of the family heard about my appointment, they were not happy either.

I left all the funeral arrangements to the extended family of Grace's late husband. There was no service. Grace had made a list of those people she wanted to enjoy her wake over a meal at an expensive restaurant. Interestingly, the extended family did not want her hairdresser to be included, although this had been one of Grace's expressed wishes, and, because of that, I had to go out to dinner with the hairdresser separately, at Grace's expense. When Grace's ashes were scattered, the extended family did not include me.

Grace left most of her jewellery and the contents of her house to a childhood friend, while small monetary gifts were given to three individuals including me. I also received a beautiful piece of jewellery and an item of furniture, as per Grace's will. The bulk of the work in relation to the house fell on my shoulders, and I spent the next three months clearing the property and getting it ready for sale. Grace's estate, with a gross total in the region of about NZ$3M, was left to various charities. The work around her estate took approximately three years to complete, and I worked hard, documenting events and, ultimately, saving the estate from paying overseas inheritance tax. I didn't receive any compensation from the estate for the vast number of hours of work I carried out on its behalf.

In around 2006, I was introduced to Kaleo, who had recently purchased a house across the road from where Jeffrey and I were living. At that time, Kaleo only spent the summer months in New Zealand and the rest of his time in Hawaii. When he was in New Zealand he would visit me and Jeffrey, chatting with us daily. Kaleo and I would go out for morning tea every day, taking turns to pay, and some acquaintances in the town thought that we were partners. Kaleo was polite, considerate, and kindness itself, and I was aware that he was gay. Although he was a generation older than me, having been born in 1938, we had a very easy friendship. He told me that he had known from the age of three that he was gay, but thought that he would 'grow out of it', which he never did. Being gay in small-town New Zealand in the 1950s was difficult for him, and he had adopted a more secretive approach to his sexuality. He had tried to fit in and had a girlfriend at one time. He introduced her sister to his brother, who later married her; they have been married for over sixty years. Kaleo would often say in a tongue-in-cheek manner to one of the daughters that he was responsible for bringing her into the world. Once Kaleo felt more relaxed with me and Jeffrey, he would talk to me about the forty-two-year relationship he had had with his late partner, Levi, whom he had supported through years of living with dementia.

Jeffrey and I later went on a memorable holiday to Hawaii and stayed at a hotel near Kaleo's home. He would turn up every day to take us around and show us the sights. On another occasion, my daughter Moira and I flew to Hawaii and had a fantastic holiday there, staying in a hotel. During that visit, Kaleo said that he would like to introduce us to two good friends of his, Saul and Barney, who had invited all of us out for breakfast. Kaleo felt that he should mention in advance that these friends were gay, though, in fact, I had probably taken that as a given, as I had had many gay friends over the years since knowing Art in London. Saul and Barney went on to become particularly good family friends with me and Jeffrey, often telephoning or Skyping for a chat. Then, they came to stay with Kaleo in New Zealand, and we all went on outings and for meals together as a group. Later, Jeffrey and I were invited to Saul and Barney's wedding in Honolulu. Both men were in their mid-to-late seventies by then. On that occasion, I travelled alone and stayed in Kaleo's apartment — he generously gave up his bed to me and slept on the living room couch — and had a wonderful time at the Hawaiian wedding.

Another couple, JJ and Jim, came on a holiday to New Zealand, and Kaleo introduced them to our family. We enjoyed a very sociable time together throughout the trip and, sometime later, Moira visited San Francisco and went sightseeing in the city with JJ. She was extremely fond of him, saying that he reminded her very much of her dad. Among other places, JJ took Moira to the Castro — one of the first gay neighbourhoods in the United States and still one of the world's most prominent symbols of LGBT activism — which did not faze her.

In 2010, Kaleo became ill in Hawaii and was diagnosed with a serious illness; he was not expected to survive, but, remarkably, he beat the odds and managed to make a full recovery over time. He and I care very much for one another and continue to be the best of friends. Kaleo brings me the daily newspaper when he has read it, and I receive vegetables from his garden; he is always welcome in our home.

Around the time that I first met Kaleo, I had my first anaphylactic shock. After using a hair dye, I had an itch on my scalp, severe headaches, and felt as if someone had hit me on the back of the neck with an iron bar. My head became completely swollen to the point that I felt I resembled a sumo wrestler, and I felt generally unwell. At that stage, I just thought I had had a bad reaction to the dye. Undeterred, sometime later I tried an organic brand of hair dye that had been recommended to me by the chemist. This time, the reaction was even more severe than the first one had been. I have learnt that I don't react immediately to a chemical; it takes around five to eight hours after use of the product before I start to feel the full effects. After the organic hair dye episode, I started to use henna and had no reaction to it.

Then, following a facial called a 'fruit acid skin peel' in 2016, I suffered a severe anaphylactic shock, and, on that occasion, I was hospitalised. The terrifying experience was life-threatening; I was subsequently told by my doctor that they'd had to do everything in their power to save my life. From that time onwards, I have been careful about what I eat or put on my skin. However, despite my vigilance, I had another anaphylactic shock after eating cucumber relish in an upmarket Japanese restaurant. Once I had recovered, I contacted the restaurant and enquired about the ingredients used in the food I had consumed and was told that everything was natural. I then requested a photograph of the ingredients used in the cucumber relish, and the packaging showed it contained FCF brilliant blue colouring (FCF was commonly used for dyeing leather.) Subsequently, I had two further anaphylactic shocks after using a scratched Teflon frying pan.

A visit to an integrative medicine practitioner suggested that my severe reaction was probably caused by PEG (polyethylene glycol), a compound derived from petroleum. Such compounds are widely used in cosmetics as thickeners, solvents, softeners, and moisture-carriers, and they are commonly used as cosmetic cream bases. They are also used in pharmaceuticals such as laxatives. I always carry an EpiPen with me now.

TWENTY-ONE
AN INTERLUDE IN TURKEY AND GREECE

The world is a book, and those who don't travel read only one page.

—St Augustine

To our mutual delight, Jeffrey and I were successful in the ballot for tickets to attend the services marking the centenary anniversary at Gallipoli in 2015. Jeffrey's grandfather had served there, and I also had a relative, a doctor, who had served in Gallipoli as a medical officer for the Australians. It was a privilege to be able to participate in such an auspicious event and to spend time with other New Zealanders and Australians who were there for the occasion and part of our tour which lasted two to three weeks.

Just as many Irish died at Gallipoli as New Zealanders. In fact, 15,000 Irish soldiers served there in total and of these, 3,000 lost their lives. The *Irish Independent* of 13 May 2014 tells the story:

On April 25, 1915, the ageing tramp steamer the 'SS River Clyde' approached Turkey's Gallipoli peninsula. On board were soldiers from two Irish regiments, the Royal Dublin and Royal Munster Fusiliers.

The British plan was to use the 'River Clyde' as a Trojan Horse, grounding the old ship on 'V Beach' and opening doors cut in its sides to let the fusiliers storm on to the sands.

But the plan went badly wrong. The beach was heavily defended by Turkish troops, and as they opened fire, shells from their German-supplied pom-pom guns began "hitting off the ship and tearing people to pieces", according to one Irish veteran. The sea turned red from the slaughter.

More fusiliers attempted to land in small boats, and eventually 200 troops got ashore, but at a terrible price — the Irish troops sustained 90 per cent casualties in the attack.

The 'River Clyde' crew were so moved by the Irish soldiers' bravery that they later presented the ship's wheel and lantern to the Munster Fusiliers. And, almost 100 years later, these artifacts are on display at the award-winning 'Soldiers and Chiefs' exhibition, at the Military Heritage of Ireland Trust in Dublin, which charts Irish military history from 1550 and has several rooms dedicated to World War I.

The Gallipoli trip was a highly enjoyable one for us, and we took the opportunity to have an extended holiday. We travelled around Turkey, one of my favourite countries, finding the people there warm and open-hearted. Starting in Istanbul, we went to see the Blue Mosque and the Hippodrome where Roman chariot races were once held and also Hagia Sophia, at one time a cathedral, a mosque, and in 2015 it was a museum. We also visited Topkapi Palace, a walled city perched above the Bosphorus and the Golden Horn and took in the Basilica Cistern. This is also known as the Sunken Palace, an underground waterway constructed by Justinian in 532, which was used as a reservoir for water storage. Shopping at the famous Grand Bazaar, with more than 4,000 shops, cafés, and tea houses was an unforgettable experience.

Sabrina and Jeffrey visiting Gallipoli for the 100 year anniversary of the ANZAC landing at Gallipoli, Turkey

From Istanbul, we crossed the Dardanelles Strait to arrive in Anzac Cove and drove along the shores of the Sea of Marmara to the peninsula of Geliboul, better known as Gallipoli. We made time to visit the site of the legendary city of Troy, where archaeological excavation has established nine levels of habitation and saw the enormous reconstruction of the famous Trojan wooden horse as well as the nearby 14th century Ottoman Murad

Hüdavendigar Mosque in Bursa. Enjoying this immersion in classical history, we continued to Mt Assos and viewed the ruins of the Doric-style Temple of Athena (530 BC) on a hilltop surrounded by olive groves; the hills offered spectacular views over the Aegean Sea and the nearby Greek island of Lesvos. Further down the coast in the Izmir province of the Anatolian region, we explored Pergamon, the seat of an ancient Hellenistic-period kingdom which had been made a UNESCO World Heritage site in 2014. Here, we visited the Acropolis, the Temple of Athena, and what is thought to be the site of the famous library, which is said to have had 200,000 scrolls and was second only in the Ancient Greek world to that of Alexandria. At the foot of the Acropolis, we toured the ruins of the Asclepium, one of the most famous shrines and therapeutic centres in the ancient world, and the 'Red Basilica', the remains of an Egyptian temple of Isis and Serapis.

Jeffrey and I then travelled on to Ephesus, one of the world's finest archaeological sites, just south of the modern city of Selçuk. Here, we walked the colonnaded Arcadian Way and enjoyed the ancient wonders, including the splendid façade of the Library of Celsus and the Amphitheatre, the largest and most impressive structure to survive from Hellenistic Ephesus. In the nearby coastal town of Kuşadası, we visited the Basilica of Saint John and the House of the Virgin Mary, spectacularly situated above the Ephesus ruins. Pamukkale, which means 'Cotton Castle', is famous for its dazzling chalk-white array of fantastically-shaped travertine terraces. This is the site of the ancient Greek city of Hierapolis, and we took in the fairyland terraces — glistening pools and cascades in scallop-shell basins — and relaxed in the warm thermal pools. Venturing further inland to the central Anatolian Plateau, we visited Konya, the old capital of the Anatolian Seljuk Empire. This is one of the oldest urban centres in the world, now

Turkey's most religious city and home of the mystic Whirling Dervish sect founded by the Persian poet and mystic, Rumi. Among the sights we took in was Rumi's tomb, which is within the Mevlana Tekke, a museum and national monument famous for its beautiful fluted turquoise dome.

No trip to Turkey can really be considered complete without a visit to Cappadocia, which is where we went next, making an excursion to Göreme in this unique region of volcanic landscapes, the famous fairy chimneys, and rock-hewn churches decorated with ancient wall paintings. In the Zelve Valley, the scenery is dotted with churches, caves, and troglodyte dwellings, and here we explored the underground city of Kaymakli and saw the Cone of Uchisar. Another memorable day included the trip to Agzikarahan, one of the best-preserved Seljuk caravanserais in Anatolia. From there, Jeffrey and I continued north to Ankara to visit the Hittite Museum and Anit Kabir, the mausoleum of Ataturk, Turkey's greatest modern leader.

Once back in Istanbul, we took a cruise along the Bosphorus waterway, travelling towards the old city from close to the Black Sea, the scenery complementing the grandeur of the old Ottoman palaces, mansions, and fortresses.

Our journey around Turkey was followed by a ten-day cruise through the Greek Islands, starting from Kuşadası on the Izmir coast, where we explored the bazaar. The cruise took in Santorini, with its famous, blue-domed churches and white cuboid houses clinging to the sheer cliffs, and from there we sailed south to Crete where we visited Knossos to see the Palace of King Minos. Next, we headed to Rhodes, the largest of the Dodecanese islands, sometimes known as 'the island of roses' and chosen by the Knights of St John for their fortified headquarters. Symi, one of the most picturesque islands in the Dodecanese, was also on our itinerary. The ship then docked at Chios before cruising on to

Mykonos where we explored the town with its winding maze of walkways, whitewashed houses, and magnificent windmills.

When we arrived in Athens, we visited many of the popular sights including the Acropolis, Syntagma Square, the Olympic Stadium, and the Phaleron War Cemetery, the final resting place of many of the men who were killed during the fighting in Greece in 1941. We also toured the WWI battleship Averof, now a museum. The cruise itinerary included a guided tour of the key sites in the Battle of Greece along the Gulf of Saros, taking in the beaches from which the retreating British and Australian troops were evacuated in April 1941, as well as the airfields from which the Luftwaffe launched the world's first-ever airborne invasion. The cruise liner entered the Corinth Canal (site of one of the desperate battles of the Greek campaign) from where there was a coach trip inland to see the archaeological gem, ancient Mycenae, and then onwards to the picturesque seaside town of Nafplion.

Back in Athens, there was a farewell dinner at a restaurant on the hills of Athens with the lights of the city providing a spectacular backdrop for the last night of what had been a trip of a lifetime. With the travel bit well and truly between our teeth, we then continued the holiday with a tour that took in Italy, Switzerland, Germany (where I traced the origins of my German refugee family roots), and the city of Prague. Visits to Britain and Ireland were included in our itinerary.

In the early 1980s, Jeffrey and I had met a man named Peter, from Czechoslovakia, at a youth hostel in Brussels. Few Czech people were permitted to leave their country in those days, and I had been fascinated as to how he had managed to be allowed out on holiday. During the encounter in Brussels, the three of us had shared stories about our skiing experiences, with Jeffrey and I talking about our trip to Kitzbühel in Austria to meet up with Jeffrey's classmate. Peter recounted a frightening experience he'd had on the mountain in whiteout conditions. We had remained friends ever since and, on the 2015 trip, Jeffrey and I met up with Peter and his wife in Prague. Despite some thirty-five years having passed since our first meeting, the four of us had a happy time together in the historic city, sightseeing, and swapping stories.

Sabrina and Jeffrey on a skiing holiday in Austria in 1980

TWENTY-TWO
SINK OR SWIM!

Be yourself; everyone else is already taken.

—Oscar Wilde

Jeffrey and I always had a firm desire to raise our children to be strong, stable, Christian adults equipped to face life and all its challenges. This was always our guiding force as parents. Of course, family life comes with its challenges, and when Moira was in her late teens, she started seeing a young man from overseas. Jeffrey and I were as supportive as we possibly could be, under the circumstances, although this relationship caused a lot of family stress, as it turned out to be increasingly troubled.

It was several years before the relationship finally ended. It has been said that leaving a violent partner is '100 times harder than quitting meth (amphetamine addiction)',[1] but Moira gained the courage to do this in her early twenties and started a new life for

---

1. 'Professor Doug Sellman, director of the University of Otago's National

herself. She enrolled at university and gained a Bachelor of Commerce, majoring in Human Resources (HR). By this point, life was looking good for her; she went on a diet and lost the weight she had gained during the stressful years in the coercive and controlling relationship.

Then, she decided to take a one-year break from her employment and travel internationally. Soon after arriving in London, where she found a job, she met her future husband, Bill. His father was a detective and his sister a detective in child protection, so policing was in their blood. At the time he and Moira met, Bill had been a police officer for some six years. He recognised almost immediately, from his experience as a police officer and from what Moira had told him, that she was a young survivor of a coercive, controlling relationship. Bill was incredibly supportive of her, providing the rock she needed, and they decided to get married. Following their marriage, Bill was keen to move to New Zealand with his new wife, and, after years of planning and emotional turmoil surrounding his own family in England, they moved in June of 2019. They had paid an emigration advisor in the UK and had also contacted the New Zealand police multiple times to try and set up a job for Bill.

It was not until after they arrived in New Zealand that Bill was given the shocking news that he would need to be a permanent resident — a process which would take more than two years to complete — in order to be able to formally apply for a

---

Addiction Centre in Christchurch, says attachments to substances can look as compelling as relationship attachments, but they aren't necessarily.

Primary relationship attachments are the most powerful attachment we humans engage in. Following on from the bond between mother and child, this intensity of attachment transfers to our primary adult relationships.

Both dependency on a relationship and dependency on a drug can look similar in terms of the life and death nature of the emotional response that can be ignited when the relationship or drug availability is threatened.

position with the New Zealand Police. After much heartache and many tearful discussions, Moira and Bill decided that he would return to the UK to his old job with a regional police force, which involved a re-application and vetting process. Moira remained working in New Zealand until this was confirmed.

From my professional experience in the 'helping' industry, I believe that the police need to, as the saying goes, 'get with the programme' and recognise that many women in abusive relationships are neither bad people nor criminals by association. The NZ Police have access to two systems, those of the Justice Department, for criminal records, and their own internal vetting system which documents all of an individual's involvement with the police, regardless of whether they have committed a crime.

In many cases where a woman has no criminal conviction, the police have put information in relation to an abusive partner on the victim's file. This gives the innocent woman, in effect, a lifelong profile as a victim or survivor, long after the abusive relationship has ended. It is not good enough to give the impression that the NZ Police are victim-focused and sympathetic to the plight of victimised women when the police HR and police organisation continue to *re*-victimise these women on internal records. Such practices need to change, and, in 2021, it was deemed illegal for the NZ Police to put warnings on an innocent person's file. As reported by *NZ Stuff*:

> *The police practice of issuing "formal warnings" to people who haven't been convicted of any crime – and sharing that information with other parties – has been found to be illegal.*
>
> *In a ruling that could change the way police officers do their job, High Court Judge, Paul Davison found that the warnings – issued 20,000 times in the past ten years – had*

no basis in statutory or common law and were a breach of the Bill of Rights Act.

The Police Association has called on police to stop issuing the warnings, which are entered into the national intelligence database and shared with other agencies and prospective employers during the police vetting process.

Davison found there was no specific police policy governing the issuing of the warnings.

"As the judge points out, by doing formal warnings without an admission of guilt ... they are playing investigator and judge really, which is inappropriate," association president Chris Cahill said.

... Warren Pyke, the lawyer who sought the judicial review for a client who had been issued with one of the warnings, said most people would have no idea that such information was kept and shared.

They would think the only thing that exists is your conviction history. But police keep a record of all their dealings with every member of the public and then when it comes to vetting, people sign up to disclosure ... and it effectively signs away their privacy.

No one was really prepared for the global COVID-19 pandemic that swept the world, starting in early 2020. As New Zealand is fairly isolated, it took a few weeks for it to reach the country, but by late March everyone was under a strict lockdown. Households were not allowed to mingle with other household 'bubbles', and the only car trips that were permitted were to buy groceries or seek medical help. Nearly all shops and businesses had to close and outdoor exercise was limited to your own neighbourhood.

On 26 March, the first day of the New Zealand lockdown,

Moira departed New Zealand bound for England, managing to get a seat on the one and only flight with British Airways from San Francisco to Heathrow. The whole event was incredibly fraught for everyone involved. Moira was pregnant with her first children (twins) and, as New Zealand's borders were closing, she made the decision to make a quick exit just in case she would not be allowed to travel to the UK later in the year to join her husband. On her departure from Wellington, Wishbone café at the airport was shutting up due to the lockdown, and the staff were giving away all the food. Moira was able to stock up on supplies for the first two sectors of her journey — Wellington to Auckland and onwards to San Francisco. She had consumed all of this food by the time she arrived in San Francisco, and the British Airways flight to London had no food onboard, other than a breakfast to be served before landing. Moira informed the attendants that she was pregnant with twins and the cabin crew managed to secure some fruit for her from one of the pilots—a kind gesture.

It took me months to recover from the painful realisation that my daughter (and future grandchildren) would not be able to live near us in New Zealand as we had all hoped. Back in 2014, over a three-month period when I was recovering from surgery, I used to listen to the New International Version of the Holy Bible read by David Suchet, the BAFTA award-winning actor who played the central character in the British TV *Poirot* series. (Suchet had had a long-held ambition to read the whole Bible and put it on MP3 and CD, once he had finished recording the Agatha Christie series.)

I found it a delight to hear his distinguished voice reading to me, and now I once again listened to him online. This was a great comfort and helped me to overcome the grief of losing my daughter back to the UK just months after she had returned home with her husband to start a new life in New Zealand. In a dream, I heard the voice say to me, 'Let her go, she is Mine', which helped me to accept that great loss. During the first COVID-19 lockdown, I went on long walks; although it was early autumn, the weather remained fine and warm, and it felt more like an enforced holiday than a 'Stay at Home' order. However, everyone kept their distance from one another, wore masks, and regularly sanitised their hands. Of course, thoughts of Moira were never far from my mind as I spent time listening to David Suchet.

Once back in the UK, Moira continued in her job for the Wellington-based IT company where she was employed, working at night to coincide with the New Zealand working week. She carried on with this arrangement until about three months before the babies' due date. Because of the COVID-19 protocols in place in the British hospitals, Bill was not permitted to visit her in hospital prior to the birth of the twins; he was only allowed to be with his wife for the actual delivery. I spent hours during the New Zealand night-time supporting Moira on the phone when she was admitted to the labour ward at Watford Hospital.

As soon as she was home from hospital with her new baby daughters, Moira and I began calling each other a couple of times a day using Viber and WhatsApp. I became Moira's emotional support, long distance. Once the babies were a few months old, I started having nursery rhyme reading and singing sessions with them nightly from New Zealand (UK morning time) for up to an hour. The babies began to recognise me on the computer screen once I came online, and I would get big smiles from them.

Not only were there births during the pandemic, there were also deaths. I attended three online overseas funerals during lockdown. One of these was for my close friend, Art, who passed away in the UK from COVID-19 and other complications in May 2020. He was seventy-nine years old. Jeffrey and I were invited to join his online funeral service, which took place many months after his death. Art's family had had no choice about when or where the service was held, simply receiving short notice that the event had been scheduled. In common with many families, they had to make the best of it and every other situation under the COVID-19 pandemic restrictions.

The most distressing online funeral was the one held for an extremely close childhood friend, Stacey, who passed away from cancer. I was invited via the internet into the hospital room as this friend passed away, and Jeffrey and I were later able to attend the funeral online. Only ten persons were allowed in the funeral home at any one time in Ireland at that stage, and as they all had to be masked, it was almost impossible to recognise the other mourners on a computer screen. However, the farewell was marked by poetry, photography, stories, and artwork by the deceased which graced the funeral parlour, and her favourite music was played. As the burial grounds had no internet, Jeffrey and I were unable to join that part of the ceremony.

The lockdown in New Zealand was extremely stressful for me from an emotional standpoint, what with the overseas births of our twin grandchildren and the death of Stacey in Ireland. I had no option but to grieve from afar. The years 2020 and 2021 were a strange time for people all over the world.

Having ample individual accommodation arrangements to offer, Jeffrey and I gave free board to three 'Brits' during the lockdown, as many overseas visitors suddenly found themselves stranded in New Zealand when the borders closed and flights ceased to operate. One lady stayed for about sixteen days, another for two weeks, and the last person, a young man, for two nights. In this way, Jeffrey and I did our bit for the stranded holidaymakers during the country's initial lockdown.

. . .

Having made Aotearoa New Zealand, 'Land of the Long White Cloud', my home, I took several trips back to Ireland when my children were young, to reconnect with my homeland, to see my father, and to allow our children to become properly acquainted with the Irish side of their family. When Jack was a young boy, he got to know his Irish grandfather. To my father's delight, Jack showed a keen interest in a hurling stick that was in the house. Years later, when he was in his early thirties, Jack went on to take up Gaelic football in Wellington, and other team members found it hard to believe that he had not played the game before, as he showed a natural skill on the field. I like to think that my father's love of traditional Irish sports has been passed on, through me, to my son. A proud graduate of Wellington College, Jack met his wife, Cara, in around 2006. They married and spent some time living and working in Perth, Australia, which they loved, before returning to New Zealand. They became parents of four children, two boys and two girls, who, along with Moira and Bill's twin daughters, are treasures to me and Jeffrey, their Nana and Poppa.

Family has always been extremely important to me, and I thought I knew all there was to know about mine. But life has a way of surprising us when we least expect it! When I checked my Ancestry account on 28 March, 2023, I was greeted by the following message:

> Hi
> *Delphine Dowling may be my maternal Grandmother.*
> *This is the story, I know:*
> *Delphine Laughton from Rimelow gave birth to Freda in 1945 in The Rotunda Hospital in Dublin. I always knew connection to Baile na Ghlic, also.*

Apparently, she worked in Clough, Co. Antrim as a house maid. The supposed father married a spinster and then adopted her [the baby?]. Her adopted mother died at forty-one years and he remarried and moved to England. Would you be able to help me with this. I have such a strong feeling; it is Delphine in your tree. I have ordered a dna test, so this should also show some connections? Many thanks, Maryjane

Over the next few months, I tried to glean information on this surprising news from relatives. It appeared that my maternal first cousins all knew about the pregnancy and the baby. Each one blamed the other for not having informed me, now that my father had passed away. As far as I know, he had also been unaware of the baby's existence.

One of my mother's nephews (my first cousin) rang over that Easter weekend and asked me if I had a support person with me, and I said yes. The news was confirmed that the information was indeed correct, that my mother Delphine had had a baby girl in 1945. It was apparently also very distressing for my mother's two sisters. Her nieces and nephews, the children of her two sisters and brother, had all known about the baby, but no one had told me.

When I asked who the father was, one cousin said he was the son of a farmer who had lived in a big house — but that would account for a large percentage of Irish men, at the time. Another said that the name of the father was Maxwell, and yet another maternal first cousin said that the father of the baby was his first cousin on his paternal side, but no one was honest.

When I started to look into Irish adoption record procedures online, I came across an article published on 12 January 2022 by

The Guardian, headlined 'Ireland to give adopted people access to birth records to end 'historic wrong'.'

Because Baby Laughton's mother — my mother — was Church of Ireland (Anglican), an arrangement had been made for her, by her two sisters, with the assistance of a Church of Ireland minister, to get Delphine into a mother and baby home in Dublin. The home was called Bethany Home, or House, and was an establishment run by the Plymouth Brethren to assist Protestant girls who were considered 'fallen women'. (Some were prostitutes or had been sent there for committing petty crime.) From there, Baby Laughton was taken to Northern Ireland, where she was adopted and brought up as a member of the Brethren.

Mrs Page, a Brethren member, was named in the Rotunda Hospital's notes as the person to whom Baby Laughton was to be adopted. (In 2011, the Irish Redress Board refused to compensate survivors of the Bethany Home in Dublin.) Then, when the little girl was five years old, her adoptive mother died, and that turned her life upside down.

Suddenly, I was reminded of the 'suitcase incident' in which Uncle Bart had taken the case filled with my mother's belongings and kept the contents, which had greatly upset her before her death. It probably contained information she had kept on her baby girl.

I tried to get information on my mother from AAI (Adoption Agency Ireland), but they were only concerned for the adopted child. I found myself waiting for almost a year to be told, when I asked why I had not received a reply to my enquiry, that 'there is nothing outstanding from AAI.'

After further communication from the agency, I received a few lines from an entry in a register giving my mother's name, age, and address and stating that she had attended the Rotunda Hospital in 1945 one month before the baby was born. It stated she 'would not stay'. One month later, there was another entry which gave her name and date of birth, which appeared to be different from the month before, and another address that was not the same as the one she had given on the previous occasion. In the notes, there was reference to a woman, Mrs Page, who was to adopt the child. Other lines were redacted. That is all the AAI would give me.

I felt that I was entitled to all the information that these agencies held relating to my late mother; I was not asking for information on the adopted child. (Using other means I had by then unearthed sufficient facts about how her life had turned out, nearly eighty years after her birth at the Rotunda Hospital.) What a great shame that Ireland is still trying to hold on to its power in not releasing information to a daughter, adopted or not, relating to her own deceased mother. Delphine was my flesh and blood, and she had given birth to a baby — my half-sister — on her twenty-second birthday in 1945. The circumstances around Mrs Page, which read, 'Particulars to whose care child is removed — Mrs Page, relationship Adopted' was all I was permitted to know.

Looking back over my life, I feel I have been an empathetic, compassionate, inclusive, resourceful, and generous person who has fought hard, against the odds, to survive. Up to the age of around twenty, I was continually overrun by others before necessity saw me become feistier from my mid-twenties onwards.

I believe I had two choices in life, to 'sink or swim'. I chose to swim — against the tide, in most circumstances. Overwhelmed at a very early age by sexual abuse and the trauma of being almost killed by a sexual predator, I then had to deal with being physically abused by Sr Cuffer four months after the rape; I had to endure the sudden death of my mother and becoming a support for my father before being made a ward of the state, all by the age of twelve. This is more than most children of that age could tolerate and survive into adulthood.

As the years went by, I could clearly see a pattern emerging wherein I would appear to attract the wrath of older women who would abuse me emotionally and add insult to injury. It was as if they understood my needs, but, instead of helping me, they chose to abuse me further. I believe there must have been a spiritual dimension to that destructive attraction.

Working and keeping myself busy prevented me from giving into suicide and drove me on to make a success of my life. My strong sense of justice and fairness meant I would go to great lengths to uphold those principles, whether in my private life or in a work environment such as the Accident Compensation Corporation's Sensitive Claims Unit. This extended to my dealings with the Employment Court.

At the heart of my adult life has been the extraordinary support of my husband, Jeffrey, whom I truly believe to have been chosen for me by God. Jeffrey has been central to my life. I have nothing but admiration for my husband and our two children, who had to witness me re-living my traumatic childhood experience when, as an adult, I 'gave birth to the monster.' They have had to weather their own long-term effects of that. I also realise how important it was for me to be able to enjoy the holiday home which Jeffrey and I own. At times, it provided my family with an escape and an oasis in the middle of what appeared to me to be a vast, stormy desert.

To both my parents, Delphine and Tony, who showed me the way to trust in God, I owe a debt of gratitude. I recognise the stability that my father provided in my life for he was, undoubtedly, my rock. He had his own difficulties, disappointments, and loss to deal with, and he suffered from depression, but no matter where in the world I found myself, I knew that he would be there in Baile na Ghlic waiting for my smiling face to arrive at the door. I could hear his voice in my head saying, 'Wait till I tell you,' an opening line he always used to start asking me questions, in an effort to get me to tarry awhile. It was my mother who instilled in me the ethics of hard work, integrity, and the importance of family life. I acknowledge the role of Biblical principles in the lives of my ancestors and the knowledge of God that I received in my life, and have passed on to my children, hopefully for generations to come.

Without any guidance, I became highly creative in my survival techniques and, using my own basic skills, learned how to endure the horror of the childhood sexual abuse and accompanying near-death experience. Against the odds, I managed to go on to have a relatively normal life, to marry, and remain married, and to bear and successfully raise two children. Over my lifetime, I have been, among other things, a successful personal assistant (PA), electrologist, teacher, a doula business owner, an NZAC counsellor, and a property developer, but I consider that my greatest achievements have been as a wife, mother, and grandmother to my dearly loved husband, children, and grandchildren.

The words 'There but for the Grace of God, go I' are sometimes attributed to John Bradford, who is said to have uttered them in the mid-16th century as he watched a group of prisoners being led to execution. (Bradford was himself executed for heresy two years later.) However, these words are Biblical in origin and a paraphrase from 1 Corinthians 15:8-10, (NIV) which states:

> *and last of all He appeared to me also, as to one abnormally born. For I am the least of the apostles and do not even deserve to be called an apostle, because I persecuted the Church of God. But by the grace of God, I am what I am,*

and His grace to me was not without effect. No, I worked harder than all of them—yet not I, but the grace of God that was with me.

All is forgiven, I hold no grudges: Psalm 34:18, *'The Lord is close to the broken-hearted and saves those who are crushed in spirit.'*

Psalm 147:3, 'He heals the broken-hearted and binds up their wounds.'

Psalm 147:11-12, 'The Lord delights in those who fear Him, who put their hope in his unfailing love.'

There, but for the Grace of God, go I.

AMEN

SAFETY NOTE

Reading this book may have touched on traumatic issues in your life. For mental health and wellbeing support, please contact an appropriate local agency who can help you with rape crisis support, sexual abuse support, suicide prevention and support, grief counselling, depression and anxiety support. Parental guidance may be needed for young people reading this book.

ABOUT THE AUTHOR

Sabrina Dowling is a businesswoman living in New Zealand's South Island. She and her husband, Jeffrey, have two adult children and six grandchildren. A lover of art, theatre, gardening, and chamber music, Sabrina also cherishes her Irish heritage and native language, Gaeilge.

She wrote this memoir to remind others that past trauma need not define the present—that healing is always possible.

Sabrina M. G. Dowling
sabrinamgdowling@hotmail.com

ACKNOWLEDGMENTS

Sabrina acknowledges with gratitude Tanya Lunn, editor, and her husband, Nicholas, for their input into producing this book.

www.ingramcontent.com/pod-product-compliance
Lightning Source LLC
Chambersburg PA
CBHW031231290426
44109CB00012B/250